9 01 mc

I0340055

EERL Withdrawn
Surplus/Duplicate

BRITISH POLITICS
AND EUROPEAN UNITY

Parties, Elites, and Pressure Groups

British Politics
and
European Unity

Parties, Elites, and Pressure Groups

ROBERT J. LIEBER

University of California Press
Berkeley • Los Angeles • London
1970

JN
329
P7
L53

PROPERTY OF
UNIV. OF ALASKA LIBRARY

University of California Press
Berkeley and Los Angeles, California

University of California Press, Ltd.
London, England

Copyright © 1970, by
The Regents of the University of California
ISBN 0-520-01675-0
Library of Congress Catalog Card Number: 70-104104
Designed by Eleanor Mennick
Printed in the United States of America

To My Parents

PREFACE

This study of British politics and European unity has a dual purpose. First, it offers a comprehensive account of the role of pressure groups and parties in the formulation of Britain's policy toward European unity; second, it puts forward the basis for a theoretical framework with which to approach some broader conceptual questions about the influence of organized economic interests on public policy, and it also raises central issues involving pressure group politics, political decision-making, and integration theory.

At the descriptive and explanatory level, this book undertakes to answer why British policy-makers conspicuously failed to come to terms with successive European developments. The period under particular scrutiny covers the years from 1956 to 1967, and it divides into three distinct phases. The first phase is that of negotiations for the Free Trade Area and the European Free Trade Association (1956-60). The second involves the Macmillan Government's unsuccessful effort to enter the Common Market (1961-63). The third deals with the Wilson Government's initial renewal of the Common Market application and ends with the November 1967 French veto. Perhaps an understanding of these years will also provide particularly useful insights as British membership in the EEC again becomes an immediate possibility.

The making of European policy is first treated (in Part II) from the perspective of functional representation. Here the subject is the formulation of sectional (i.e., economic) pressure group attitudes and the methods with which these groups communicated their positions to governmental authorities with the aim of influencing Britain's European policy. From this standpoint, the evidence indicates a significant pressure group influence, or "concurrent majority," in policy-making toward the FTA, the EFTA, and in the first period of negotiations for Common Market entry. The subject is then analyzed (in Part III) from the perspective of party government, which involves the political parties, promotional pressure groups, press, and public opinion. In this sector there existed an initially low level of party and public attention to European unity which, when combined with the conscious choices of governmental leaders, made possible the crucial pressure group influence. As a result, and until a relatively late date, public policy formulation took place more on a basis of profit and loss calculations than in terms of a more generalized public interest.

At the theoretical level, the discussion is set in the context of British collectivist politics. A number of propositions are then developed concerning group influence in order to clarify the relationship between interest politics and the decision-making process within the British system of government. Among the central findings which emerge are the following: that pressure groups have played a crucial restraining role in Britain's movement toward Europe; that group influence is limited when an issue receives political treatment, or becomes "politicized"; and that at crucial moments political authority, motivated by considerations of national interest rather than material advantage, has ultimately exercised responsibility for national policy.

By way of acknowledgement, I wish to express my thanks to those institutions, organizations, and individuals whose assistance has made this study possible. A Harvard University Knox Travelling Fellowship supported me for a year of research and interviewing in London during 1966-67, and I later benefited from a Research Training Fellowship of the Social Science Research Council. The following organizations kindly permitted me to use library and other facilities: London School of Economics, University of London, Royal Institute of International Affairs, Confederation of British Industries,

National Farmers' Union, Trades Union Congress, Labour Party, and Conservative Party Research Department. The Confederation of British Industries allowed me to quote from its files, and Social Surveys (Gallup Poll) Ltd. has granted permission to use figures from the *Gallup Political Index*.

I am indebted to the leaders and staff officials of the major pressure group and party organizations, as well as senior civil servants, former Cabinet ministers, Members of Parliament, and journalists with whom I conducted more than sixty lengthy interviews. Considerations of propriety make it impossible to thank them by name for their time and candor. At each stage of my research and writing I have benefited from a great deal of comment and criticism. The pressure group portions of this work have been read by Eric Felgate (of the Confederation of British Industries), Geoffrey Redmayne (formerly of the National Farmers' Union), and R. Colin Beever (research officer of the National and Local Government Officers' Union). They have been quite helpful in their comments, but I must emphasize that their scrutiny by no means implies agreement with the conclusions I have drawn. I also wish to thank Sir Michael Frazer, Lord Netherthorpe, Sir Norman Kipping, and Professors Leon D. Epstein, and Karl W. Deutsch. On more general grounds of intellectual stimulus I ought to mention William L. Smith, William W. Bingham, M. David Gordon, Peter Cheeseman, and Nancy I. Lieber.

It is a particular pleasure to acknowledge my debt to Samuel H. Beer and S. E. Finer, who directed my original research. Both men have been of the greatest help at the conceptual level as well as in making suggestions involving more mundane matters of organization and research. Nonetheless, the responsibility for matters of fact and interpretation must remain entirely my own.

Robert J. Lieber

St. Antony's College
Oxford
March 1970

ABCC	Association of British Chambers of Commerce
ACML	Anti-Common Market League
BEC	British Employers Confederation
BOT	Board of Trade
CBI	Confederation of British Industries
CEIF	Council of European Industrial Federations
CIA	Commonwealth Industries Association
CMC	Common Market Campaign
DEA	Department of Economic Affairs
ECSC	European Coal and Steel Community
EEC	European Economic Community
EFTA	European Free Trade Association
ERO	European Regional Organization of the ICFTU
THE FIVE	Member countries of the EEC, excluding France
FTA	Free Trade Area
FBM	Forward Britian Movement
HMG	Her Majesty's Government
ICFTU	International Confederation of Free Trade Unions
NEC	National Executive Committee of the Labour Party
NEDC	National Economic Development Council
NFU	National Farmers' Union
NUM	National Union of Manufacturers
OEEC	Organization for European Economic Cooperation
OTHER SIX	Member countries of the EFTA, excluding Portugal
PLP	Parliamentary Labour Party
SEVEN	Member countries of the EFTA (Britain, Switzerland, Austria, Sweden, Denmark, Norway, Portugal)
SIX	Member countries of the EEC (France, Germany, Italy, Belgium, Netherlands, Luxembourg)
TUC	Trades Union Congress

CONTENTS

PART 1

INTRODUCTION

RASMUSON LIBRARY
UNIVERSITY OF ALASKA-FAIRBANKS

Chapter 1

Introduction

For years, considerable attention and research have been devoted to the relations between Britain and Europe, mainly in the form of detailed and useful accounts of negotiations and the development of official views.[1] The present study seeks to employ the development of British policy toward Europe as a means of raising some fundamental questions concerning the operation of the British political system and, by implication, the process of policy-making in democratic and industrialized countries. Specifically, it undertakes to analyze the effect of the major pressure groups and political parties on a key area of British policy formation and from this to generalize about the role of these groupings in the making of foreign policy. This effort differs from previous pressure group case studies in that it examines neither an important piece of legislation,[2] nor the administration of an existing program.[3] Rather it deals

---

[1] See, for example, Miriam Camps, *Britain and the European Community, 1955-63* (Princeton: Princeton University Press, 1964); *European Unification in the Sixties; From the Veto to the Crisis* (New York: McGraw-Hill, 1966); Nora Beloff, *The General Says No* (Baltimore: Penguin, 1963).

[2] E.g., James B. Christoph, *Capital Punishment and British Politics* (London: Allen & Unwin, 1962); and H. H. Wilson, *Pressure Group: The Campaign for Commercial Television* (London: Secker and Warburg, 1961).

[3] E.g., Harry Eckstein, *Pressure Group Politics* (Stanford: Stanford University Press, 1960).

with the formation of a policy, and one which has as its subject foreign rather than domestic concerns.

CORPORATIST POLICIES IN BRITAIN

The British political process has been aptly described by Samuel Beer as one of "collectivist politics."[4] Its novel features are the two channels through which society and the Government interact. On the one hand, there is the system of *party government*. Development of the Welfare State and the realities of winning power have required that the political parties (each influenced by its distinctive conception of the common good)[5] bid for the votes of consumer groups (i.e., blocs of voters), who thereby exercise their influence through the electoral process.

The second channel linking society and the Government is that of *functional representation*.[6] Here, as development of the Managed Economy involved the Government in extending its control over the economy, the realities of governing in a free society necessitated that it bargain for the active cooperation of the major interests involved.[7] Pressure groups have become the embodiment of these interests. Indeed, they have become so important that Robert McKenzie has observed: "Pressure groups, taken together, are a far more important channel of communication than parties for the transmission of ideas from the mass of the citizenry to their rulers."[8]

---

[4] Samuel H. Beer, *British Politics in the Collectivist Age* (New York: Knopf, 1965), esp. Chap. 12.

[5] *Ibid.*, p. 352.

[6] As S. H. Beer defines it, the notion of functional representation is one which "finds the community divided into various strata, regards each of these strata as having a corporate unity, and holds that they ought to be represented in government," *Ibid.*, p. 71.

[7] *Ibid.*, p. 321.

[8] R. T. McKenzie, "Parties, Pressure Groups and the British Political Process," *Political Quarterly* 29, no. 1 (January-March, 1958): 10.

Pressure groups are seen to enjoy such prominence in the political process because of the fading of major class and ideological contours and the emergence of a general policy consensus which relegates conflict to matters of detail.[9] This general situation lessens the intensity and importance of party competition and enhances the role of pressure groups. Several specific bases of group influence emerge. To begin with, pressure group *advice* is essential in order for government to obtain basic information and technical knowledge, without which economic regulation would be impossible. Next, *acquiescence* is a necessity if government programs are to operate successfully. Thus, for example, any hope of a viable prices and incomes policy requires business and trade union support. Finally, the *approval* of the groups concerned is required if particular government policies affecting them are to be regarded as legitimate.[10] This last consideration reflects a basic collectivist ethos which is shared by the Labour and Conservative parties. In Labour's case it is expressed in terms of "Socialist Democracy" and for the Conservatives it is embodied in traditions of "Tory Democracy," elements of which include strong government, paternalism, and the organic society.[11] The Collectivist theory of representation, which sets both parties apart from the nineteenth-century political individualism of the Liberals, is an intrinsic part of twentieth-century British political culture.

What is meant by the term *pressure group*, which will appear so frequently throughout this study? A lush terminology of labels and definitions has grown up to classify interest or pressure groups. For present purposes, a relatively simple definition and classification will suffice; that of S. E. Finer seems the most straightforward. Pressure groups will be taken to mean those organizations which are "occupied at any point of

---

[9] Eckstein, *op. cit.*, pp. 18-19.
[10] Beer, *op. cit.*, p. 329. Beer provides a detailed treatment of these bases of pressure group power, pp. 320-331.
[11] *Ibid.*, p. 68.

time in trying to influence the policy of public bodies in their own chosen direction; though (unlike political parties) never themselves prepared to undertake the direct government of the country."[12]

In addition, major differences exist between types of pressure groups and a dual classification of pressure groups will be employed here. *Promotional* will designate those groups organized around attitudes or points of view, and which generally seek to persuade people without regard to their sectional affiliation.[13] It is characteristic of the promotional groups to operate via the process of party government or to organize public campaigns rather than to work through administrative agencies. This is natural because they lack the ability to represent a corporate sector, and thereby to withhold services or invoke threats. Accordingly, in promoting their causes, they are usually less powerful than those groups which operate through the process of functional representation.

Sectional will describe those organizations whose political task it is to reflect the interests of the economic or occupational sectors they represent. Unlike the promotional groups they do not direct their attention to the parties, Parliament, or the electorate, which make up the party government sphere. Instead, as a result of governmental structure, activities, and

---

[12] It must be noted that Finer uses the term "The Lobby" to describe these organizations. He rejects the label "pressure group" as implying the threat of a sanction if demands are refused, and also observes that even groups which do use pressures do not do so at all times. Furthermore, he finds "interest group" too narrow because it omits those gathered in support of a cause, e.g., Peace Pledge Union. S. E. Finer, *Anonymous Empire* (2d ed rev.; London: Pall Mall Press, 1966), pp. 2-3.

I find Almond and Powell's definition of the term "interest group" to be far too broad, since it does not imply the necessity for conscious organization and activity. It is "a group of individuals who are linked by particular bonds of concern or advantage, and who have some awareness of these bonds." Gabriel A. Almond and G. Bingham Powell, Jr., *Comparative Politics: A Developmental Approach* (Boston: Little Brown, 1966), p. 75.

For other usages see Allen Potter, *Organized Groups in British National Politics* (London: Faber and Faber, 1961); Peter Self and Herbert

attitudes, the sectional pressure groups almost always concentrate their efforts on the administrative departments of government.[14] Thus they normally operate through the functional representation process. The bargaining power of these groups ultimately rests upon their performance of crucial productive functions in the society and is distinct from any position they may have in the system of party government. To the extent that government commits itself to intervene in the economy it must obtain their cooperation. This need can be minimized in a totalitarian system, but in a free country the government has little choice but to secure a large measure of voluntary cooperation from the bodies being regulated.[15] The actual mechanisms for group operation via functional representation are both formal and informal. They include numerous official advisory committees upon which sectional groups are represented as well as close personal contact between representatives of the interests and their opposite numbers in the Civil Service.[16]

Despite their economic basis, there are several reasons why the sectional pressure groups do not function entirely on the basis of unrestrained economic self-interest.[17] First, these bodies seek to justify themselves with some notion of broader national interest which their actions are designed to advance.

J. Storing, *The State and the Farmer* (Berkeley: University of California Press, 1963); H. H. Wilson, *op. cit;* Christoph, *op. cit.,* and Eckstein, *op. cit.*

[13] See Allen Potter, "Attitude Groups," *Political Quarterly* 29, no. 1 (January-March, 1958): 72. Potter actually uses the term "attitude" rather than "promotional," which is Finer's expression. McKenzie categorizes pressure groups into "sectional," "promotional," and "other," *op. cit.,* p. 11.

[14] See Eckstein, *op. cit.,* pp. 16-17.

[15] Beer, *op. cit.,* p. 321.

[16] For a detailed treatment see Political and Economic Planning, *Advisory Committees in British Government* (London: Allen & Unwin, 1960).

[17] Self and Storing resist the dichotomizing of groups into promotional and sectional categories because they argue that sectional interests hold general social views, *op. cit.,* pp. 212-213.

The Federation of British Industries (FBI), National Farmers' Union (NFU), and Trades Union Congress (TUC) all pitch their demands above the level of mere advantage for businessmen, farmers, and trade unionists; nonetheless, conceptions of free enterprise, agricultural prosperity, and working-class advancement still fall short of a more or less universalistic public interest. Second, the role of sectional pressure groups depends on competence in specialized areas. They therefore concentrate their attention overwhelmingly on matters of a technical nature rather than on overall policy. Third, these groups expend a great deal of their energy on organizational self-maintenance. This takes the form of providing information and services, as well as seeking to hold together a huge and heterogeneous membership. The latter problem frequently makes it difficult to formulate a business, agricultural, or labor view at the national level (though this obstacle is frequently exaggerated by group officials). Fourth, leadership is a crucial variable. A change in individuals may produce an entirely different organizational policy. Thus a non-activist FBI president, a staunchly anti-European NFU president, and a pro-Common Market TUC leader were responsible for organizational viewpoints less likely to have been adopted under different leadership.

Whatever the limitations upon them, the fact is that the sectional pressure groups have come to occupy a position of great power within Britain's quasi-corporatist system. Perhaps the best characterization of this role is that of S. E. Finer. He finds that organized capital and labor do not dictate public policy, but because of their position in the economy, their cooperation must be won. The essence of this relationship is that "they do not direct but they may veto."[18] Put another way, Britain has reached the position wished for by John C. Calhoun more than a century ago. Calhoun had dreaded the prospect of the "numerical majority" getting control of the

---

[18] Finer, *op. cit.*, p. 27.

government by means of its majority status, then using its authority to oppress minority sections. To forestall this situation he sought to have government regard interests as well as numbers, allowing each a concurrent voice in the making of laws or a veto in their execution. In Finer's estimation, the major sectional groups have attained exactly this "concurrent majority" status.[19]

A basic object of the present study is, therefore, to analyze the operation of sectional groups and determine whether, and under what conditions, their position of power in domestic politics, expressed by the notion of a concurrent majority carries over into the formulation of major departures in British foreign policy.[20] The study will also pose the fundamental question of whether policy-making in an industrial democracy can or should be reduced to an interplay among organized interests and party factions reflecting interest coalitions. The analysis entails a division into spheres of functional representa-

[19] *Ibid.*, pp. 133-134. Formulating group influence in this manner, by identifying a veto power, may be one way of dealing with LaPalombara's objection, from the Italian experience, that it is impossible to measure influence of groups over administrative decisions. See Joseph LaPalombara, "The Utility and Limitations of Interest Group Theory in Non-American Field Situations," in *Comparative Politics*, eds. Harry Eckstein and David Apter (Glencoe: The Free Press, 1963), p. 425. The application of Dahl's criteria for the measurement of power is an alternative conception. See below, Chap. 10.

[20] Major alternative dimensions of analysis do exist, and while they lie beyond the scope of this work, their existence merits acknowledgement. In particular there is the obvious relevance of integration theory, as set forth in such works as Ernst Haas, *The Uniting of Europe* (Stanford: Stanford University Press, 1958) and *Beyond the Nation State* (Stanford: Stanford University Press, 1964); Karl Deutsch, *et al.*, *Political Community in the North Atlantic Area* (Princeton: Princeton University Press, 1957); and Amitai Etzioni, *Political Unification* (New York: Holt, Rinehart and Winston, 1965). The conclusions of the present study, which posit an inverse relationship between pressure group influence and progress toward European unity, also raise serious questions about the applicability of David Mitrany's functionalist thesis, particularly the proposition that the surest route to political integration is through de-politicization and a concentration on economic or technical issues.

tion and party government. In the former area, treated in Part II, the focus is upon the three dominant sectional groups, the FBI, NFU, and TUC. In the case of the party government function, treated in Part III, the analysis covers the political parties, promotional groups, the press, and the expression of public opinion in polls and by-elections. Within this framework, four particular cases are considered: first, the ultimately unsuccessful negotiations for establishment of a Free Trade Area (FTA) during 1956-58; second, the establishment of the European Free Trade Association (EFTA) in the period 1958-60; third, the Macmillan Government's decision to apply for membership in the Common Market, and the subsequent negotiations during the years 1961-63; and fourth, the Labour Government's resumption of the Common Market application in 1966-67.

PRESSURE GROUPS AND EUROPEAN POLICY

An analysis of Britain's European policy-making between 1956 and 1967 indicates that the role of sectional pressure groups declined over this period of time. The thesis of the present study is that the change was caused by *politicization* of the European issue; that is, by an increase in the perception and treatment of European unity as a matter of major national importance rather than as a relatively specialized or economic question. The essential feature of politicization is that the subject is transferred from consideration by the processes of functional representation, where sectional pressure groups are dominant, to the channel of party government, where parties play the leading role. This does not require that the issue be subject to partisan dispute, though it may be.

Normally, in operating through the functional representation process, sectional pressure groups concentrate on questions of a technical nature. As Harry Eckstein notes in the case of the British Medical Association (BMA), group political power is based on "the non-controversial character" of the public policies and on the closed relationship between pressure group and Government ministry.[21] But politicization precludes the possibility of a closed administrative relationship; it lifts an issue into a less specialized and more public realm, one which implies wider attention, participation by political parties, and often controversy. This is what determines whether the sectional groups' concurrent majority power extends to the making of European policy.

It should be made clear that the term politicization will be applied when the overall *treatment* of European policy merits the label. The reason for this is that, in a sense, all the interactions analyzed here are political in their *content,* as for example Almond and Powell argue in their definition of the political system:

When we speak of the political system we include all the interactions which affect the use or threat of use of legitimate physical coercion. The political system includes not only governmental institutions such as legislatures, courts and administrative agencies, but *all structures in their political aspects.* Among these are traditional structures such as kinship ties and caste groupings; and anomic phenomena such as assassinations, riots and demonstrations; as well as formal organizations like parties, interest groups, and the media of communication.[22]

As a result, the usage adopted in this study can be regarded as only a specialized case within Almond and Powell's all-encompassing framework.[23]

To be more systematic, it seems useful to identify three

---

[21] Eckstein, *op. cit.,* p. 92. Potter makes basically the same point, *op. cit.,* p. 233.

[22] Almond and Powell, *op. cit.,* p. 18.

[23] Employment of the term *politicization* invites possible misconception. In order to clarify the terminology, it should be understood that politicization applies here to the status of those issues which enter the realm of diffuse or general purpose politics. Non-politicization applies to issues treated in the context of specific or special purpose politics. S. H. Beer has suggested "publicization" and "privatization" as alternative designations. It must also be emphasized that politicization is not synonymous with partisan dispute since there are circumstances in which bi-

necessary indicators of politicization. The *first* of these is the handling of the issue by primarily political ministries (such as the Foreign Office) rather than by economic ones (such as the Board of Trade and the Treasury). There is little provision for formal consultative processes in the former case, while in the latter arrangement groups are normally accorded an intimate corporate role. Although the Foreign Office may receive deputations from groups such as the TUC, these are heard as bodies of standing within the country rather than in their capacity as sectional representatives. Under these circumstances such groups are far less likely to influence the making of foreign than domestic policy.[24] The *second* indicator is the existence of involvement by the broader public. At a minimum it implies that an issue passes from the exclusive scrutiny of an elite or specialized audience to the notice of the attentive public.[25] This is reflected in the activity of promotional pressure groups and attention to the issue in the communications media (including the mass press) and in by-elections and opinion polls. The significance of such involvement is that it

partisan or tripartisan accord exists over manifestly politicized issues. This point is elaborated upon in Chapter 10.

"Politicization" is also used in different contexts, but with related meanings, by Karl Deutsch, *et. al., op. cit.,* pp. 46-47; and by Ernst Haas and Philippe Schmitter, "Differential Patterns of Political Integration in Latin America," in *International Political Communities* (Garden City, New York: Anchor, 1966), pp. 261-262.

[24] One listing of 700 central advisory committees presented to the House of Commons in 1949 included only two attached to the Foreign Office and both of these were highly specialized. The two committees were both in the Foreign Office's German Section: the Book Selection Committee and the Scientific Committee for Germany. Potter, *op. cit.,* pp. 223-225.

[25] "Elite" and "attentive public" are here used in the manner of Gabriel Almond's basic approach. The "Attentive public" is "informed and interested in foreign policy problems, and . . . constitutes the audience for the foreign policy discussion among the elites." The "policy and opinion elites" are "the articulate policy-bearing stratum of the population which gives structure to the public, and which provides the effective means of access to the various groupings," *The American People and Foreign Policy* (rev. ed.; New York: Praeger, 1960), p. 138.

conflicts with the essentially private process of bargaining between government and sectional pressure groups. The *third,*
and most important, of the indicators is the participation of
the political parties. Since public opinion sets few limits upon
foreign policy[26] the crucial element in politicization, and in
the limitation of group influence, becomes the political parties.
This is so because party involvement interferes with the exclusively technical consideration of an issue in a closed relationship between administrative department and sectional
pressure group. It also provides the opportunity—though certainly not the assurance—that judgments may be rendered on
the basis of an interpretation of broad national interest rather
than on mere cost-benefit calculations of importance mainly to
sectional interests.

If the above three factors are indicators of politicization,
what are its causes? The onset of politicization appears to be
determined by a combination of external events and conscious
choices. Thus a pressing international situation may thrust a
subject into the forefront of national attention, or at least
make such treatment possible. What events do is to create a
propensity toward politicization. They are at least the necessary, if not always the sufficient, condition. Internally, a conscious choice by political or governmental figures is almost
always essential before politicization can occur. For example,
despite the importance of the EEC, neither Conservative nor
Labour leaders consciously chose to treat European unity as a
salient political matter until 1961.

There is also a normative aspect to the present study. It is
an implied preference that parties rather than interest groups

---

[26] British voters tend to be bipartisan on foreign policy, and concentrate their attention on domestic matters. Their tendency to vote on
the basis of domestic issues is analyzed in Max Beloff, *New Dimensions
in Foreign Policy: A Study in British Administrative Experience, 1947-
1959.* (London: Allen and Unwin, 1961), p. 15; Jean Blondel, *Voters,
Parties and Leaders* (Harmondsworth, Middlesex: Penguin, 1966), pp.
75-87; and Kenneth Younger, "Public Opinion and British Foreign
Policy," *International Affairs* 40, no. 1 (January 1964): 22-25.

play the greater role in the shaping of public policy. Thus politicization is viewed as desirable because it transfers consideration of an issue from a situation where pressure groups normally enjoy a corporatist relationship with the administrative departments to one in which parties possess the dominant voice, or at least create the discretionary powers for leaders to make independent judgments reflecting their own assessment of where the general interest lies. This is not to say that pressure groups do not perform essential functions. Without question they are necessary in promoting interchange between society and government and in furnishing advice, acquiescence, and approval. Yet, although pressure groups successfully perform a representational function, there are ways in which parties fulfill the role in a more complete manner.

One way of evaluating the difference between pressure groups and parties is to make reference to the functions which parties perform, then seek to judge whether pressure groups can carry out these same tasks. Almond offers a useful categorization of functions,[27] but a slightly different classification will be employed here. According to Sigmund Neumann,[28] parties perform four functions: first, organizing the public will; second, educating the private citizen to political responsibility; third, constituting a connecting link between government and public opinion; and fourth, selecting leaders. Of these tasks, pressure groups cannot necessarily be said to carry out the second (educating the citizen), nor do they fully carry out the fourth (selection of leaders). But the most important difference between pressure groups and parties is that parties aggregate interests along with at least an implicit conception of the public interest,[29] whereas pressure groups—whatever

[27] Almond cites the functions of interest articulation, interest aggregation, political recruitment and political socialization, *op. cit.,* pp. 98-107 *et passim.*

[28] "Toward a Comparative Study of Political Parties," in Sigmund Neumann (ed.), *Modern Political Parties* (Chicago: University of Chicago Press, 1956), p. 397.

[29] The term "public interest" is, as Finer observes, a "social fiction,"

their notions of free enterprise, agricultural prosperity, or working class advancement, as mentioned above—are not readily suited for taking into account such broad purposes.[30] Thus it will be argued that, because of their difference of interest and perspective, the predominance of sectional interests in the early formulation of European policy inevitably complicated Britain's efforts to come to terms with European unity.

---

but a beneficial one. In this context it is employed in a restrained version of Rousseau's General Will, meaning the overall interest of society, rather than the Benthamite notion of the sum of sectional satisfactions, Finer, *op. cit., pp.* 108-111. The concept of common good is in the nature of party government, according to both R. T. McKenzie and S. H. Beer.

[30] The limitations are not confined to the sectional groups, but extend to the nature of the functional representation channel in which they operate. In general, functional representation tends to manifest a static bias, is essentially non-responsible, provides bargaining advantages for those interests which are better organized, and minimizes more diffuse considerations of public benefit. The main sectional groups play little role in the overt democratic process conducted by elected representatives of the public, yet they maintain an essential and often secretive dialogue with government officials. Frequently, the outline of legislative proposals is thus determined before they reach Parliament. See Andrew Shonfield, *Modern Capitalism* (New York: Oxford University Press, 1965), p. 389. Bernard Crick has also criticized functional representation on the basis that compromises hammered out between groups and the Administration may be excessive, and ministries and civil servants in dealing privately with interest representatives tend to treat their attitudes as fixed, hence become pessimistic on the possibilities of change. *Observer* (London), October 23, 1966.

Chapter 2

The Contemporary Historical Record

The contemporary record of proposals for British participation in a unified Europe[1] begins with Prime Minister Winston Churchill's dramatic wartime offer of June 15, 1940, "that Britain and France should become one nation with a common citizenship."[2] The offer was made at the instigation of Jean Monnet and Charles de Gaulle, approved by the Cabinet, and aimed at bolstering the sagging morale of French Prime Minister Paul Reynaud and the French people. Reynaud's Cabinet greeted the proposition with overwhelming suspicion, and soon afterward, France negotiated a separate peace with the victorious Germans.[3]

The next initiative came little more than a year after the end of the war, when Churchill called for the building of a

---

[1] For more detailed treatment of the history of British policy toward European unity, see Nora Beloff, *The General Says No* (Baltimore: Penguin, 1963); Emile Benoit, *Europe at Sixes and Sevens* (New York: Columbia University Press, 1961); Miriam Camps, *Britain and the European Community, 1955-1963* (Princeton: Princeton University Press, 1964); Uwe Kitzinger, *The Challenge of the Common Market* (4th ed.; Oxford: Basil Blackwell, 1962); George Lichtheim, *The New Europe* (New York: Praeger, 1963); John Pinder, *Britain and the Common Market* (London: Crescent Press, 1961); Michael Shanks and John Lambert, *Britain and the New Europe* (London: Chatto & Windus, 1962).

[2] Quoted in *Hansard, Parliamentary Debates* (Commons), Vol. 413 (August 16, 1945), c. 88-89.

[3] For an intriguing discussion of the June 1940 proposal see N. Beloff, *op. cit.*, pp. 43-45.

United States of Europe in his Zurich speech of September 1946. This speech did much to move European opinion in favor of integration, but the Europe he described was one in which Britain's involvement would be less than total. "In all this urgent work France and Germany must take the lead together. Great Britain, the British Commonwealth of Nations, mighty America, and I trust Soviet Russia . . . must be the friends and sponsors of the new Europe and must champion its rights to live and shine."[4] Advocacy of a united Europe thus was based on the assumptions that Britain remained a great power on the level of the U.S. and U.S.S.R., that Britain's Commonwealth relationships were paramount, and that Great Britain was to be a sponsor or well-wisher rather than a participant.

The reasons for British aloofness from involvement were abundant. The country had emerged from the war as one of the three major victorious powers. In striking contrast to the Continental states, she had been neither defeated nor occupied, her political and economic structures were intact, she headed an Empire and Commonwealth of three-quarters of a billion persons, and she maintained a close relationship with her American ally. Union with a prostrate and demoralized Europe offered no visible material advantages to Britain and her transoceanic involvements seemed to preclude any participation in a solely European grouping. Britain's immediate postwar posture is best described by the "three circles" concept, first enunciated by Winston Churchill. One Conservative leader later described it in the following way. "The position of Britain . . . is . . . quite unique, for we are a part, and an essential part, of . . . the three great unities of the world. The unity across the Atlantic, the unity within the British Commonwealth and Empire, and the unity with Western Europe."[5]

---

[4] Quoted in Hans J. Heiser, *British Policy with Regard to the Unification Efforts on the European Continent* (Leyden, The Netherlands: Sythoff, 1959), p. 25.

[5] H. A. Nutting, Joint Under-Secretary of State for Foreign Affairs, *Hansard,* Vol. 494 (Novembere 20, 1951), c. 237.

An overwhelming majority of British leaders subscribed to this view; it furnished the operative principle for Britain's world role until at least the late 1950's. Not only was the "three circles" notion dominant, but within it, the place accorded Europe was clearly of lesser priority than that of the Commonwealth or U.S. In January 1944 at Marrakech, Morocco, Churchill made this brutally clear when he said to de Gaulle, "How do you expect that the British should take a position separate from that of the U.S.? . . . each time we must choose between Europe and the open sea, we shall always choose the the open sea. Each time I must choose between you and Roosevelt, I shall always choose Roosevelt."[6]

As Churchill expressed it a few years later, the Empire and Commonwealth came first in Britain's thoughts; next, fraternal association of the English-speaking world; and, only then, the creation of a United Europe. Britain should help forward all efforts toward European unity, but must keep her role in all three of these groups in mind.[7]

The basic orientation of the Labour and Conservative parties largely coincided, despite considerable partisan disagreement over specific policies toward Europe. In addition to supporting the three circles concept, leaders of both parties, such as Clement Attlee, Ernest Bevin, Winston Churchill, Anthony Eden, and R. A. Butler heartily advocated European unity—but only in the most general terms. They also tended to agree that the desired form of partnership was intergovernmental cooperation along the lines of the Organization for European Economic Cooperation. It was crucial to them that final responsibility must rest with the national governments of the countries involved.

Chief among the considerations shaping the European policy of the 1945-1951 Labour Government was the fear that by participating in a European system in which important areas

---

[6] Quoted in David P. Calleo, *Europe's Future, The Grand Alternatives* (New York: Horizon Press, 1965), p. 124.

[7] *Hansard,* Vol. 476 (June 27, 1950), c. 2157-2162.

of national policy were surrendered to a supranational authority, Britain would find herself faced with a permanent anti-
Socialist majority. This concern became especially important
after 1947-48, when the right gained political domination in
Italy and France. While the Labour Party claimed to be guided
by the "firm conviction" that Britain must play a leading part
in the necessary close cooperation of the European peoples, it
held the view that any complete economic or political union
of Western Europe must be excluded because it would demand an unalterable uniformity within each participant country.[8] The Party's document on European policy stated in 1950,
"The Labour Party could never accept any commitments
which limited its own or others' freedom to pursue democratic
socialism, and to apply the economic controls necessary to
achieve it."[9] At most, Britain might consider the step-by-step
functional cooperation enunciated by the Foreign Secretary,
Ernest Bevin. Clearly, Labour's first priority was to carry
through its postwar social revolution; Europe was of decidedly
lesser importance.[10]

Despite the Conservatives' repeated condemnation of Labour's failure to advance the European cause in the period
from 1945 to 1951, their basic orientation was not in fact
far different from that of the Labour Government. Thus
Churchill opted for a rather spiritual kind of unity which
would involve sentiment and culture, but not constitutional,

---

[8] The Labour Party, *European Unity, A Statement by the National Executive Committee* (May, 1950), p. 8.

[9] *Ibid.,* p. 4.

[10] Even when Bevin was reported to have been leaning toward creation of a customs union with France in August 1947, officials of the Board
of Trade and Treasury were obstinate in their opposition to any closer
collaboration. Duff Cooper, then British Ambassador to France and a
staunch advocate of European unity attributes this "pig-headed" refusal
to two departmental principles: first, that in such a union Great Britain
stood to give to France in material terms more than she got back; and
second, that "nothing in the world matters except dollars, and that therefore no country counts except the United States," Duff Cooper, *Old Men
Forget* (London: Rupert Hart-Davis, 1953), pp. 376-381.

economic, or military matters. In 1950, he defined his view with consummate vagueness: "I do not wish to fall into generalities. Let me, therefore, express our policy as I see it in a single sentence. Britain and France should stretch out hands of friendship to Germany, and thus if successful, enable Europe to live again."[11] Churchill's unwillingness to commit himself to a concrete plan of British participation in a united Europe is at least partially attributable to his obsession with regaining power. While European unity was desirable, it did not appear to him as a winning election issue.

In the years following World War II, a multitude of European organizations were proposed or established. The first important step took place in 1947 when Britain, France, Belgium, the Netherlands, and Luxembourg signed a defense pact, the Brussels Treaty. This foreshadowed the establishment of NATO in 1949 and eventually led to the Western European Union as the vehicle for rearming Germany in 1954. In April 1948, the Organization for European Economic Cooperation was established to carry out the Marshall Plan. Then, following a 1948 Congress of Europe at The Hague, the Council of Europe was formed in May 1949. This organization joined the U.K. with most of the non-Communist European states,[12] and reflected an emergent European idealism. However, the differences of view concerning the organization's structure clearly reveal the divergent conceptions held by British and Continental leaders. While Ernest Bevin paid tribute to the idea of European unity, he resolutely opposed any federal arrangements. As a consequence, the Council of Europe came into being as an intergovernmental body, with its Committee of Ministers acting only on the basis of unanimity. Complete responsibility therefore remained with the member governments, and the organization possessed little power.

Nothing better illustrates the nature of Britain's European

---

[11] *Hansard,* Vol. 515 (May 11, 1953), c. 891-892.

[12] The original signatories were Britain, France, Belgium, Netherlands, Luxemburg, Denmark, Norway, Sweden, Ireland, and Italy.

policies and the underlying kinship of Labour and Tory attitudes than the developments accompanying the formulation of the Schuman Plan. On May 9, 1950, French Foreign Minister Robert Schuman put forward a proposal "for placing the whole of the Franco-German production of coal and steel under a common high authority in an organization open to other countries of Europe."[13] This arrangement implied the subjugation of the member states' coal and steel industries to a supranational authority and aimed at tying France and Germany together so as to make future war between them a virtual impossibility. Ultimately a Treaty setting up the European Coal and Steel Community (ECSC) was signed in April 1951 by France, Germany, Italy, and the Benelux countries; a few years later these same countries would join in creating the Common Market.

Britain had been approached during early 1949 by Jean Monnet, the originator of the proposal and the driving force behind European unity. In April, Britain's Chancellor of the Exchequer, Sir Stafford Cripps, sent three of his economists to a confidential meeting with Monnet and two of his associates at a villa near Paris. The meeting was a failure. One of the participants is later reported to have observed, "the British were talking in terms of a little extra French beef. . . . The French were talking about a supra-national edifice to merge the two economies into one."[14] Once it was clear that British leaders such as Bevin, Morrison, and Attlee opposed association on anything more than a most-favored nation basis, Monnet determined to go ahead in his project without Britain.[15]

---

[13] Quoted in *European Community* (June 1967), p. 4.

[14] N. Beloff, *op. cit.*, p. 54.

[15] Raymond Aron contends that the Schuman Plan was put forward so as to invite a refusal from London, *Observer*, April 3, 1960. At least one other scholarly interpretation also claims that the French preferred to keep Britain out, Ulrich Sahm, "Britain and Europe, 1950," *International Affairs* 43, no. 1 (January 1967): 12-24. Kenneth Younger disputes this contention and cites a persistent British "myopia" toward Europe, lasting until 1961, as the reason the U.K. did not seek to join in the Schuman Plan, *ibid.*, pp. 24-25. I am inclined to agree with Younger.

The official British response to the Schuman proposal came in a statement to Parliament by Prime Minister Attlee in June 1950. He observed that the French had required that Britain accept two principles as preconditions for negotiation: (1) the pooling of resources and (2) creation of a high authority whose decisions would be binding. Attlee refused to accept or to reject these conditions in advance, therefore the Government regretfully found it impossible to associate itself with the negotiations.[16] The Labour Party's National Executive Committee (NEC) put this rejection more forcefully, noting that "no Socialist government in Europe could submit to the authority of a body whose policies were decided by an anti-Socialist majority."[17] The Government's negative stand thus vitiated Bevin's claim that Britain was ready to participate in functional cooperation.

The Conservatives in the House of Commons excoriated the Government for its negative attitude and introduced a motion (also supported by the Liberals) urging that Britain accept the invitation to the Schuman talks, while reserving its freedom of action if discussions showed the plan not to be practicable. Eden praised the Schuman plan as important to peace, and claimed that it should even have been acceptable to Labour under the terms of a resolution carried at that Party's Annual Conference in 1948.[18] In turn, Churchill urged British participation in the negotiations and stated that the Conservative and Liberal parties were prepared to consider the abrogation of national sovereignty, provided they were satisfied with conditions and safeguards.[19]

---

[16] *Hansard*, Vol. 476 (June 13, 1950), c. 35-36.

[17] Quoted by Arthur Koestler, who adds the comment that this amounts to a "mild British version of the Russian 'Socialism in One Country' policy," in Lewis Galantière (ed.), *America and the Mind of Europe* (London: Hamish Hamilton, 1951), pp. 53-54.

[18] The Conservative proposal foresaw Britain's participation in the talks on the same basis under which the Dutch had accepted participation. *Hansard*, Vol. 476 (June 26, 1950), c. 1907-1922.

[19] *Ibid.* (June 27, 1950), c. 2157-2162.

As a result of Churchill's European speeches and the Party's position on the ECSC, the Conservatives came to be regarded on the Continent as the European Party. However, once they regained power in November 1951, they did not take long to confirm their basic policy agreement with Labour. By merely endorsing friendship and a desire for close association with the ECSC, rather than offering to participate fully, the new Government made clear that Britain under the Conservatives was no more ready to offer its full commitment to Europe than Britain had been under Labour.[20]

Policy toward the European Defense Community followed a pattern not unlike that toward ECSC. In August 1950, Churchill had successfully moved a resolution in the Assembly of the Council of Europe, advocating establishment of a European army subject to a European Minister of Defense and to European democratic control. Then in October, French Prime Minister Réné Pleven obtained approval in principle from the National Assembly for just such a European army "under a single European political and military authority."[21] There followed an attempt at creating a European Defense Community (EDC), also known as the Pleven Plan. Britain, still under the Labour Government, supported EDC but refused to participate, citing the arrangement as excessively federal and insufficiently Atlantic.[22] At the same time, the Government's position owed something to a general antipathy toward Germany and German rearmament, particularly within the Labour Party. However the Opposition Conservatives forthrightly advocated British participation of some kind, and Churchill's son-in-law, Duncan Sandys, termed the proposal "undoubtedly the most important recommendation which the

---

[20] See the statement to Parliament by H. A. Nutting, *Hansard,* Vol. 493 (November 12, 1951), c. 7-8.

[21] Quoted in *European Community* (June 1967), p. 4.

[22] See, for example, the comments of Ernest Bevin, *Hansard,* Vol. 481 (November 29, 1950), c. 1172-1174; and Kenneth Younger, *ibid.,* Vol. 484 (February 12, 1951), c. 156-157.

European Assembly has made."[23] Eden, and Churchill himself, added their support."[24]

The new Conservative Government therefore stunned the
Europeans when, despite the impression left by previous statements, it refused to join the EDC. As put forward by Foreign
Minister Eden, this rejection was phrased not negatively but
through a pledge of wholehearted support for the EDC within a broad Atlantic framework; the EDC treaties were too
supranational for Britain's taste.[25] Churchill justified his Government's policy by saying that his original idea had lacked
the objectionable supranational features, which the EDC proposals contained; other Tory spokesmen argued it was now
too late to reshape EDC arrangements, or that doing so would
produce a delay disastrous for European defense.[26]

In an effort to overcome the supranational obstacles to
Britain's participation in the ECSC and EDC, Eden made a
proposal in March 1952, which provided that the Council of
Europe be reorganized in order to provide the institutions for
these and other future organizations. At the same time the
Council of Europe would continue to function as a channel
for Western European intergovernmental cooperation.[27] The
Eden Plan failed completely, the Europeans viewing it as a
method of granting Britain the advantages of participation
without its responsibilities. Eventually, the EDC proved impossible to salvage, and it collapsed when the French National
Assembly rejected the proposal in August 1954. At that point,
Eden was instrumental in establishing the Western European
Union as a substitute framework for German rearmament,
linking Britain with the Six. Once again, Britain had found
a means for associating herself with the Continent without

---

[23] *Hansard*, Vol. 480 (November 13, 1950), c. 1415.
(February 12, 1951), c. 50.
[24] See *Hansard*, Vol. 481 (November 30, 1950), c. 1333; and Vol. 484
[25] *Hansard*, Vol. 496 (February 28, 1952), c. 1467-1468.
[26] *Hansard*, Vol. 500 (May 14, 1952), c. 1580.
[27] *Hansard*, Vol. 498 (March 24, 1952), c. 32-33.

participating in a European federation or altering her role in the Atlantic framework. Obviously, as Churchill had put it, Britain was still "with," but not "of" Europe.[28]

June 1955 marks a watershed in Britain's relations with Europe. It was on this date, less than a year after the failure of EDC, that the Foreign Ministers of the six ECSC countries began their talks at Messina with a view to establishing what was to become the European Common Market. Although Britain was represented at first by an observer from the Board of Trade (BOT), he withdrew in November, and Britain played no part in the Spaak Committee's drafting of the arrangements for the Common Market and Euratom, nor in the drawing up of the Treaties of Rome which the Six signed on March 25, 1957. The Government disliked the Common Market proposal because it cut across the existing OEEC arrangements, contained supranational features, and appeared to conflict with Britain's Commonwealth and Atlantic ties. Britain was willing to consider only limited free trade, not the common external tariff and institutional arrangements envisaged by the Six. What is more, most officials held the view that this was merely another elaborate paper scheme of the Continentals, and nearly certain to fail.[29] In the House of Commons there was an almost complete absence of reference to the subject until July 1956; the fact that the Europeans were engaged in a dramatic departure involving merger of their economic systems and the aim of eventual political integration seems to have been appreciated by neither British political leaders nor the public.

In late 1955, the British had withdrawn from the meetings of the Six after Belgium's Paul-Henri Spaak confronted them with an ultimatum to negotiate or get out. Beginning in early 1956, the question of Britain's relations with the Six was taken

---

[28] *Hansard*, Vol. 515 (May 11, 1953), c. 891-892.

[29] This skepticism, often privately expressed in earthy language, was widespread among civil servants and others who dealt with European matters.

up by an interdepartmental committee led by R. W. B. Clarke of the Treasury, and under explicit instructions to concentrate on problems for the British economy and to avoid high politics.[30] Eventually the committee brought forth a list of recommendations, including one which later led to the proposed Free Trade Area. Later, in mid-1956, the Government passed over a renewed opportunity to negotiate with the Six in establishing the Common Market. Yet again, Britain would respond to European proposals by seeking an arrangement giving her associational entrée without the commitment of full membership, but this time she would be painfully unsuccessful.

What conclusions can be drawn from statements during the period 1945 to 1956? Basically, successive British governments never seriously entertained European proposals and radical departures. Although continually claiming to be pro-European, Britain managed to find objections to each European initiative. Her policy became one of minimal concessions at each step, and of associational status rather than full membership in the various groupings. Even those in Britain who favored unity were anti-federal, and generally stressed the need to enter talks in the formative stages in order to shape the organizations away from a supranational orientation. A Great Power illusion also played a large part in the British attitude, especially until the October 1956 Suez crisis, and it contributed to a general consensus on European policy. If the U.K. had her own world role, then she could only be "in" but not "of" Europe.

With the exception of the consistently pro-European Liberals, party differences were determined by circumstances and partisanship rather than any fundamental divergence of outlook. The major disagreements developed within rather than between the parties. Both Labour and the Tories basically rejected participation in federal arrangements, but each party

---

[30] See N. Beloff, *op. cit.,* p. 75.

did so for its own reasons. The dominant sentiment was one of great hesitation toward any sort of European venture. Indeed, in later trying to come to terms with the Six through the device of the FTA, the Government would face more opposition from those who felt this was going too far than from those who believed it was not going far enough.

PART II

FUNCTIONAL REPRESENTATION AND
EUROPEAN UNITY

Chapter 3

The Free Trade Area

Britain's first major effort to come to terms with the emergent unity of the Six, which were then in the early stages of establishing the European Economic Community, was to seek creation of a wide Free Trade Area (FTA) to link the newly formed Common Market group with the other Western European members of the OEEC. This chapter will set out the complex sequence of events, then deal with the role of each of the major British sectional pressure groups (Trades Union Congress, National Farmers' Union, and Federation of British Industries) in the formation of Britain's policy toward the FTA. The picture which emerges here, as well as in Chapter 6 (which analyzes the same period in terms of the party government perspective), is one of an almost entirely non-politicized treatment of European unity, in which the FTA was dealt with as a basically economic and technical matter and the sectional groups exercised substantial influence in shaping and restricting the terms of the British approach.

THE SEQUENCE OF EVENTS

The conception of the Free Trade Area formally originated in a report by a group under the chairmanship of the Belgian Foreign Minister, Paul-Henri Spaak, which was presented to the Foreign Ministers of the Six on April 21, 1956. The Spaak

Report set out the framework and philosophy for the Common Market and largely established the basis for negotiating the Treaties of Rome, but it also provided for an arrangement whereby other countries might join with the Six in a free trade area.[1]

While the process of drafting treaties for the establishment of the EEC began, the Council of the OEEC decided in July 1956 to study possible forms of association between the proposed customs union and other OEEC members.[2] The organization therefore set up a working party including members from all seventeen OEEC countries under the direction of Baron Snoy of Belgium. In January 1957 this group published its report stating that establishment of a free trade area was technically feasible.

Meanwhile the British Government had undertaken a reappraisal of its European policy and accompanying hostility toward the Common Market. After consultations with the Commonwealth countries and major domestic interest groups in industry, agriculture, and labor, the Government formally decided in November 1956 that it would be desirable to enter negotiations for establishment of an industrial free trade area in Europe. In early February 1957, the Government published a White Paper setting out its views, and circulated this to the OEEC.[3] The British proposal provided for the eventual establishment of free trade in industrial goods through the removal of restrictions on trade such as tariffs and quotas. Unlike the proposed Common Market, it made no provision for economic integration, harmonization of financial and social policies,

---

[1] For a complete chronology see *Negotiations for a European Free Trade Area, Report on the Course of Negotiations up to December, 1958* (Cmnd. 648, Her Majesty's Stationery Office, January, 1959). Also see accompanying Documents (Cmnd. 641).

[2] The Six included Belgium, France, Germany, Italy, Luxemburg, and the Netherlands. Other members of the OEEC were Austria, Denmark, Greece, Iceland, Ireland, Norway, Portugal, Sweden, Switzerland, Turkey, and the U.K.

[3] *A European Free Trade Area* (Cmnd. 72, HMSO, February 1957).

strong institutions, or the inclusion of agriculture. The White Paper also required that Commonwealth preference remain unaltered. Although the British regarded the FTA as a bold move toward Europe, some OEEC members remained unsatisfied. Agriculture exporters, such as Denmark, Holland, Italy, and France, opposed the exclusion of agriculture from the proposal and argued that the U.K. sought to open European markets to her industrial exports while denying Britain's agricultural market to the Europeans.

Under the chairmanship of Peter Thorneycroft, then Chancellor of the Exchequer, the OEEC Ministers met on February 12 and 13 and decided to go forward with a free trade arrangement. The Council unanimously adopted a resolution that negotiations should begin "in order to determine ways and means on the basis of which there could be brought into being a European Free Trade Area."[4] However, Britain failed to get agreement on working toward an exclusively industrial FTA; indeed, the resolution drew special attention to the objective of expanding agricultural trade on a non-discriminatory basis. The resolution also left unanswered the questions involving external territories, colonies, and institutions.

On March 8, the OEEC Council set up three working parties. The first of these was to determine the conditions for establishment of an FTA, the second to deal with agricultural trade, the third to examine problems of the less developed European countries. The Six meanwhile had completed their own negotiations, and on March 25, 1957, they signed the Rome Treaties establishing the EEC and EURATOM. HMG[5] officially welcomed these signings, but sought rapid progress toward establishment of the FTA, hoping to see negotiations reach a successful conclusion early enough so that the first tariff cuts could begin simultaneously with those of the Six. The Prime Minister held separate talks with French and Ger-

---

[4] Cmnd. 648, p. 3.

[5] *HMG,* Her Majesty's Government, is the commonly used abbreviation for the British Government.

man leaders, who acknowledged the importance of the FTA. However, in May, France requested a delay in negotiations until ratification of the Rome Treaties had made substantial progress.

Eventually the OEEC Council met again on October 17, and unanimously passed a resolution declaring its determination to secure the completion of an FTA associating the EEC with other members and taking effect parallel to the Rome Treaty on January 1, 1959. The Council established an Inter-Governmental Committee at ministerial level to carry on negotiations, and on October 18 this group held its first meeting under the Chairmanship of the Paymaster General, Reginald Maudling. By this time it had become clear to the British Government that there was no possibility of reaching agreement on the simple FTA outlined in its February White Paper. Hence, the area of discussion in the Inter-Governmental Committee went well beyond the mere elimination of tariffs and quotas, to include rules for administering the definition of origin of industrial products, rules of competition, agriculture, coordination of economic policy, harmonization of legislation, payments, coal and steel, nuclear materials, movement of labor and capital, transport, and the position of overseas territories.

Britain now made certain concessions on agriculture. These were put forward by Reginald Maudling in a statement to the OEEC Committee in October and were later expanded and circulated in January 1958 as part of a draft outline of an agreement.[6] The new proposals provided for freer and increased agricultural trade and an annual review system. But although HMG was now willing to discuss agriculture, its proposals met with little response from the Six because Britain still wished to retain agricultural tariffs and Commonwealth agricultural preference.

There were further delays in the spring of 1958 while the

---

[6] Cmnd. 641, pp. 190-192.

Six prepared proposals of their own and while the French political crisis took place. Disagreements also developed over external tariffs, Imperial Preference, and French demands for special exemptions. The Inter-Governmental Committee met again in July, October, and November 1958, but on November 14, M. Jacques Soustelle announced to the press that France was formally rejecting the Free Trade Area, saying "it is not possible to create the FTA as wished by the British— that is, with free trade between the Common Market and the rest of the OEEC, but without a single external tariff barrier round the seventeen countries and without harmonization in the economic and social spheres."[7]

In the absence of unanimous determination to achieve an agreement, the talks were ended shortly afterward. The three broad areas of disagreement remaining were external tariffs, internal economic and social policies, and institutional arrangements.

During the two-year period (November 1956–November 1958) in which establishment of an FTA had been a British policy objective, a considerable shift in the Government's attitude took place. Originally, it had sought to confine arrangements to the removal of barriers to industrial trade. It sought to limit cooperation in economic policies and in agriculture to the existing OEEC mechanisms, and to exclude supranational elements from any free trade area treaty. With time, the British negotiators came to accept an increased role for institutions, some majority voting, arrangements for agriculture, and more extensive economic cooperation. However, this shift came too slowly and grudgingly.

Ironically, although originally France had been the country most anxious to ensure that at least some features of the tight institutional framework of the Common Market should be taken over into a free trade area, her attitude shifted in the opposite direction to Britain's. In a virtual reversal of position,

[7] *Financial Times* (London), November 15, 1958.

France moved in the fall of 1958 to the principle of unanimity in decision-making within FTA institutions. She felt that the FTA provided one-sided advantages for Britain, and that if Britain wanted advantages, she needed also to accept obligations of unity similar to those in the Common Market. Because France could not get her way in the FTA arrangements, she decided to protect her interests through use of escape clauses and preservation of her veto power.

This, then, was the external sequence of events and policies during the two years of active consideration of a Free Trade Area. Within this context, how did the major British interest groups operate and what role did they play in shaping Britain's FTA policy?

THE TRADES UNION CONGRESS

In order to consider the role of the Trades Union Congress (TUC) it is first necessary to examine the organization itself. The operation of the TUC in the formation of European policy will then be treated under three subsequent headings: policy, channels, and effectiveness.

Organization.—The TUC was established in 1868, and it is now the national coordinating body for most of organized labor in Britain.[8] Its total membership includes 176 unions with over 8½ million of the country's 9½ million trade unionists. This concentration is remarkably high compared to Continental standards, and can be measured by the indicators of *density* (percentage of potential membership actually belonging) and *amalgamation* (extent to which the organized have been brought into one body).[9] In terms of density, 42 percent

---

[8] For a more detailed treatment of the TUC and its operation as a pressure group see Samuel E. Finer, *Anonymous Empire* (2d ed. rev.; London: Pall Mall Press, 1966), p. 11; Henry Pelling, *A History of British Trade Unionism* (Baltimore: Penguin, 1963); Samuel H. Beer, *British Politics in the Collectivist Age* (New York: Knopf, 1965), pp. 334-336; Trades Union Congress, *ABC of the TUC* (London, 1965).

[9] Beer, *op. cit.*, p. 332. The notion of "density" comes from S. E. Finer.

of the total working population of Britain belong to trade unions (the TUC comprising slightly under 90 percent of those unionized). As far as amalgamation is concerned, the TUC has never been seriously challenged in its primacy as the foremost union organization; the only body of any consequence remaining outside it is the National Union of Teachers.

Since 1921 the executive body of the TUC has been the General Council. Its members are elected by an annual Congress and its purpose is to act as "the General Staff of Labour,"[10] giving centralized leadership to the trade union movement as a whole. In carrying out its responsibilities the General Council maintains regular contact with the Government, with employers' organizations and with a great number of advisory and consultative bodies dealing with social and economic matters. Indeed, the TUC is represented on more than sixty different public bodies, as well as forty private ones, ranging from the National Economic Development Council to the Employment of Prisoners Advisory Council.[11]

In exercising its influence, the TUC utilizes two major channels. One of these consists of intimate association with the Labour Party, which, as in the case of the Cooperative Societies, has often been regarded as "simply one wing of the Labour movement."[12] The trade unions possess 88 percent of the votes at the Party's Annual Conference, elect 18 of 28 members on the National Executive Committee (NEC), and, in 1959, sponsored 93 of 258 successful Labour candidates for the House of Commons.[13] Despite this strength, the unions usually work through the TUC's General Council rather than the Labour Party's NEC, and this is where the second channel comes into importance. The General Council has established

[10] Finer, *op. cit.*, p. 11.
[11] *ABC of the TUC*, p. 11 and pp. 22-23.
[12] Richard Rose, *Politics in England, An Interpretation* (Boston: Little Brown, 1964), p. 124.
[13] *Ibid.*, pp. 124-125.

its right to governmental consultation on all ministerial actions, legislation, and administrative processes which affect
the interests of workers. This emphasis on consultation tran-
scends older notions and sharply diverges from the European
syndicalist tradition. As George Woodcock (the TUC General
Secretary) had said, "We exist to be near Government. Our
place is not on the soapboxes in Trafalgar Square but in the
Chancellor's private office, and we can't be both places at
once."[14]

Despite a trend toward increased authority, the TUC lacks
extensive powers over individual unions, the largest six of
which make up two-thirds of its total membership. It is thus
unable to intervene in wage policies of individual unions, to
effect changes in union structure or to intervene in interunion
disputes.[15] As a confederation, the TUC therefore tends to
avoid making formal recommendations of specific actions to
its affiliates. Given the somewhat archaic structure of British
trade unions, this has prompted criticism that the TUC is unable to keep order in its own house.[16] Nonetheless, the TUC
does function effectively in representing and in voicing concern for the interests of organized labor in Great Britain.

Policy.—It is not difficult to evaluate and understand the
position of the TUC on the FTA question. The reason is that
the criteria of full employment and improved living standards
governed its approach throughout the period. In this sense,
the TUC's concern was thoroughly pragmatic and economic.

From the start, the TUC's General Council regarded the
FTA proposal as one which merited careful and detailed
examination. In fact, its 1957 Annual Report judged that the
FTA was the "biggest issue on the economic front" which the

---

[14] Quoted from the *Observer*, September 1, 1963, in Lord Windlesham, *Communication and Political Power* (London: Jonathan Cape,
1966), p. 163.

[15] Beer, *op. cit.*, p. 336.

[16] See, for example, the criticisms of Michael Shanks, *The Stagnant
Society* (Baltimore: Penguin, 1961), pp. 75-78.

TUC needed to face during the year.[17] This contrasted strikingly with the relative lack of attention paid to Europe by the political parties.

The first formal statement of TUC policy emerged from a joint meeting of the Economic and International Committees of the General Council on November 2, 1956. Its main points were, first, that Britain could not become a full member of the EEC; second, there would be serious economic and political disadvantages if Britain stayed entirely aloof; third, an FTA along "progressive lines" could improve living standards and decrease national antagonisms in Europe; fourth, the Government must keep the General Council regularly informed and fully consulted on matters under negotiation; and fifth, there should be reasonable safeguards for working people in Britain and the other countries, and the Government must be willing to take necessary action to mitigate any internal hardships caused by the transition to an FTA. The General Council forwarded this statement to the Government, which was then still in the process of policy formulation.

As a means of implementing its policy the TUC submitted to the Government, in June 1957, a draft clause on full employment for inclusion in the proposed FTA Treaty. The clause called on each member government to formulate a full employment objective, to present an annual report to a Central Authority on measures taken to implement full employment, to take powers to influence consumption and investment, to secure a balanced distribution of industry, and to develop maximum use of national employment services. Member governments were to interpret other treaty provisions in light of full employment programs.[18] The TUC persisted in its demand for a formal Treaty commitment to full employment, and this later became a central element in TUC policy toward EFTA and the Common Market.

---

[17] Quoted in *Financial Times*, August 30, 1957.

[18] TUC, *Report of Proceedings at the 89th Annual Trades Union Congress* (1957), pp. 270-276.

On balance, the TUC favored British membership in the FTA—as did the Labour and Conservative parties, and the FBI. The debate at the September 1957 Annual Congress made this clear. Though no vote was taken, supporters out-numbered critics. Spokesmen for the General Council ex-pressed the belief that the FTA would offer economic expan-sion and higher efficiency, which would in turn promote full employment and better living standards. Perhaps the stress put by the leadership on full employment explains the easy approval the FTA received. Opposition came from those whose own industries might be threatened. Thus the two members of the General Council most opposed to the FTA were L. T. Wright (Weavers) and J. E. Newton (Tailors and Garment Workers), both of whom represented workers whose industries expected harm from FTA entry. There was also a brief attack on the FTA as a capitalist device.

One other rather theoretical consideration governed TUC policy toward European unity at this time. This was the fear that the Common Market would be a first step toward com-plete integration and the development of a central authority which could overrule national governments on important economic matters. TUC leaders felt such a change would be undesirable since they viewed most governments of the Six as having less favorable ideas on economic and social policy than the British Government, albeit a Conservative one. Even more important for the TUC—as for other sectional interest groups—was the structural change involved. A transfer of authoritative decision-making power to a supranational body would drastically weaken the effective influence of the TUC. In a new European Community, the sectional veto which British labor unions often hoped to exercise upon their own Government's policies would no longer be so significant. That is, even though operation of a concurrent majority might persist at the national level, its existence would be far less im-portant because the determination of economic policies would have been removed to a supranational authority upon which the British Government—and the British public—would possess only partial influence.

Integration theorists such as Leon Lindberg have observed that Community-wide pressure groups have emerged to exert their common interests upon the EEC at Brussels as the Community organs have taken on decision-making functions in areas once exclusively the province of national governments.[19] Although still in its preliminary stages, this process is regarded as offering a new channel for sectional groups to influence policy outcomes. On the other hand, even in some future federal Europe with effective transnational interest groupings, the influence of a single national trade union organization (e.g., the TUC) still would be considerably less than in a national context. It is thus readily understandable that the TUC preferred European cooperation to proceed along the intergovernmental OEEC pattern. Pressure group concerns of this nature emerge again later, for example, on the part of the NFU over the Common Market question.

Channels.—Communication between the TUC and Government took place mainly through meetings and correspondence between the Government's Economic Ministers (President of the Board of Trade, Chancellor of the Exchequer, Paymaster General) and the Economic Committee of the TUC's General Council, led first by W. L. Heywood, then by J. Alan Birch.

The impetus for direct TUC-Governmental consultation came from the General Council. In October 1956, shortly after the Government had announced it was considering association with Europe, the General Council wrote the Chancellor of the Exchequer, Peter Thorneycroft, requesting information about the proposal.[20] Accordingly, the Economic Committee had the first of many meetings with Thorneycroft and the President of the Board of Trade, David Eccles, on October 23. The

---

[19] *The Political Dynamics of European Economic Integration* (Stanford: Stanford University Press, 1963).

[20] TUC, *Report* (1957), p. 268.

TUC representatives asked for clarification of the Government's intent on minimizing any difficulties in U.K. industry during a transition period. They also sought to determine whether the Government would reserve the right to promote particular economic or social policies, and what provisions there would be for action to secure fair labor standards and full employment. In turn, the Chancellor of the Exchequer explained the benefits of associating Britain with Europe, assured them that no decision had yet been taken on the form of association, and stressed the Government's wish for the fullest consultation with the TUC on all aspects of the proposals.[21]

The next set of exchanges coincided with the issuing of the February 1957 White Paper. The Economic Committee held talks with Peter Thorneycroft, David Eccles, and the Economic Secretary to the Treasury, Nigel Birch. This meeting produced Government reassurances that full employment was an objective of the European proposals and that measures would be taken to provide alternative employment for workers displaced through the lowering of tariffs. The Ministers again reassured the TUC leaders that they would be kept informed as the negotiations proceeded.

In March, the TUC issued its first demand for formal inclusion of full employment as an article of the proposed Treaty. This took the form of a long and detailed memorandum, which the TUC sent to the Chancellor of the Exchequer. The Government replied in detail in April, and late the following month the Economic Committee met with the President of the Board of Trade—again on full employment. This meeting led to the TUC's submitting its draft treaty clause to the Chancellor of the Exchequer in June. Subsequently the TUC pushed this demand in meetings with Britain's chief negotiator, Reginald Maudling (then Paymaster General). In October 1957, and again in January, July, and October 1958, members of the Economic Committee had further lengthy

---

[21] *Ibid.*

meetings with the Paymaster General, who also drew up written statements for them on developments in the FTA negotiations.

The one other channel of communication between TUC and Government provides an interesting example of how a domestic interest group can avail itself of foreign leverage to apply pressure on its own Government. In mid-May, the Fourth European Regional Conference of the International Confederation of Free Trade Unions (a body known as the European Regional Organization, or ERO) was held at Brussels. The TUC was represented there by four members of the General Council: W. L. Heywood, Frank Cousins, Sir Charles Geddes, and W. E. Jones. The conference discussed FTA Treaty provisions, and adopted a resolution stressing the need for full employment, increased living standards, and the right of unions to be consulted at every stage in negotiation and implementation of the Treaty. Copies of this statement were sent to the Chancellor of the Exchequer and the President of the Board of Trade. Thus when the TUC put forward its draft clause on full employment in June, it could muster whatever additional influence there was in the fact that it was following common views established within the European union movement as a whole.

Similar developments took place during and after the Fifth ERO Conference at Brussels in May 1958. As well as deciding to strengthen ERO machinery for coordination of trade union policy on the FTA, the conference adopted a strong resolution on the need for the establishment of institutions to secure full employment. In August, the ERO sent its policy statement to the Chairman of the OEEC negotiating committee (Reginald Maudling), as well as to member governments. At its October meeting with the Paymaster General, the TUC stressed its agreement with the ERO position.

The importance of this ICFTU channel does not seem to have been very great, though it provided some reinforcement of TUC pressures. Its real significance lay in the framework which it established for eventual trade union policy coordination within the expected FTA. In this respect, the unions found themselves ahead of the farmers and industrialists in organizing international cooperation with their European counterparts. While this situation does not seem to have concerned the Government or other sectional groups, the labour correspondent of *The Director,* the influential journal of the Institute of Directors, expressed his fear of a powerful international labor cartel within the FTA. After attacking the TUC's insistence that full employment and rising living standards must be maintained (demands which he felt they had been making *ad nauseam),* he went on to gauge the implications of the TUC's efforts, saying "the road from the TUC to the Treasury is worn smooth by union leaders seeking information and imposing conditions which, if conceded altogether, would hamstring negotiations."[22]

Effectiveness.—What, then, was the actual outcome of the TUC's policies and with what success did it pursue these through the channels mentioned above? First, the TUC succeeded in obtaining substantial and continued consultation. In essence, this process involved the supplying of information, explanation, and reassurances by Government Ministers to the TUC's Economic Committee. Yet while the Government listened seriously to the TUC's reservations and proposals, there is no evidence that Britain's position in the negotiations was modified as a result of trade union pressures.

Second, the TUC obtained assurances on national policies which were definitely in line with TUC aims on full employment, improved living standards, and other safeguards. Although the TUC was not fully content with measures short of a formal treaty commitment, its representations to the Government on employment were at least successful in eliciting pledges that necessary steps would be taken on a national level and later in coordination with other FTA members.

---

[22] "The Workers' Cartel in Europe," *The Director* (February, 1958), p. 304.

Third, the soundings both revealed and developed a substantial area of agreement between TUC and Government. They shared the view that the FTA would be broadly beneficial for Britain's economy and that it would be harmful for the U.K. to remain aloof from association with Europe. The Government also reassured the TUC that European cooperation would not be pursued along Common Market lines.

Despite HMG's refusal to push for the inclusion of full employment in the Treaty, the TUC was likely to have supported membership had the Free Trade Area negotiations succeeded. J. A. Birch candidly put this point during the debate at the TUC Congress in September 1958, when he stated that the General Council was continuing to urge its full employment position upon the Government, but that he rejected the idea that Britain should not negotiate if the provision were not in the treaty.[23]

THE NATIONAL FARMERS' UNION

Organization.—The NFU was established in 1908, and now contains more than 200,000 farmers, or between 75 and 80 percent of the potential membership in England and Wales.[24] Whereas the TUC, powerful as it is, represents less than 40 percent of the total working population, and the FBI has had to share business and industrial leadership with several other peak organizations, the NFU enjoys the most impressive sectional concentration in terms of both density and amalgamation. Indeed, unlike the large unions such as the Transport and General Workers' Union (T&GWU) or the large firms such as Imperial Chemical Industries (ICI), which function as powerfully independent voices within their respective spheres, few groupings exist to detract from NFU pri-

---

23 TUC, *Report of Proceedings at the 90th Annual Trades Union Congress* (1958), pp. 446-447.

24 Finer, *op. cit.*, p. 9. Scotland and Ulster have their own organizations, which closely cooperate with the NFU.

macy.[25] It is no exaggeration to describe the NFU as the embodiment of the agricultural sector.

Prior to 1945, the NFU maintained ties with the Conservative Party, though on a considerably looser basis than those of the TUC with the Labour Party. Following World War II, however, the NFU adopted a position of strict electoral neutrality, determining to work with whatever Government held power. First the experience of wartime cooperation and then the 1947 Agricultural Act gave the NFU an exceptionally intimate position in relationship to the Ministry of Agriculture. This channel of communication and influence was far more important than the channel the Union continued to maintain with the parliamentary agricultural committees of the major parties. The Agricultural Act specifically named the NFU as the spokesman for agriculture in the Ministry's Annual Review of the industry. This led to a situation in which the Union was able to pressure the Government to shape the agricultural program in the direction of its wishes and to require a formal NFU endorsement for each year's final settlement. These circumstances produced professionalization within the NFU,[26] and also increased its power over its own membership to an extent considerably greater than that prevailing in the TUC or FBI. Even more than in the other sectional groups, leadership constituted a highly important independent variable in the determination of the NFU's role, and Sir James Turner (later Lord Netherthorpe) guided the organization with great skill and subtlety during his tenure from 1945 to 1960.

In consequence of the extremely intimate relationship of consultation and bargaining with the Administration, the Union's overt political activity decreased substantially. None-

---

[25] There are other bodies such as the Country Landowners Association and the National Union of Agricultural Workers, but they lack the structure and resources of the NFU.

[26] See Peter Self and Herbert J. Storing, *The State and the Farmer* (London: Allen & Unwin, 1962), p. 63; and Finer, *op. cit.*, p. 38.

theless, it continued to benefit from the inherent place of agriculture within the ethos of the Conservative Party. During a 1962 Conference debate on Common Market entry, a Tory MP, Sir Harmar Nicholls, could quite naturally observe "this is a Conservative Conference. We are the farmers' party."[27] The NFU also benefited from the social structure of the Conservative Party, which produced over a score of large landowners as MP's, and greater numbers of others who dabbled in farming or exhibited a sentimental attachment to it. In addition, the Conservative Party relied to some extent on the agricultural vote, holding, as it did in 1956, 76 of 80 English agricultural seats.[28]

Perhaps surprisingly, the fact that farmers voted overwhelmingly Conservative did not prevent Labour from courting the farm vote. This was partly a function of the thin margins upon which British politics operate, partly a result of the way in which the Party, in Self and Storing's words, "seems almost to have been hypnotized by the image of agriculture held up by the Farmers' Union."[29] Whereas the NFU sought to exert political pressure by influencing Conservative MP's when a Tory Government held power, it concentrated on the Minister of Agriculture whenever Labour was in office. Tom Williams, Minister of Agriculture in the 1945-51 Government, maintained unusually close relations with the Union, and in 1950 the Labour Government went so far as to increase food prices rather than cut agricultural income.[30] Even Fred Peart, Minister of Agriculture in the Wilson Government, tended to take the side of the agricultural producers more readily than that of agricultural workers or consumers.

The NFU, as a sectional group representing the definite

27 National Union of Conservative and Unionist Associations, *81st Annual Conservative Conference* (Llandudno, October 10-13, 1962), p. 55.

28 Self and Storing, *op. cit.*, pp. 194-196.

29 *Ibid.*, pp. 203-204.

30 Roland J. Pennock, "The Political Power of British Agriculture," *Political Studies,* 7, no. 3 (October, 1959): 291-292.

economic interest of its members, also succeeded in linking agriculture with the public interest. Given the fact that only 4 percent of the British working population and the same percentage of the GNP are accounted for by the agricultural sector,[31] such a tie-in was a necessity if the NFU were to exert political influence. Not only did the Union promote the belief that "what is good for agriculture is good for the nation," but it also succeeded in tying support for agricultural policies to such unquestionably national concerns as the balance of payments, living costs, export competitiveness, and Commonwealth trading relationship. The record of British policy toward the Free Trade Area and the Common Market reflects this linkage.

Policy.—The National Farmers' Union did not oppose the Free Trade Area *per se,* but rather the inclusion of agriculture in any such arrangement. It argued that for foodstuffs, drink, and tobacco to be covered by the FTA would damage British agriculture and harm Commonwealth Preference. If the U.K. were to abolish tariffs and subsidies on agriculture, the home industry would lose considerable ground to European exports in Britain's home market. Since Britain was the world's largest importer of food, reversal of trade liberalization (e.g., by importing French wheat above world prices) would result in deterioration of the balance of payments, and increased food costs to the consumer. Britain would be required to support the agriculture of others while some of her own farmers suffered. Furthermore, if the U.K. withdrew preferences granted to agricultural imports from the Commonwealth, the Commonwealth in turn could be expected to withdraw preferences granted to British industrial exports. This point was of genuine importance, since at that time nearly half of Britain's total exports went to the Commonwealth, while only 13½ percent went to the Six and 14½ percent to the other Euro-

---

[31] Figures based on 1.09m. of a 24.6m. working population and GNP for 1958. Self and Storing, *op. cit.,* p. 15.

pean countries of the OEEC. The NFU did not object to international cooperation and consultation, but this could be done best through existing arrangements of the International Federation of Agricultural Producers (IFAP) and the OEEC Ministerial Committee for Agriculture and Food.[32]

The NFU mounted a strong case, and, as we shall see below, one which the Government and most leading sections of British opinion supported. But the case was rather too categorical in its refusal to consider any agreement on agriculture. Most European farmers did not seek free trade in agriculture. What they and their governments—especially those of Denmark, Holland, Italy, and France—did want was an agreement short of complete free trade. British agriculturists, however, feared that once they entered a Free Trade Area which had provision for agriculture, the logic of the new arrangements would change the minds of British politicians and the cherished support structure embodied in the 1947 Agriculture Acts would collapse, taking with it the subsidies and tariffs encouraging high U.K. output.

Eventually, the British Government found it necessary to modify its position in order to meet widespread European demands for the establishment of a regulated market in agriculture. In October 1957, HMG proposed that there be a separate agricultural agreement outside the FTA. The proposal involved arrangements in line with a May 1956 OEEC report, and included European consultations on price supports, coordination of policies to avoid stimulating marginal production of agricultural surpluses, integration of imports, and the abandoning of dumping and export subsidies.[33] The main aim of British policy was to avoid encouraging increased uneconomic production at home. Meanwhile, it had become more evident that the farmers' fears were misplaced, and after consultations with the Government, the NFU "welcomed"

---

[32] National Farmers' Union, *Information Service,* Vol. 12 (1957), p. 66.

[33] *Financial Times,* November 8, 1957.

the October statement. With tenuous justification the NFU maintained that, all along, it had been willing to see agriculture included in a separate agreement outside the FTA.[34]

Channels.—First, as one would expect given the NFU's exceptionally close relationship with the Ministry of Agriculture, there were discussions about the FTA at Ministerial level. These contacts took place through the Ministry's External Relations Division. The NFU also participated in talks at the Board of Trade and was consulted while the Government worked out details of proposals to break the FTA impasse in October 1957.[35]

Secondly, and as in the case of the TUC, the NFU made use of the European Conference of its International Organization, in this case the IFAP and its European Regional Committee. This body met at Brussels in April 1958. The main points emerging from its meetings concerned the need for reasonable agricultural living conditions, extended trade within Europe and with the outside world, and possible commodity arrangements. There was also a statement that agriculture should not be regarded as the main obstacle in the setting up of the FTA. Steps were taken to "acquaint" the British Government with the terms of an IFAP Resolution and to make it aware of the high degree of unanimity among European farmers on the need for a separate agricultural agreement.[36]

Whereas the TUC had exercised its influence mainly through the types of Ministerial and European levels mentioned above, the NFU also employed a third method: pressure from within major business groupings, particularly by means of its membership in the Federation of British Industries. Farmers constituted a very important market for industries such as chemical fertilizers and tractors, and their influence benefited from the activities of the NFU President, Sir James Turner, who established effective leadership on

---

[34] "Annual Report, 1958," *British Farmer* (January 10, 1959), p. 13.
[35] NFU, *Year Book* (1958), p. 18 *et passim*.
[36] *British Farmer* (January 10, 1959), p. 17.

agricultural matters within the FBI Grand Council. To the extent that agricultural concerns could be shown to involve important consequences for industry, as well as for Britain as a whole, the NFU acquired powerful leverage in adding the voice of the FBI to its own.[37] From the start, the NFU actively participated in the work of FBI committees concerned with overseas trade policy. To the special panel examining the original Messina (Common Market) proposals, the NFU explained why these were completely unacceptable for British agriculture and horticulture. The FBI acknowledged this exclusion.[38] Later the NFU expressed its position on the FTA in discussions of the Grand Council and in the Committees on Economics, Taxation and Transport. The NFU also participated in the important Common Market Working Party established jointly by the FBI, National Union of Manufacturers (NUM), and Association of British Chambers of Commerce (ABCC). The NFU Annual Report noted with satisfaction that these three business organizations supported the exclusion of food, feed, drink and tobacco from the FTA.[39]

Effectiveness.—How influential was the National Farmers' Union in shaping British policy toward the FTA? Certainly the Government did intially adopt the exact position—total exclusion of agriculture—urged by the NFU. Indeed, this was made a condition of negotiations by Harold Macmillan,

---

[37] The NFU successfully influenced matters only remotely related to agriculture, as for example when it managed to have the agricultural support program omitted from FBI criticisms of excess government spending. Self and Storing, *op. cit.*, pp. 208-209.

[38] NFU, *Year Book* (1957), p. 14.

[39] Two other avenues of agricultural influence also existed. One was the National Union of Agricultural Workers, under Harold (later Lord) Collison, which took a position similar to the NFU. This attitude was understandable since anything affecting the prosperity of agriculture would have direct impact on the welfare of farm workers. See *The Times* (London), March 4, 1957. The other method consisted in the interviewing of MP's and candidates by NFU branches, though this was less important on the FTA issue than at the time of the later Common Market debate.

then Chancellor of the Exchequer, when he said "I repeat, the exclusion of foodstuffs, drink and tobacco from the FTA is quite crucial for the UK. Unless such an exclusion is accepted, we could not proceed with any such negotiations.[40] Welcoming this statement, the NFU proclaimed a "complete identity of view on this question between HMG and the Union."[41]

There were certain factors in existence which influenced governmental policy in the same direction regardless of the existence of an organized agricultural interest group. The most important of these complementary pressures was concern for the Commonwealth. Since the bulk of Britain's Commonwealth imports consisted of agricultural goods and raw materials, establishment of an FTA confined to industrial products would leave 90 percent of her Commonwealth trade unaffected. A second complementary factor in the exclusion of agriculture was reluctance on the part of the Government to see the whole postwar agricultural support system upset. As it existed since 1947, the policy was aimed at combining the purchase of cheap farm products from the Commonwealth, low food prices for British consumers, and support of a prosperous domestic agricultural industry. Any disturbance in the existing arrangement was likely to cause problems in at least one of these spheres. Thirdly, the idea of confining a free trade arrangement to industrial products had simplicity on its side, and HMG desired a speedy agreement.

What effect on Government policy did the NFU then have? Despite other reasons for the initial exclusion of agriculture from the FTA, the NFU does indeed seem to have been the critical factor. Had the Union, by some transformation, become a positive advocate of a common agricultural policy, there would have been little likelihood of agriculture remaining outside the European arrangement. Indeed, Britain would

---

[40] *Hansard,* Parliamentary Debates (Commons), Vol. 561 (November 26, 1956), c. 39-42.

[41] NFU, *Year Book* (1957), p. 13.

have been more favorably disposed to Common Market membership itself. Commonwealth pressures did not have nearly so much relevance. At meetings in mid-1957, Commonwealth representatives even told HMG that they were not opposed to including agriculture in the FTA provided there were safeguards against dumping. They implied that Britain's agricultural reluctance was the consequence of powerful pressure by U.K. farmers rather than the result of Commonwealth loyalty.[42]

In influencing Britain's policy, the NFU thus exercised an indirect effect on the FTA negotiations. The Government was squeezed between European desires and Commonwealth and British farming interests. On the one hand, the French National Assembly was told by Christian Pineau that an FTA without agriculture was unthinkable. On the other hand, Sir James Turner, NFU President, declared himself satisfied with "unreserved assurances" he had received from the Government, but added that while Britain had so far preserved mastery of her own destiny, the agricultural industry needed to exercise unceasing vigilance.[43] By toughening Britain's original bargaining position, the agricultural interests made a European agreement more difficult. It is true that the collapse of the FTA talks in late 1958 was also due to questions of external tariffs, definition of origin of goods, and the role of France. However, the NFU certainly contributed to major delays, and to the situation whereby Britain overplayed her own bargaining position in the negotiations.

Another identifiable effect was in influencing FBI policy. The FBI held a dim view of agriculture's place in an FTA, and the NFU took credit for this attitude. "At every available opportunity, both at home and abroad, the Union's representa-

---

[42] *Observer* (London), August 4, 1957.

[43] *The Times,* October 18, 1957. Pineau, then Foreign Minister, made his statement on July 6, 1957, in the French National Assembly debate on ratification of the Rome Treaties. See Miriam Camps, *Britain and the European Community, 1955-1963* (Princeton: Princeton University Press, 1964), p. 89.

tives have maintained this policy. In the FBI and in the British national Committee of the International Chambers of Commerce, *the Union has been able to exercise a significant influence whenever the subject of the FTA has come up for discussion.*"[44]

This influence is all the more noticeable because the FBI had much more in common with the TUC. The two sides of industry would have been affected similarly by the establishment of a Free Trade Area, and since industry as a whole was expected to benefit, it would have been in the FBI's own interest to indicate greater flexibility on the question of agriculture. Certainly the TUC took a more moderate position, arguing that agriculture ought not be included in free trade, but noting that agricultural give and take was possible.[45]

THE FEDERATION OF BRITISH INDUSTRIES

Organization.—The FBI was established in 1916 to meet the need for a central body of manufacturers through which the Government could mobilize industrial production for full-scale war. However, once wartime urgencies were gone, the Federation encountered difficulties because many industrialists disagreed with the need for such a central council of industry.[46] Eventually the economic problems of the Depression, early Government efforts at economic management, and then World War II confirmed the necessity for the FBI and insured the acceptance of its role. The Federation flourished under the managed economy of the postwar decades, and by 1964 it grouped a total of 9,166 member firms and 272 trade associations.[47] Directly or indirectly, the FBI thus represented approximately 50,000 firms, or about 85 percent of all those

---

[44] *British Farmer* (January 10, 1959); italics added.
[45] TUC, *Report* (1957), p. 427.
[46] *FBI Review* (October, 1960), p. 29.
[47] See FBI, *48th Annual Report of the FBI, for the year ending December 31, 1964.*

employing more than eleven workers.[48] Despite this high density of membership, the process of amalgamation had not gone far enough in the industrial sector to give the FBI the unchallenged predominance enjoyed by the TUC or NFU. The reason for this was the existence of several other smaller but substantial peak organizations, including the National Union of Manufacturers (5,110 small- or medium-sized firms and 53 trade associations), the British Employers' Confederation (54 autonomous employers' associations, accounting for the employment of two-thirds of those working in the private sector), the Association of British Chambers of Commerce (60,000 members including manufacturers, banks, shippers, and insurance firms), the National Chamber of Trade (10,000 firms, mostly retailers), the Institute of Directors ("the bosses' trade union"),[49] and the Commonwealth Industries Association. However, in August, 1965, amalgamation in this sphere increased when the FBI, NUM, and BEC merged to form the Confederation of British Industries (CBI).[50]

As a voluntary organization, the FBI needed to proceed in a relatively consensual manner, sometimes on the basis of unanimity. Competition from the smaller peak associations as well as the existence of larger member firms with independent resources dictated this course. However, the permanent staff officials, led by the Director-General Sir Norman Kipping, did possess the ability to shape policy and lead the Federation in desired directions, especially in the making of policy toward Europe.

In its relationship to the Government, the FBI operated, as did the NFU, so as to concentrate its attention upon the administrative side. The Federation possessed exceptionally close formal and informal links, especially with the Board of Trade

---

[48] Finer, *Anonymous Empire,* p. 10.

[49] Institute of Directors, *The Director,* Annual Conference (Report of Speeches) Supplement, Vol. 7, no. 3 (December, 1955), p. 466.

[50] For details of the various organizations making up the business lobby, see Finer, *op. cit.,* p. 8 ff.

(BOT) and Treasury, and therefore it generally de-emphasized parliamentary and party channels. By means of these contacts, as well as by its membership on scores of governmental and other committees,[51] the FBI exercised a consultative and bargaining function. The relationship between the FBI and Government was of course a two-way process, with the Federation making representation to Ministers on matters affecting industry and the various Government departments soliciting advice and cooperation almost daily from the FBI. The bulk of items under consideration involved various technical details rather than broader policy questions, but industry's role in policy implementation, as well as occasional consultation in policy formulation, gave the FBI a position of great importance.

Politically, the FBI maintained a role of formal neutrality, but one tending to closer sympathy and greater influence with a Conservative Government. This was inevitable given the FBI's basically "free enterprise" ethos.[52] The Federation also claimed to decide its policies in light of the national interest, rather than being guided by naked self-interest. At the same time, this found expression in the notion that, in export-oriented Britain, what was good for industry was good for the country.

Policy.—During the period (1961-63) of Britain's attempt to enter the Common Market, industry as a whole adopted a favorable view toward Europe, and by the time of the 1966-67 effort, the CBI was a vociferous advocate of Common Market entry. Inevitably, this produced the impression that industry had long been in the vanguard of the pro-European movement. In fact, this has not always been so. Certainly as far as the FTA was concerned, British business and industry showed considerable initial hesitation. This was evident in the case of the FBI, though the Institute of Directors (generally pro-

---

[51] For a partial listing of these committees see *ibid.*, pp. 31-32; for a more complete listing see FBI, *48th Annual Report, 1964.*

[52] Samuel E. Finer, "The Federation of British Industries," *Political Studies,* 4, no. 1 (February, 1956): 76.

Europe), and the Commonwealth Industries Association[53] (strongly anti-) provide a contrast.

To begin with, the FBI was slow in awakening to the European unity movement. Although the discussions for what was to become the Common Market began in the spring of 1955, and the Messina Conference of the Six (with Britain participating as an observer) took place in June, it was another year before the Federation actually began to study the Common Market. As late as November 1955, the FBI's Southern Regional Council held a conference on exports, attended by representatives of the Board of Trade, merchant banks, and the Export Credits Guarantee Department, yet the meeting gave no attention to the Common Market and European unity.[54] The first mention of the Common Market in the FBI's journal came only in September 1956, as did the first reference in the Director-General's *aides-mémoire* to member trade associations.

Not only was the FBI slow to pay attention to Europe, but when it did so its position was exceptionally cautious and hedged with conditions. The Federation envisioned an FTA which would be far different from the Common Market and which would contain none of its economic integration or supranational institutions. What is more, while industrial leaders were generally favorable toward the FTA, few were vociferously so. There were three bases for this lack of enthusiasm. First, the FBI approved the FTA for rather negative reasons. Business leaders disliked the idea of membership in the Common Market, but they saw disadvantages in being shut out of Europe altogether. Second, business viewed the FTA as an economic proposition, and for some industries there were

---

[53] It was known as the Empire Industries Association and the British Empire League until late 1958 when it became the Commonwealth and Empire Industries Association. In 1961 it was renamed the Commonwealth Industries Association.

[54] A lengthy report on the conference in the *FBI Review* contained no mention of the Six or Messina.

definite risks. Third, the FBI was in a ticklish position. The larger firms and the FBI leadership were quite favorable to European free trade, but much of the membership was unenthusiastic. Given the nature of the FBI as an organization, this meant that its policy had to remain a cautious one.

In May 1956, a European Integration Panel began a study of the Spaak Report for the Overseas Trade Policy Committee of the FBI. To determine the effects of the Spaak proposals upon British industry, the Panel examined three alternatives for the U.K.: abstention from Europe, participation in the Common Market, and membership in a Free Trade area. The Panel concluded that the long-range effects of the Common Market could be disastrous for industry if Britain did nothing.[55] To stay out would leave Imperial Preference and the domestic market undisturbed, but would involve losses in the fast-expanding export market of the Six and severe competition in third markets. There was also the danger that others (Scandinavia, Switzerland, Austria) might associate with the Six by means of the FTA regardless of Britain's choice, thus further damaging her export future. On the other hand, actual Common Market membership would mean the end of Imperial Preference, and while the Panel recognized that the benefits of Imperial Preference were no longer substantial and that they were likely to wither further, there was no evidence that British industries wanted to sacrifice the residual advantages. Membership would also result in Britain's losing control of her external tariffs against other countries and require her to face unwelcome harmonization of social legislation and the free movement of capital and labor.

In its report, made to the Overseas Trade Policy Committee in early September, the Panel found the FTA to be the best choice. The proposal offered protection from the Common Market threat and contained positive benefits. British manu-

---

[55] FBI European Integration Panel, Memo: "Economic Integration of Western Europe," prepared for Overseas Trade Policy Committee, D/9989A, September 3, 1956.

facturers would obtain free entry into the expanding Common Market as well as a voice in shaping it and, at the same time, Britain would retain her external tariffs and reciprocal preferences with the Commonwealth. There would also be advantages of scale in third markets. The price was that Britain would have to grant free access to her own market at a substantial cost to some sectors of industry. It would be necessary to shield British agriculture and vulnerable industries, as well as obtain various other safeguards, but subject to these reservations, the FTA would put Britain in a position of trade leadership.

This was substantially the case put before the FBI's Grand Council in October 1956. Meanwhile, during the summer, the Federation had been asked by the Government to ascertain the views of industry on the FTA proposal and report back by October. Although the Federation poll of the membership revealed widely differing reactions, the weight of opinion was clearly in favor of negotiations, subject to adequate safeguards against unfair trade practices. Among the FBI rank and file, individual firms answered more favorably than did member trade associations. The position of the latter toward the FTA was often a form of the words "no, unless . . . , " whereas the former generally responded "yes, but . . . ." The reason for this divergence was that trade associations themselves were subject to internal differences and tended to reconcile these on the basis of a lowest common denominator.[56] Objections came mainly from those industries expecting direct economic danger from an FTA (e.g., paper, timber, cotton spinning, jute, and hand tools). The main safeguards suggested in the FBI survey were continuance of Imperial Preference, exclusion of agriculture, tight rules against dumping and unfair trade practices,

---

[56] A total of 479 of 663 firms answering the questionnaire gave favorable replies, *Times Review of Industry*, Vol. 2, no. 122 (March, 1957), p. iv. Of 94 trade associations reaching decisions 67 were favorable provided safeguards were established, 9 opposed unless safeguards were assured, 18 unconditionally opposed, *Financial Times*, November 7, 1957.

safeguards on currency and exchange matters, protection of strategic industries and harmonization of costs of taxation, transportation, and labor. The report also suggested the establishment of machinery to enable the Federation to develop its points on essential safeguards for fair trade and thus to guide the Government in future negotiations. On behalf of the Government, the president of the Board of Trade willingly accepted this recommendation and undertook to consult the FBI and various industries on the progress of negotiations.[57] Accordingly, in December, a small FBI working party under Sir William Palmer, a former official at the Board of Trade, was set up to maintain contact with the Government, and the ABCC and NUM were invited to participate.

Once it became official Government policy to work toward the establishment of an FTA, the role of the FBI shifted subtly. HMG was going ahead with its plans, and the task of the FBI became one of shaping the FTA in the interests of British industry. This meant that those within the FBI who were opposed to free trade would have to come to terms with it. The debate was no longer on whether to enter, but on what terms.

Although pressing for safeguards was its main task, the FBI also spent considerable time educating its own membership about the FTA proposals.[58] Thus the Palmer working party not only maintained consultation with the Board of Trade and Foreign Office, but considered numerous technical questions such as tariff reduction, quota restrictions, escape clauses, rules of competition, institutions, patent legislation, transport, restrictive business practices, and the position of overseas territories. The working party's first report was a useful and well-written pamphlet which appeared in April 1957. Entitled *European Free Trade, a Survey for Industrialists,* it offered a comprehensive explanation of the Rome Treaty and the FTA

---

[57] *FBI Review* (January, 1957), p. 18.

[58] Later, at the time of the EFTA and Common Market negotiations, this educative role offered opportunities for the FBI leadership to shape organizational opinion along lines slightly more favorable to European unity.

proposals for British businessmen, and set forth a list of safe-guards.[59] The pamphlet took pains to point out that there had been no attempt to formulate a common policy on this issue; instead the FBI had taken exhaustive efforts to learn the views of its members and communicate them to the Government.

During the spring of 1957, shortly after the FTA negotiations began, business circles began to voice considerable unrest over the speed at which the FTA was proceeding. In accord with views expressed at the FBI's Grand Council meeting in April, Sir Norman Kipping met with the Chancellor of the Exchequer on April 18 to raise matters over which much of his membership was uneasy. These included concern over a lack of detailed information on FTA proposals, demands for reassurances for those who feared their industries would be hard-hit, and complaints of seemingly headlong speed with insufficient time for discussion. While the Government sought to reassure the business sector, Kipping was told that HMG was unwilling to voice publicly its reasons for speed, for fear that this would threaten its bargaining position. The Government feared that once the Rome Treaty was ratified, Britain would be in difficulty due to her exclusion from Common Market trade and disadvantage in third markets. Continental non-members would be pulled into the Common Market, and Britain would find herself seriously isolated economically and militarily. The result of lost markets would be a decline in overseas earnings which would directly precipitate a fall in Britain's living standard. What this meant for the negotiators was that Britain had a weak hand on some essential conditions, such as the exclusion of agriculture, and that rather than being "graciously pleased to come in on such terms" as she wished, Britain faced a hard struggle.[60]

---

[59] These included tax reform and depreciation allowances, transport efficiency, disadvantages due to the 1956 Restrictive Trade Practices Act, dumping, and help for hard-hit industries, FBI, *European Free Trade Area, A Survey for Industrialists* (April, 1957), pp. 59-61.

[60] FBI, *Director-General's Aide-Memoire to Member Trade Associations*, D/1290, no. 77, May 21, 1957.

During the first half of 1957, the Palmer working party had been preparing a major report, which was to precede the FBI's taking an official position on the merits of the Free Trade Area. This study was completed in late August, and after some modification, was publicly issued in September as the Joint Report of the FBI, ABCC, and NUM.[61] The report presented a lengthy statement of the cases pro and con and stressed that there was no consensus in the working party, nor in industry or commerce generally, because of the hypothetical nature of the FTA and the different effects it would have on different industries, firms, and even branches within firms. It therefore expressed no opinion on the relative weights of the arguments, but set out several basic requirements to which it attached the utmost importance. These were generally the safeguards requested a year previously in the FBI survey, but the report stressed that equality of manufacturing conditions in employment and social policies required an integration which would be too high a price for Britain to pay. This point was especially important because it meant a complete refusal to accept the kind of organization which the Six were creating in the Common Market. The report was candid in recognizing this implication, and stated that it meant there would be limits to the number and extent of safeguards that could be sought within the concept of an FTA rather than a fully integrated EEC. Safeguards would thus depend heavily on the domestic policies of HMG.

The Joint Report on the Free Trade Area also contained a remarkably explicit statement of industry's claim to participate in a concurrent majority in regard to the Government's

---

[61] FBI, ABCC, NUM, *A Joint Report on the European Free Trade Area* (September, 1957). Note that the term "EFTA" was widely used from 1956 onward in referring to the proposed Free Trade *Area*, which was to include the Six plus most other OEEC countries. After the negotiations for this collapsed in November 1958, the European Free Trade *Association* was successfully established by the Seven, and has since been known as "EFTA." To avoid semantic confusion, I have used "FTA" to apply to the earlier arrangement, and "EFTA" to the latter.

FTA decision. The statement was occasioned by the subject of hard-hit industries, an item of considerable, and sometimes emotional, importance to many industrialists. Simply put, the position was that it would be wrong for HMG to proceed with the FTA without first having satisfied industry on this problem. "No government should contemplate a decision of this magnitude without a reasonable measure of support from industry; and we do not believe that, until the problem of hard-hit industries has been publicly faced, HMG can claim to have the confidence of industry in proceeding with its proposals."[62]

From September to November, trade associations within the FBI undertook an intensive survey of their members' views. Then, on November 13, the 400-member Grand Council of the FBI finally recorded its opinion as being, on balance, in favor of the Government's policy provided important safeguards were secured. The resolution was sent to HMG, the FBI membership, and the press. The safeguards and conditions cited were generally those of the Joint Report. Given the cautious nature of this welcome to the FTA, it is scarcely surprising that the resolution was endorsed by a large majority. The only major industry opposed was paper, which feared a serious threat from Scandinavia. Probably most firms and trade associations felt the risks of staying out exceeded those of entry, but there was no enthusiasm.

Channels.—As in the cases of the TUC and NFU, the FBI operated through multiple channels of influence. In addition to close contact with HMG at all levels, the FBI made use of joint efforts with the ABCC and NUM, the Council of European Industrial Federations (CEIF), and an informal grouping of the industrial federations and employers' organizations of the "Other Six."

In its close relationship with HMG, especially through the Board of Trade, the FBI leadership functioned as the key link in a two-way process involving the interchange of informa-

---

[62] *Ibid.*

tion, education, and pressures between the Government and the membership of the FBI. The dual role of the FBI leadership was, on the one hand, to convey to its member firms and trade associations information concerning the nature of the free trade proposals and, on the other hand, to formulate and transmit to the Government a coherent presentation of industry's position and its concern for safeguards. Had the European impetus lain with the FBI, the Federation would have taken the initiative in communicating its position to the Government. It is thus significant that the first contact between Government and FBI was the request from the Government that the Federation determine its members' views on the proposed Free Trade Area. The primary means by which consultation was maintained was through the FBI working party under Sir William Palmer. This body was established in late 1956 and later expanded to include representatives of the NUM and ABCC. The working party functioned in making representations to the Government on matters of general policy and in preparing a substantial number of reports and position papers for the information of British business and industry. Although it maintained constant contact with the Board of Trade, particularly on the safeguards required by British industry, the Palmer working party left individual trade associations to deal with matters affecting particular industries.[63] On this subject, the FBI was very careful to satisfy its own members by keeping them fully informed on the negotiations and by offering to assist individual industries to make their own representations to the Government.[64]

Throughout the period of FTA consideration, the FBI maintained close contact with HMG. Thus when the Grand Council finally offered its cautious approval of the FTA in November 1957, its statement especially welcomed the undertaking by the President of the Board of Trade to consult the

---

[63] FBI, *Annual Report* (1957), pp. 8-9.
[64] *FBI Review* (April, 1957), p. 26.

FBI if material changes in the safeguards developed. The 1958 Annual Report mentioned frequent *ad hoc* consultations with Ministers and officials, meetings between Board of Trade representatives and members of the Palmer party, and three meetings of the Consultative Committee for Industry presided over by the President of the Board of Trade or the Minister of State and attended by Britain's chief FTA negotiator, Reginald Maudling, who gave a personal account of the FTA talks.[65]

As the outlook for the FTA worsened in 1958, the FBI made efforts to coordinate policy with its European counterparts; it thereby also established the basis for what later became the European Free Trade Association (EFTA). Although the Federation made a number of contacts among industrialists of the six Common Market countries, it concentrated its attention on industrial and business organizations of Austria, Denmark, Norway, Sweden, and Switzerland (a grouping which, together with Britain, became known for a time as the *Other Six*). A certain community of interest among these Other Six industrialists first emerged at a London Conference called by the U. K. Council of the European Movement in February 1958. This led to further discussions and the publication in April 1958 of a joint statement by these groups agreeing on the terms of an FTA which they could support.[66] The statement was close to the views put forward in the October 1957 Joint Report of the FBI, ABCC, and NUM. These groups then made unsuccessful efforts through the CEIF in seeking to move from their own statement to a common line of policy with the Rome Treaty Six. While some of the Common Market countries' industrial organizations were amenable, the French *Patronat* thoroughly disliked the whole idea.

Within British industry as a whole, a substantial body of

---

[65] FBI, *Annual Report* (1958), p. 10

[66] *Free Trade in Western Europe,* A Joint Statement by the Industrial Federations and Employers' Organizations of Austria, Denmark, Norway, Sweden, Switzerland, and the U.K. (Paris, April 14, 1958).

opinion existed apart from the dominant voice of the FBI. Individual firms, as well as trade associations ranging from the Silk and Rayon Users' Association to the Shoe Manufacturers, voiced their positions on the Free Trade Area. Among the most significant of the other comprehensive business groups, the views of the Commonwealth Industries Association (CIA) and the Institute of Directors merit some attention. In particular, the CIA resolutely opposed any European participation and consistently advocated the alternative of British Empire self-sufficiency. The group invoked the ideas of Joseph Chamberlain and warned of the harm which European free trade would do to the Commonwealth. The Association also cautioned that too much attention was being paid to the strictly economic implications of the FTA and not enough to the disadvantages of the European integration toward which this was leading.[67] Lacking the importance and easy governmental access of the FBI, the CIA publicized its position through a monthly bulletin, by public speeches, and in letters to British newspapers. By contrast, the Institute of Directors—or at least its President and its journal[68]—were early advocates of European association. Their method of communication was predominantly via *The Director,* with its prestigious circulation. Characteristically, *The Director* was critical of the Joint FBI, ABCC, NUM Report (the CIA had cautiously welcomed it) for being concerned almost entirely with safeguards for the manufacturer instead of showing faith in the increased competition that would follow.[69]

Effectiveness.—It is obvious that throughout the two years in which the FTA underwent active consideration, the FBI operated as more of a brake than a stimulus in relation to the Government. There is no reason to disagree with the comment of the *FBI Review* that "the main task of the Federation

---

[67] *Monthly Bulletin* No. 199 (November, 1957), p. 3.

[68] The Institute of Directors does not itself adopt policy positions on matters of this sort.

[69] *The Director,* Vol. 10, no. 5 (November, 1957) pp. 262-263.

has been to impress upon the Government the conditions and safeguards that would be necessary if the FTA came into being with Britain as a constituent member."[70]

Perhaps the role of the FBI is best understood as being governed by the necessity to come to terms with the Government while operating to obtain the most favorable outcome possible within the given situation. Since, for reasons going beyond narrowly economic considerations, HMG wished to reach some kind of agreement with Europe, industry sought to shape the arrangements rather than oppose them outright. The importance to the FBI of maintaining a favorable relationship with HMG is evident in the Federation's recognition that British industry would be heavily dependent upon the Government's domestic cooperation because many safeguards could not be written into a treaty. This basic outlook was put quite candidly by the Director-General in a May 1957 *aide-mémoire* to member trade associations:

> The objectors face, then, a not unfamiliar situation in which the Government of the day announce their intention of taking a course which is heavily disliked by many people in industry (past examples are nationalizations or the Restrictive Trade Practices Act) but which at a certain stage it becomes useless from a practical point of view to oppose, and the time comes when the best thing to do is to negotiate for the best possible terms.[71]

The Federation was quite open in basing its judgment upon narrowly economic terms; industries which stood to lose from FTA membership were urged to demand more reassurances than they had yet received.[72] At one point the FBI even suggested to the Chancellor of the Exchequer that the British official delegate be accompanied by an assessor drawn from in-

---

[70] *FBI Review* (January, 1958), p. 22.

[71] FBI, *Director-General's Aide-Memoire*, D/1290, no. 77, May 21, 1957.

[72] *EFTA, A Survey for Industrialists*. At one point, Sir Norman Kipping agreed that there was something to the contention that efficiency of a firm could be judged by its reply to the FTA inquiry, *Financial Times,* October 2, 1957.

dustrial ranks. This assessor would be familiar with industrial views, so he could "jog the elbow" of the delegate when he felt insufficient concern was being given to industrial difficulties.[73]

The essential difference between industry and the Government was in their order of priorities. The eventual action of the Government in shifting position to accommodate European views is clear evidence that it set first priority on reaching some sort of association with Europe. Political (as well as long-range economic) considerations directed this choice. Industry, on the other hand, was very divided in its own priorities. Less dynamic firms and many of the trade associations specifically preferred no agreement to one which lacked adequate safeguards. In fact, the Joint Report came near to expressing this position. Some large firms and important individuals (including the FBI leadership) did share the Government's desire for a European agreement, whether because they took a broader view, were personally committed to free trade, or merely were confident that their own industries would fare well within the proposed FTA. But the effect of business restraint upon the Government remained considerable. This influenced HMG's initial bargaining position and also made it slower and less open in modifying its terms than political considerations alone would have dictated.

CONCLUSION

In analyzing the group context of Government action during this period, it seems fair to characterize the situation as being similar to the usual relationship in domestic politics. That is, the sectional (or "producer") groups exerted influence because the executive found it necessary or desirable to bargain

---

[73] FBI, *Director-General's Aide-Memoire.* D/1026, no. 76, March 7, 1957.

for their cooperation. Though the groups paid more attention to technical aspects than to overall policy, this was consistent with the customary pattern of operation on domestic
matters.

The major groups in fact took care to remind HMG of the
necessity for acquiring their assent. For example, the TUC
General Council consciously enunciated the concurrent majority conception in sending its November 1956 policy statement to the Government: "Observance of these principles is
necessary *if there is to be in this country that measure of national agreement which a long term commitment of this kind
requires.*"[74]

At various times the FBI and NFU made similarly explicit
statements. In addition, since these groups were aware of their
own domestic importance, none of them wished to see Britain
conclude a European agreement involving supranational arrangements. Any removal of final decision power to a central
European authority would eventually lessen their influence
because the British Government, with which they maintained
such close and even corporate relationships, would no longer
determine economic policy.

The Free Trade Area never became a politicized matter
within Britain. Neither the Conservatives nor Labour chose
to make the FTA a public issue, perhaps because they were
divided internally and their leaders were basically in agreement. The public did not become involved, and the fact that
the Board of Trade, rather than the Foreign Office, conducted
the FTA negotiations reflected the fact that the Government
viewed Europe as more of a trade or economic issue than a
political one. Because of this non-politicized treatment, policy-
making proceeded through the functional representation
channel rather than that of party government, and therefore
sectional pressure groups played the dominant role in internal

---

[74] TUC *Report* (1958), pp. 446-447; italics added.

politics. Given a context in which trading was regarded as the chief consideration, the cooperation of British industry, as embodied in the FBI, would necessarily have to be bargained for since it was this sector which would be involved in carrying out the business of importing and exporting. Similarly, agriculture could not easily be dealt with without the consent of the NFU. A broader political judgment, which would have relegated the groups to a lesser role, was lacking. Agriculture, business, and labor judged the FTA in terms of commercial gain and loss, and expressed their group interest heavily on the side of safeguards. The Government was concerned to get approval from those groups which might be hurt and which were politically powerful. Under the circumstances, prospective and diffuse public benefits attracted less interest and publicity.

At times the Government made certain judgments which transcended the narrowly economic plane. In modifying Britain's terms of association and in agreeing to changes on institutions, majority voting and agriculture, HMG made obvious political judgments. But because the FTA issue remained largely within the realm of functional representation, the pressure groups exerted a major restraining influence upon Governmental policy.

Domestic considerations directly shaped Britain's conduct of the actual FTA negotiations. There is every reason to judge, as Miriam Camps does, that HMG felt its main task lay in defeating internal opposition to free trade and in winning over business and labor rather than concentrating on persuading the Six.[75] The Government's decision to exclude agriculture from the initial proposals prompted a very explicit acknowledgement of the groups' importance from a Labour MP, who said, "The only really effective argument which I have heard for excluding foodstuffs from the scheme is that if we are going to have trouble with pressure groups and with the FBI, why should we have trouble at the same time with

---

[75] Camps, *op. cit.*, pp. 104-105.

the NFU? From a tactical point of view, there is much to be said for taking on these pressure groups one at a time."[76]

The ultimate effect of group pressures was to place the Government in the position of being squeezed between French intransigence and group demands. Because of group pressures, HMG entered the FTA talks asking too much from the Europeans. Although the negotiations eventually broke down over external tariffs and definition of origin, there is a real possibility that had HMG been able to show flexibility earlier the FTA talks might have succeeded.

[76] Fred Mulley, *Hansard,* Vol. 561 (November 26, 1956), c. 80.

Chapter 4

Pressure Groups and the European Free Trade Association

INTRODUCTION

Collapse of the FTA negotiations produced no basic shift in the substance of Britain's European policy, and the treatment of the issue remained non-politicized. While the interruption of the talks was dramatic, it did not convince British leaders in government or industry that the European choice had become one of Common Market membership versus Common Market exclusion. Instead, they persisted in the belief that a wide European trade agreement along OEEC lines remained possible, and they maintained intermittent contacts with the Six for several additional months.

Reginald Maudling, who remained the chief Government spokesman on European unity, enunciated this policy continuity in a speech to the House of Commons in February 1959. While maintaining that Britain was not hostile to the Rome Treaty, he believed the FTA principle was still best for Europe. Britain desired a 17-nation multilateral association within the principles of the OEEC. She could not contemplate Common Market membership because this would involve a number of unacceptable features: the determination of commercial policy by majority vote, the end of Commonwealth free entry, the breaking of Commonwealth agreements and of Government obligations to British farmers, movement toward political federation, and harmonization of social policies.[1]

During the Maudling Committee negotiations, the Other Six, especially Britain and the Scandinavian countries, had found themselves in frequent harmony over the FTA conception, and they began to concert their actions by meeting informally together before each bargaining session.[2] This grouping was hardly surprising since it comprised all the highly developed countries of the OEEC which did not already belong to the Common Market. After the Soustelle veto, Government representatives of the Other Six quietly met for exploratory talks in Geneva on December 1, 1958, at the invitation of the Swiss. (Portugal unexpectedly attended this meeting, thus raising the number of participants to seven.) Without governmental commitments, these seven met again at Oslo on February 21 and then at Stockholm on March 17 and 18. At the latter meeting, a Swedish official and a Norwegian official were designated to prepare detailed plans and to travel to each of the seven countries for further talks.

Meanwhile, in mid-May, the British press gave prominent mention to concrete plans for a rival European organization which might be established in the event that the deadlock could not be broken in talks with the Six.[3] On May 27, Sweden officially invited Austria, Denmark, Norway, Portugal, Switzerland, and the U.K. to join with her in exploring a possible free trade area. Talks took place at a resort near Stockholm from June 1 to 13, with the U.K. delegation led by Sir John Coulson (then Maudling's advisor) and composed of senior officials from the Treasury, Board of Trade (BOT), and Min-

---

[1] *Hansard, Parliamentary Debates* (Commons), Vol. 599 (February 12, 1959), c. 1368-1380, 1489-1494.

[2] In the case of Britain and the Scandinavian countries there was a background of cooperation from at least 1951 and the UNISCAN payments arrangement.

[3] *Financial Times* (London), May 11, 1959.

istry of Agriculture. Then from July 20 to 22, Ministers
of the Seven met at Stockholm and formally agreed to the
establishment of a European Free Trade Association (EFTA)
by July 1 of the following year. Drafting of the actual Convention began on September 8, and the completed document
was initialed by Ministers on November 20. Britain officially
signed the Stockholm Convention on December 29, 1959, and
the first EFTA tariff cuts of 20 percent took place on July 1,
1960.

The aims of the Association which Britain had joined—
namely, free trade in industrial products, an absolute minimum of institutions and integration, and the isolation of agriculture in an appendix to the Convention[4]—were precisely
those she had envisioned in the initial negotiations for the
FTA. Despite the increasingly important international implications of European developments, the treatment of European unity within Britain proceeded largely on the same non-
politicized basis as had been the case for the Free Trade Area.

THE FBI AND THE ORIGIN OF THE EFTA

The role played by the FBI in the establishment of EFTA
was a prominent one. Not only did the Federation lead the
Government on this issue, but it provided an important impetus for the whole arrangement. When HMG adopted the
policy of negotiating to bring about EFTA, it was following a
course urged upon it by the FBI leadership and working with a
blueprint which the FBI and its Scandinavian counterparts had
drawn up. The situation was nearly unique, since on only one
other postwar occasion (involving currency holdings and export subsidies through the CEIF in 1950)[5] had the FBI ever

---

[4] See A. C. L. Day, "The European Free Trade Association," *London
and Cambridge Economic Bulletin,* in *The Times Review of Industry,* 13,
no. 155 (December, 1959).

[5] In 1950, the FBI succeeded in getting the industrial organizations
of Denmark and Germany to join in the abandonment of practices which

exerted leadership on a foreign policy issue.

On a policy level, the FBI maintained the kind of European position it had held for the previous two years. For channels, it utilized direct contacts with the Other Six industrial and employers' organizations and consultation—especially via the Palmer working party—with the Board of Trade, the Treasury, and a few Ministers. In terms of effectiveness, the FBI was successful in securing the agreement of its European counterparts and in seeing the commitment of the British Government to the desired approach.

What is of most interest here is the FBI's active role in the formation of the EFTA. The community of interest between the FBI and its counterparts initially emerged at the London Conference called by the U.K. Council of the European Movement. Nine months before the collapse of the negotiations, over a hundred industrial and union leaders from fifteen countries gathered to discuss the FTA at a three-day meeting beginning February 19, 1958. The FBI and British Employers' Confederation (BEC) at first hesitated to participate, and ultimately did so at least partly to avoid embarrassment. Their delegations included members both pro- and anti-FTA. Somewhat surprisingly at the time, the conference revealed considerable harmony among business and industrial leaders of Britain, Austria, Switzerland, and the Scandinavian countries. Perhaps the opposition of the French to the FTA had much to do with this, as Sir Norman Kipping later described it to FBI members: "We were told (a) that you could not find two dozen deputies in France who would vote for it, and (b) that for the first time in history the Conseil National du Patronat Français (our opposite numbers) were completely unanimous —in opposing any EFTA."[6]

---

were harmful to the interests of all concerned. The British Government then stepped into the picture by officially agreeing to the arrangement with the governments of these countries.

[6] FBI, *Director-General's Aide-Memoire to Member Trade Associations*, D/3946, no. 80, March 14, 1958.

The immediate outcome of this "Other Six" solidarity was an agreement among the Federations, at the suggestion of the Swedish Federation of Industries, to meet for exploratory talks in Paris during mid-March. Sir Hugh Beaver (FBI President), along with P. F. D. Tenant (Overseas Director), Lincoln Steel (Chairman of the Overseas Trade Policy Committee), and representatives of the BEC attended the meeting. According to the FBI President, these men played a leading part in a series of discussions which culminated in April in the publication of a joint statement indicating agreement on the terms of an FTA.[7] This statement later helped to serve as the basis for the seven-nation EFTA. Although it ostensibly aimed at preventing a European split, it had obvious implications, which *The Times* noted: "It is not the beginning of a new block. But it shows that a new block is not to be ruled out."[8]

The purpose of the signatories, who sent the statement to their own governments and to the OEEC, was to help forward the FTA negotiations by showing what kind of agreement was feasible. They expressed basic accord on the previously troublesome questions of definition of origin, institutions, and the Commonwealth. Their approach mirrored the U.K.'s overwhelmingly economic and commercial view of the FTA. Only on agriculture and institutions did their report differ somewhat from HMG's position. The whole statement reflected the FBI's influence and its conception of Europe as set out in the October 1957 Joint Report (with the ABCC and NUM), and in the Palmer Report. Indeed the FBI president drew attention to this likeness in the Federation's Annual Report.[9]

The FBI had been eminently successful in influencing and coordinating policies of the industrialists of the Other Six, but proved less so in achieving a common line of policy between this group and the industrialists of the Six, with whom it met under the auspices of the CEIF. The FBI put Britain's case

---

[7] FBI, *Annual Report* (1958), p. v.

[8] *The Times* (London), April 19, 1958.

[9] FBI, *Annual Report* (1958), p. ii.

through the annual conference of the Directors of the European Industrial Federations and through informal contacts. It presented factual reports on such things as the nature of U.K.-Commonwealth relations, and held talks with some of the Six's industrial federations on a bilateral basis. All this was to little avail. The French—for various reasons—were hostile to Britain's FTA conception, and although the industrial groups of the other five Common Market countries were more favorable, their loyalties lay with the Rome Treaty when it came to a choice between Britain and the Common Market.

As the ill-fated Maudling Committee negotiations resumed for the last time, in early November 1958, the Other Six industrialists met again in Paris at the suggestion of the FBI and BEC. The aim of the meeting was to discuss their common attitude toward the negotiations and to reaffirm their desire for an all-European FTA. However, given the expectation of an imminent collapse, the implication of a common position was a separate European agreement.

One week later M. Soustelle interrupted the FTA talks with his announcement. The logic of the Other Six industrialists' position became obvious. Less than a week afterward the organizations were in touch concerning an alternative arrangement. While official representatives were not involved in these soundings, HMG definitely had "no objection" to the FBI and BEC going ahead on their own.[10] The most important period in the establishment of the EFTA now began, and it was here that the FBI played its key role in helping to initiate the scheme. It did so by consolidating the Other Six and pushing the project at the Board of Trade during the winter of 1958-59.

The first overt move to bring together these like-minded countries came with the trip to Stockholm of the FBI President and the Director-General at the invitation of the Swedish Federation of Industries. On December 17, they held an "in-

---

[10] *Financial Times,* November 20, 1958.

formal exchange of views," then issued an important communique. Since progress on a wider FTA no longer appeared likely, and since the two Federations deemed inaction unadvisable, they decided to launch a detailed study at industrial level for a trading association among the Other Six countries. This study was to be based on the April 1958 report of the industrial federations and to be ready by April 1, 1959.[11]

On January 5, four days after the official initiation of the Common Market, the FBI leaders held another crucial set of talks at Copenhagen. Accompanied by NFU representatives, they discussed the impact of the Common Market with their Danish agricultural and industrial counterparts. The importance of these meetings was that the Danes were torn between their two major trading partners, Britain and Germany, and hence were extremely reluctant to join a group which would separate them from one of the two. The talks were difficult, and the Danes remained very reluctant. This meeting left the FBI pessimistic about the chances of establishing the limited EFTA, and in a February *aide-mémoire* to member trade associations, the FBI Director-General expressed gloom about the prospects for an Other Six trade association as well as concern about serious tariff disadvantages and the diversion of investment likely to result from the establishment of the Common Market.[12]

At the same time as it sounded out the Scandinavians, the FBI was pushing its views before the BOT. There was nothing exceptional in close contact between business groups and the BOT; however, in this case, the foreign policy initiative of the FBI was unusual. Certainly the Government found it useful to have the EFTA arrangement explored in this manner without becoming committed in advance. Thus Mr. Maudling could tell Parliament that a number of industrial organiza-

---

[11] *Ibid.*, December 18, 1958.
[12] FBI, *Director-General's Aide-Memoire*, D/343, no. 83, February 16, 1959.

tions were canvassing the idea, and the Government would certainly keep an open mind.[13]

In mid-March, a reversal of roles began which ended the FBI's task in policy innovation. The Other Six Federations were holding another round of exploratory talks, this time in London, when the Government advised the FBI President that it was now seriously considering the formation of a free trade area, after having previously held discussions among Government officials of these countries.[14] The Government move came just as the FBI effort was faltering: the Copenhagen meeting had made it seem that the FBI leadership and staff had over-reached themselves, a non-activist FBI President (at least in contrast to his predecessor) had taken office, and the FBI membership showed signs of hesitation. These difficulties were substantially a result of the FBI trying to exert the kind of policy leadership for which it was ill-suited, in contrast to its more customary role of bargaining and veto power.

Once the Government seized upon the EFTA idea (and it picked up the project so suddenly that some industrial leaders were not told), the FBI trailed well behind on European policy and remained in that position even during the 1961-63 Common Market moves. Nothing illustrates this reversal of initiative more clearly than the fact that in May, HMG turned to the FBI asking it to ascertain industrial reaction to the proposal. Whereas the situation had been one where the FBI urged the establishment of EFTA and sought to pressure the Government toward that policy, the lead now passed to HMG. Industry, through the FBI, sought certain reassurances, and the Government was careful to make sure that its EFTA policy would have industrial support.

The FBI Grand Council held lengthy meetings in May and June. The main objective of British industry remained the negotiation of a European-wide trade agreement to include

---

13 *Hansard,* Vol. 599 (February 12, 1959), c. 386.
14 FBI, *Annual Report* (1959), p. 7.

the Six, and opinion in industry now appeared divided as to whether EFTA would contribute to this.[15] The Federation had mailed a questionnaire to all member trade associations, and in mid-June, it sent the survey results in confidence to the Government. At the same time, the Grand Council issued a statement in which it said that the majority of British industries were actively pro or would acquiesce because they felt EFTA would facilitate ultimate agreement with the Common Market: "The FBI therefore would support HMG in a policy of seeking to conclude an FTA Convention with the countries of the Outer Seven on the basis that every effort should be made to give it a form which would as far as possible assist the negotiation of an acceptable association with the Six."[16]

In addition to citing the overwhelming importance of avoiding the division of Europe into two camps, the Grand Council also stressed the necessity for close and early consultation with industries and pointed to the need for Government help on taxation and general domestic policies. Although a substantial section of the FBI majority also saw merit in the EFTA on strictly economic grounds, a number of industries opposed it because of the consequences for themselves.[17]

Throughout the remaining few months of negotiations for EFTA, the FBI played the sort of role it had during the FTA talks. That is, it kept members fully informed of developments, helped them to make their views known to the authorities, and exercised a watchdog role on general policy matters. In its close bargaining relationship with the Government, the FBI often worked through the small liaison group led by Sir William Palmer.

A statement in the Annual Report by William H. McFadzean clearly reveals the extent to which the new FBI president

---

[15] *Financial Times,* June 3, 1959.

[16] FBI, *Annual Report* (1959), pp. 7-8.

[17] The industries opposed included paper and board, timber, woodwool, woodworking machine tools, cotton spinning, jute, hard fiber cordage, mats and matting, and hand tools, *ibid.*

took a restricted view of his position in contrast to that of his predecessor, Sir Hugh Beaver. It is worth quoting the words at length because of what they omit from a comprehensive description of the FBI's role:

During the lengthy negotiations which preceded the signing of the Stockholm Convention we were constantly called upon to assist industry to formulate its views. While our work helped to crystallize opinions, complete unanimity was not to be expected; and besides representing the views held by the great majority on this issue, we were at pains to see that the opinions of the minority were put before HMG and that individual industries had every opportunity to make known their particular difficulties. At the same time, we were in close and frequent contact with the industrial federations of the Outer Seven and also with those of the Six in order to play our part in the endeavor to prevent the splitting of Western Europe and to achieve a framework in which trade can flourish and expand.[18]

From this statement, one would never know that 1) the FBI had been strongly pro-EFTA and 2) the organization had taken the initiative in establishing the Association with its Other Six counterparts.

Given the shift in the FBI's function, it requires some care to evaluate its role and importance in policy-making. Three kinds of questions deserve scrutiny. First, at whose bidding did the FBI meet with its Scandinavian counterparts? Second, how did the FBI itself function during the period of policy leadership? Third, can it be said that, in relation to governmental policy and the establishment of EFTA, the FBI's role was one of direct causation?

On the first point, the consensus of those involved is that the FBI went on its own, but kept HMG informed. There appears to have been tacit approval on the part of the Government. Certainly the FBI went neither as a "catspaw" for HMG nor entirely divorced from official contact. The relationship was best described by Sir Hugh Beaver (then Presi-

---

[18] *Ibid.*, p. v.

dent) in explaining the Stockholm trip: "Though we speak only for industry, the British Government is well aware of our action."[19]

Second, there is the question of the FBI's organizational role. The leadership exercised an important educative function for the membership, and at the same time led it in the direction of EFTA. Indeed, the leadership's initiative was such that, as one participant in the events put it, "Norman Kipping was sometimes dangerously in the lead." In any event, this initiative only lasted a few months, and the FBI reverted to its customary place behind rather than in front of HMG and bargaining with the Government over details rather than pushing policy innovation.

As for the third question, the answer is that while the FBI exercised a striking degree of initiative, this was not the same thing as direct causation. The striking similarities between the actual nature of EFTA, the April 1958 statement of the Other Six industrial federations, the September 1957 Joint Report of the ABCC, BEC, and FBI, and the FBI's August 1957 Palmer Report obviously indicate a considerable amount of FBI involvement. There are two reasons, however, why one must be careful to avoid an exaggeration of the FBI's causal influence. In the first place, the FBI and the British Government—along with most of the industrial federations and Governments of the Other Six—shared a view of what the principles for a European arrangement should be: free trade in industrial products, a minimum of institutions, no harmonization of economic and social policies or of external tariffs, no integration, and minimal arrangements for agriculture. Secondly, while the FTA negotiations went on, the FBI's Palmer working party met approximately fortnightly with representatives of the BOT and Treasury. HMG sought to test the sensibility of its detailed FTA proposals in these meetings, and found it a convenient way quickly to learn the views of in-

---

[19] *Financial Times,* December 18, 1958.

dustry on the effects of various features as these came up in the negotiations. Both sides learned from these frequent, effective, and confidential consultations; it was almost inevitable that their views should tend to converge on details as well as principles.

Pressure group influence is exceedingly difficult to measure in any case, and the circumstances here do not warrant the conclusion that the FBI alone caused EFTA to be established or the British Government to adopt the EFTA scheme as its aim. Whether the EFTA would have been established without the actions of the FBI is another matter. Here the Federation unquestionably played a vital role in arranging and calling attention to a viable policy option. What is more, the Federation certainly retained its concurrent majority status; HMG could not have joined EFTA over the opposition of the FBI.

THE NFU AND NEGOTIATIONS FOR EFTA

The most important part of the NFU's role in the EFTA arrangements revolved around the January 1959 trip to Copenhagen and the subsequent agricultural concessions made to Denmark. On January 5, three NFU leaders[20] accompanied Sir Norman Kipping to Copenhagen for talks with Danish industrial and agricultural organizations. The NFU participated on a basis similar to the FBI, in that it went largely on its own.

The reason for the Copenhagen trip was that Denmark needed reassurances on the agricultural arrangements in any free trade association. Unlike the U.K., where agriculture made up approximately 4 percent of GNP, Denmark's agriculture represented about 40 percent of GNP. Hence a strictly industrial arrangement with the Seven would not satisfy

---

[20] The three were Sir James Turner, President, Asher Winegarten, Chief Economist, and Geoffrey Redmayne, a staff member.

Denmark, especially if the Common Market tariffs were to cut into her agricultural exports. Accordingly, the NFU and FBI each held meetings with their opposite members, then met jointly to discuss the situation—the first time the Danish industrial and farm organizations had ever met together. The talks involved plans for a *quid pro quo* for Danish EFTA membership in the form of unilateral British agricultural concessions to Denmark.

Agricultural Ministers of the two countries met in June and July for negotiations on these concessions and eventually reached agreement. Britain abolished duties on Danish blue vein cheese and canned cream, and agreed to a 10 percent cut in the tariff on bacon and canned pork luncheon meat. Interestingly, HMG had been somewhat slow in taking up the negotiations where the NFU had left off, and arranged slightly less beneficial terms for British agriculture. The United Kingdom NFU team, led by Sir James Turner, had succeeded in getting the Danes into a frame of mind to concede that Britain should retain 44 percent of the domestic bacon market, but HMG, after several months delay, had to settle for a figure of only 36 percent.[21]

Once the terms became public, however, the Union described as misconceived "any attempt to buy Denmark's entry into the proposed Outer Seven FTA by agricultural concessions."[22] After "strong representations" by the NFU, the Government agreed to certain safeguards, and arranged that the $20 million cost of the concessions would fall on the Exchequer and not the farmers.

It appears that the NFU objections were *pro forma* and mainly for the attention of the membership. As in virtually any sectional interest group, the leadership needed to be seen as fighting—even if unsuccessfully—for the interests of the body. The facts remain that the NFU went to Copenhagen in

---

[21] Personal interview, February 9, 1967.
[22] *Financial Times*, July 2, 1959.

January 1959, acquiesced in the unilateral concessions to Denmark and accepted the establishment of EFTA.

The explanation for these actions throws some interesting light on the operation of a powerful sectional group. Basically the NFU gave way gracefully on an issue of limited importance. The concessions to Denmark were on matters of quantity, not of principle, and related to temporary tariffs which dated only from 1956. The issue was small compared to that of accepting the Common Market's Common Agricultural Policy, which the NFU so resolutely fought from 1960 to 1963. The NFU saw the handwriting on the wall and gave in because it would certainly have been beaten. By doing so, and by cooperating in the Copenhagen talks, the Union accomplished two important things. First, through helping to secure the esablishment of EFTA which industry very much wanted, it avoided antagonizing industry. In beating a tactical retreat, the NFU acquired capital for use on later issues of vital importance. Secondly, by cooperating, the Union was able to shape the concessions in accord with its own interests.

One other aspect of the NFU's operation which deserves attention is the leadership situation. As in the case of the FBI, the NFU leadership felt the need to avoid getting too far out in front of its own organization. Thus at the February 1958 Conference held by the U.K. Council of the European Movement, Sir James Turner avoided chairing a committee on agriculture, and instead the position was taken by an NFU Council member. The NFU President was being careful not to appear too friendly to European unity.

There was more potential room for leadership in the NFU than in the FBI because the advantages of the leadership were relatively greater in terms of education and resources. Large industrial firms had the ability to prepare sophisticated analyses of complex situations on their own, independent of whatever the FBI advocated. Few farmers possessed this kind of facility. Another factor was that Sir James Turner (later Lord Netherthorpe) held a unique position in the NFU. As President from 1945 to 1960, he shaped the Union and enjoyed a remarkable ascendency there.[23] He also maintained a friendly personal relationship with Sir Norman Kipping, the FBI Secretary-General. Turner thus was able to bring his organization along a path which a weaker leader would have found difficult. His successor in January 1960 as NFU President, Sir Harold Woolley, was less sympathetic to European unity, and took the organization into a quite hostile position toward the Common Market.

Clearly, leadership proved to be a most crucial variable in the operations of the FBI and the NFU. In the case of the former, the change in the presidency from Sir Hugh Beaver to William McFadzean brought a lessening in FBI activism; in the case of the latter, the accession of Sir Harold Woolley meant a shift in policy.

THE TUC AND THE OPERATION OF EFTA

Unlike the farmers and industrialists, the trade unionists had little to do with the EFTA negotiations. They were not deeply engaged in soundings, as the FBI, nor was their consent to specific concessions required. The TUC's early role consisted mainly of maintaining sporadic contacts with its European opposite numbers and with the Government.

In January 1959, the TUC met representatives of the French socialist labor union (CGT–FO) in London and explained why Britain felt she could not join the Common Market; however, the TUC representatives did stress their continued interest in a Common Market–FTA link. Later, in mid-August, unions of the Other Six met in London at the TUC's Congress House headquarters to reaffirm their FTA policies. The by now familiar points included full employment, economic planning, and the rights of unions to influence economic

---

[23] See Peter Self and Herbert J. Storing, *The State and the Farmer* (London: Allen & Unwin, 1962).

policy. The unions also welcomed their governments' stress on FTA as a bridge to a wider European economic association.

Meanwhile the TUC Economic Committee met with Reginald Maudling several times during the late spring and summer. Alan Birch, the Committee Chairman, mainly sought information on the negotiations, and the Paymaster-General undertook to keep in close consultation.[24] As the talks drew to a successful conclusion, the General Council representatives met again with Maudling, who reassured them that a commitment to pursue full employment would appear in the Convention.[25]

The TUC's main involvement came only after publication of the EFTA Convention in November 1959, and concerned the Economic Committee's displeasure at the neglect of social provisions and especially the arrangements for union representation. At their August meeting, and again at Stockholm in late October, unions of the Other Six had given considerable attention to securing a permanent place in EFTA's institutions for labor unions on a basis of equal representation with employers. They had gone into great detail in describing the machinery to insure that this was achieved.[26] The TUC General Council found that the Convention's overwhelming stress on trade accorded neither with its stated objectives nor with the expressed intent of HMG. It also disliked the lack of explicit provision for the representation of national trade union centers in the EFTA institutions.

To express these views, TUC representatives met with Maudling (who had now become President of the BOT) in early January 1960. He explained that due to the speed of negotiations, little attention had been given to union representation, but that something might be set up under terms of the Convention which provided for the establishment of ad-

---

[24] TUC, *Report* (1959), p. 279. There were meetings on May 6 and 26, and on June 24.

[25] TUC, *Report* (1960), p. 262.

[26] TUC, *Industrial News*, No. 16 (August 28, 1959).

visory bodies to the Ministerial Council. The next move came when the EFTA unions met again at Vienna in early March. As well as conferring briefly with EFTA's Council of Ministers, they prepared a memo urging creation of a Joint Advisory Committee (JAC, later the "Consultative Committee"), half of whose members would be appointed by employers' organizations and half by free trade union centers. The Committee was to include one industrialist and one unionist from each country, each representative to be accompanied by a technical advisor. The JAC would have access to the EFTA Secretariat and to the Council.

The proposal seemed to bear fruit when, in May, Maudling wrote the TUC asking that it nominate two representatives. However, a clash developed between business and labor groups. Employers' organizations objected to the arrangements, and in July they requested the presence of one representative of banking and finance in addition to their own two nominees, thus making for a total of five representatives from each country on the Committee. Supported by the unions of Sweden, Austria, Switzerland, and Norway, the TUC objected strenuously, replying that this would create a substantial Committee majority for non-union interests. In the interim, the TUC refused to nominate its two representatives to the Consultative Committee and continued to press its case with the President of the BOT.

The impasse was finally resolved in December, with the TUC backing down and accepting Maudling's explanation that his consultations with employers' organizations had convinced him of the necessity for a banking and finance representative. Union leaders also decided it was important to have a voice on the Committee in order to express their views before the Council of Ministers. They nominated J. A. Birch and Harry Douglass as their representatives and Harold Collison and Frank Cousins as substitutes. The representation issue faded away, especially as in practice the finance nominees often failed to attend meetings, and the unions turned their attention to seeking better machinery for the Committee.

What stands out about this episode of TUC involvement in EFTA is the nature of the disputed issues. That is, the subject of controversy was less substantive than procedural. The best explanation is that, because of the limited scope of EFTA, there was little the unions could seek from it—whether in terms of pressuring the Association to do or to stop doing something. Furthermore, since the issues involved were ones of low visibility and only peripheral importance, the TUC found it easy to retreat from its position without a ripple of discontent from within its own ranks.

CONCLUSION

The most significant aspect of the role of sectional pressure groups in this period is that it was the one time in which a group actually moved ahead of the Government on European policy. In this case, through the Palmer working party and meetings with the Scandinavian federations, the FBI played a substantial part in pushing the Government toward the EFTA policy option and in shaping the terms of the Association.

This initiative does, however, require careful definition. Owing to the nature of the FBI as an organization and to the governmental policy-making process, there were basic limits on the FBI's actions. Its precise role was in overtly seeking the establishment of EFTA at a time when Government probings were still discreet and without commitment. The FBI's activities gave prominence to the EFTA option, and a variety of Government motives coincided with the opportunity offered by the Federation's European soundings. At the very least, the FBI's advocacy made it possible for the Government to proceed with the EFTA option in the knowledge that such a course of action would benefit from firm FBI support. In the face of industrial disapproval, the EFTA choice would have been most unlikely.

As in the case of the Free Trade Area, the EFTA issue re-

mained almost entirely non-politicized.[27] Because of the economic and commercial treatment throughout 1959, the FBI's
involvement and importance came naturally. To say that
HMG took the more narrowly economic view is no idle gener-
alization. In their failure to adopt a wider outlook, British
leaders paid little attention to the political dynamic which
infused the Common Market; they seldom displayed awareness of the Continentals' sense of building Europe and of
ending the antagonisms which had caused the two World
Wars. They did not choose to make EFTA an issue of public
political importance within Britain, and all three indicators
reflect this treatment. First, the Foreign Office did not handle
the negotiations; instead, the Board of Trade took charge, and
many of the details were worked out at the Treasury. Second,
there was little public attention to the European question.
Third, the parties did not become deeply involved and themselves did not choose to make Europe an important matter.

But while EFTA received treatment as an economic issue,
the implications of it were quite political. By establishing the
Association, Britain preserved bargaining power and prevented the member countries from coming to terms one by
one with the Six. Those who had become involved in Britain's
conception of the FTA wished to show such a scheme could
operate successfully, whatever the criticisms of the French.
"Bridge-building" between the Six and Seven was a major objective of EFTA, and most opinion leaders in Britain saw the
new organization as a useful means to this end. (Though perhaps wrong, this was a widely shared rationalization at the
time.) Eventually, the Association complicated Britain's task
in seeking Common Market membership, both on a technical
level, and as it contributed to the Six's suspicion of British
motives. A more searching political judgment at the start
might have avoided this difficulty, or at least weighed the
eventual political costs along with the economic calculations.

---

[27] For a more detailed treatment of the EFTA from the party government perspective, see Chapter 6.

Chapter 5

Pressure Groups and the Common Market

Even while negotiators were applying the finishing touches to the EFTA arrangements, the Prime Minister and those at the highest levels of Government were reconsidering Britain's policy toward the Common Market. Close associates of Macmillan indicate that he decided during the 1960 Christmas holidays that Britain should seek membership. After various consultations within the country and among the Europeans, Macmillan announced to the House of Commons on July 31, 1961, that HMG would apply under Article 237 of the Rome Treaty to begin negotiations to see if satisfactory arrangements could be made for the special interests of Britain, the Commonwealth and EFTA. The actual negotiations opened with a speech by Britain's chief negotiator, Edward Heath, to the Ministers of the EEC member countries at Paris on October 10, 1961. Talks continued at Brussels for well over a year until they were broken off by the French two weeks after President de Gaulle's celebrated press conference of January 14, 1963.

This chapter deals with the relationship of the major interest groups to Britain's Common Market policy in two distinct periods: one involving the decision to apply for entry, the other covering the subsequent negotiations. Group influence varied significantly between these two phases, and an examination of the policies and operations of the FBI, TUC, and NFU during the years between 1960 and 1963 reveals a great deal about their influence and limitations, as well as the way in which organizational and attitudinal factors shape these groups' conceptions of their own interests.

THE FBI, BRITISH BUSINESS, AND COMMON MARKET ENTRY

Since the time of the Messina negotiations in 1955, the FBI had been reacting to the pressure of European events, rather than anticipating developments. Although many critics of Britain's entry shared the view that "the pro Common Market campaign in Britain has been led by the giant firms, hungry for their share of the European pickings,"[1] the initial attitude of business actually was reserved. There were, however, substantial differences in business attitudes between the period in which the decision to seek accession to the Common Market was made and the actual negotiation phase.

BUSINESS AND THE COMMON MARKET DECISION

The relatively restrained role played by the FBI in the movement toward Common Market entry can be explained by a combination of business ideas and organizational structure. To begin with, the general business ethos in Britain had been such as to create an obsession with safeguards in the 1956-60 period. Business looked upon European developments not as an opportunity but as a threat.[2] The roots of this outlook lay in generalized factors, such as the political culture of the country, the natural conservatism of British business and in-

[1] William Pickles, *Not With Europe: the political case for staying out* (London: Fabian International Bureau, April, 1962), p. 19.
[2] As early as September 1956, the FBI's European Integration Panel reported that the Six's plan of integration "could have gravely injurious repercussions on British industry." See "Economic Integration of Western Europe," prepared for Overseas Trade Policy Committee, D/9989 A, September 3, 1956.

dustry, and a traditional wariness of foreigners, as well as in specific conditions such as Britain's privileged trading position with the Commonwealth and the existence of a generation of protectionist tariff policies which had created an easy domestic market.

The FBI leadership, although relatively broad-minded and imaginative in its international outlook, held views which accorded more with an FTA or EFTA type of solution than with the EEC scheme. Since 1946 these leaders had worked for trade expansion on the basis of liberal free trading and intergovernmental arrangements of the OEEC pattern; later they developed strong personal commitments to the EFTA, which they had done so much to create. They and other business leaders distrusted the Common Market as an overly idealistic conception and as a restrictionist grouping which turned its back on the developing nations. They also had no readiness to face integration and interference in the British economy. Business only began to support entry when it became evident that the European choice for Britain was one of membership versus complete exclusion, but the November 1958 collapse of the FTA talks did not make this choice evident. The FBI-supported establishment of EFTA was meant to facilitate a wider European "bridge-building," and it was not until 1960-61 that industry—and Government—realized that no EEC-EFTA association would be possible.

During the 1959-61 period, a shift in attitude occurred as the largest British firms began to view the Common Market in a more favorable light. Among the most important reasons for this increasingly European view were Britain's trade figures. While exports to the Sterling area had stagnated (rising by only 1 percent between 1954 and 1960), exports to Western Europe climbed by 29 percent in the same period.[3] Moreover, the country was approaching a watershed (which it reached in the first quarter of 1962) when, for the first time, exports to

---

[3] *The Guardian* (London), June 29, 1961.

Europe would surpass those to the Commonwealth. Business also looked to the Common Market for a competitive stimulus. In the words of an FBI Deputy President, "Our young men are not at full stretch. The Common Market will provide the market and the competition. You will find that the opportunity will be eagerly grasped and the Dunkirk spirit recaptured."[4]

For the large firms, economies of scale and the expectation of a huge tariff-free market made Britain's Common Market entry an attractive prospect. Given their own size and resources, any short-term readjustments required in adapting to the EEC did not present insuperable difficulties. The smaller firms and trade associations were either hesitant or opposed because of their own greater vulnerability in the domestic market and often less imaginative leadership. Their fears tended to find expression in political rather than economic terms because commercial arguments against Common Market entry began to be seen as admissions of inadequacy and because there were greater advantages in playing upon public concern for the Commonwealth and British sovereignty. Accordingly, while Lord Chandos (a representative of big business, as head of the Institute of Directors) favored Common Market entry, he concentrated on economic reasons and explicitly opposed any movement toward political integration. By contrast, the Commonwealth Industries Association (an organization composed mainly of small industrialists and businessmen) hammered away at the political implications of membership and argued that Britain must not choose Europe over the Commonwealth.

As the Common Market choice matured, the FBI leadership found itself in a delicate position. Being the dominant spokesman for industry, and representing greater numbers and larger firms than the ABCC or NUM, the Federation moved toward a slightly "European" policy. However, serious strains

---

[4] P. F. Runge, *FBI Review* (September, 1962), p. 24.

existed within the organization. The 200 largest firms tended to become increasingly outspoken advocates of accession to the EEC, while the small firms and trade associations took a more hesitant view. Indeed, the *FBI Review* itself called attention to the necessity for the Federation to work within a broad mandate laid down by the members, even though private views of the staff might diverge from those of the membership.[5]

The positions taken by the major business associations and firms during the run-up to Macmillan's July 1961 announcement reflect the divergence of views between big business and the FBI. As early as June 1960, articles in *The Director* (Journal of the Institute of Directors) asserted that the wider free trade arrangement was no longer a possibility and described the choice before Britain as one of Common Market entry versus total exclusion. The journal also argued that business opinion was moving increasingly to the acceptance of full membership, and that it was time the Government made up its mind. British industry, it said, had decided to go into Europe, whether or not it left the Government "waving goodbye from the dock"; yet Government policy remained approximately "We don't know what we are not going to do and we don't know why we are not going to do it."[6]

By the early months of 1961, large firms were making it clear to the Government just how important they felt the Common Market to be. ICI announced the intention of investing £100 million in the Common Market during the next decade, the Chairman of the General Electric Company (Arnold Lindley) expressed alarm at the U.K.'s exclusion from the Common Market, a National Export Council team reported on the tariff threat to Britain in the Dutch Market, the head of the National Coal Board (Lord Robens) urged that Britain join Europe in order to sell her coal, and the managing director of

---

[5] *FBI Review* (February, 1961), p. 33.

[6] *The Director* (June, 1960), p. 483; and (September, 1960), pp. 419-420.

the British Motor Corporation (the U.K.'s largest automobile manufacturer) described it as "madness" to stay out of the Common Market.[7]

While the biggest firms were making these judgments independently, the FBI had also been exploring the Common Market option. In August 1960, at FBI initiative, the industrial federations of the EFTA began examining the Rome Treaty to see which of its provisions would be acceptable; and in July 1961, just two weeks prior to the Prime Minister's announcement, the FBI Grand Council published its own policy statement. It emphasized two fundamental points. First, the FBI would not support any solution which required the Commonwealth to pay a substantial part of the price for Britain's association with the Common Market; and second, Britain's contractual and moral obligations to EFTA must be honored in full. But these were not the only reservations. The Grand Council found many aspects of the Community's agricultural policies unacceptable, and preferred cooperation between sovereign governments rather than the use of common institutions. It also cited a host of lesser industrial problems such as restrictive practices, social policy, and "dumping," but described these as negotiable.[8]

By issuing this policy memo, the FBI had changed its FTA and EFTA position in only one major respect: it was now willing to accept in principle a common external tariff. Even this concession was only in response to a position already taken by HMG, and was couched in negative terms.[9] The whole tenor of the document was legalistic and parochial, yet Sir Norman Kipping expressed disappointment that some press reports described the FBI document as too negative[10]—more

---

[7] *Financial Times* (London), March 1, 1961, May 4, 1961, May 5, 1961; *Sunday Times* (London), May 21, 1961; *Sunday Telegraph* (London), June 18, 1961.

[8] FBI, *British Industry and Europe* (London, July, 1961).

[9] "In principle we do not oppose the suggestion for a common or harmonized tariff put forward by HMG" *ibid.*, p. 3.

[10] *The Times* (London), July 21, 1961.

appropriately, he might have expressed surprise that not everyone did so. While the FBI's wish for an early end to the division in Europe may have been genuine, the FBI terms were scarcely reconcilable with Common Market membership. The statement admitted that the Six probably saw the agricultural policy and common institutions as of overriding importance, yet it expressed major reservations on both points. Moreover, the statement itself had emerged from a Byzantine debate over wording, in which those reluctant to consider Common Market entry had gained the upper hand. The conclusion of the document stipulated that the FBI should not "become committed *to* formal negotiations with the Six until existing differences . . . have been narrowed as to offer the prospect of a satisfactory outcome."[11] The "Europeans" had sought unsuccessfully to replace "to" with "in."

There is no doubt that in the crucial phase of decision-making the FBI as an organization lagged behind the British Government. The role of individual firms is another matter. The result of a *Sunday Times* survey of 130 top firms published about the same time as the FBI statement certainly indicated a more favorable business attitude than that shown by the FBI.[12] The largest manufacturers were under-represented on the Grand Council, and by late May not only were they almost uniformly in favor of full Common Market membership for Britain, but some smaller high-cost businesses in protected industries appeared to be following the lead of big business rather than lobbying against entry.[13]

---

[11] FBI, *British Industry and Europe, op. cit.,* p. 5; italics added.

[12] *Sunday Times,* July 16, 1961.

[13] The large banks did not visibly play a strongly pro-European role. An examination of the Annual Reports of the Chairmen of Barclays, Martins, Westminster, Midland, National Provincial, and Lloyds in the years 1955 through 1961 indicates only moderate support for the FTA (in 1956-57). Later (1958-60) they also supported the idea, widely held in government, politics, and industry, of some kind of associational arrangement to link the EFTA and EEC countries. Not until the year-end statements for 1961 did *any* of these reports advocate outright Common Market entry. Source: annual reports printed in the *Economist*.

The forces which were moving Britain in the direction of the Common Market, and the causes and nature of the Prime Minister's decision, will be discussed later (Chapter 7); however it is appropriate to note here the direct relationship of British business to the Government's decision to seek admission to the Common Market. Although Macmillan made the choice in advance of opinion within the Conservative Party and the country at large, important and informal high-level consultations did take place between the Prime Minister, the Chancellor of the Exchequer and individual industrial leaders. The first of these meetings came several months after the October 1959 General Election victory of the Conservatives, and involved a mutual exchange of views. Originally, and on basically political grounds, the Prime Minister took more of an interest in the Common Market than did the industrial leaders, but during 1960 they began to see just how the EEC was developing and to calculate the advantages of entry and the risks of staying out. They also became increasingly aware that basic changes would take place in industry whether or not Britain entered the Common Market. During the year these leaders met again with the Prime Minister, urging upon him more rapid progress toward a European arrangement. They were told in effect that he would seek to make Common Market entry the policy of HMG if they would work to bring along the small firms and trade associations.

The movement of industrial leaders toward Europe thus appears to have been roughly concurrent with the development of Macmillan's own position. Their crucial importance lay not in pressuring the Government toward this course of action, but first, in assuring the Prime Minister that in proceeding he would do so with their support, and second, in actually working to convert the "soggy lump" of British industry to the European cause.

Business and the Negotiation Period

If business played a decidedly subsidiary part in the circumstances surrounding the British decision to seek Common Market membership, it did attain increased importance during the 18 months in which the country stood poised on the threshold of Europe.

The July 1961 FBI policy statement reflected only a minimum position within the organization. With time, the FBI's interest and enthusiasm in the Common Market grew, and by the following spring, the just-retired FBI President was asserting that "British industry has nothing to lose and everything to gain by getting into these markets now. . . ."[14]

As an organization, the FBI's formal task during the period of negotiations was in many respects similar to what it had been during the EFTA negotiations two years previously. Accordingly, the FBI Annual Report listed the Federation's functions:

to ensure that members were kept informed of developments as they arose, to maintain a two-way flow of information and advice with HMG on national issues, and to ensure that where the interests of individual industries were affected, they should have the fullest opportunities of direct consultation with the appropriate Government departments.[15]

As usual, there was more in substance to the FBI's role than it was politic to cite. The FBI undertook its first function, information for members, as a massive exercise in education and persuasion. In meetings, literature, special handbooks, a monthly European integration supplement, and a host of miscellaneous ways, the FBI successfully educated the bulk of its member firms and trade associations to both the facts and desirability of the Common Market. The FBI and the numerous promotional groups also made considerable use of special

---

[14] Sir William McFadzean, *The Guardian,* June 3, 1962.
[15] FBI, *Annual Report* (1961), p. 10.

PROPERTY OF
UNIV. OF ALASKA LIBRARY

conferences in introducing and indoctrinating businessmen to the Common Market. Thus the *Observer's* business correspondent wrote:

If any British businessman has not yet attended a Common Market conference, it can hardly have been because of lack of an invitation. Scarcely a day passes without news of some fresh gathering to discuss the effects of 'going into Europe,' whether it is a mass jamboree by the seaside or a select houseparty of two dozen industrialists in a provincial city.[16]

The thoroughness of the FBI in paying full heed to the formal Common Market terms actually gave concern to industry within the Six. Operating on the assumption that entry would occur, the Federation produced a booklet on Article 85 of the Rome Treaty (restrictive trade practices)[17] and began explaining to firms how to register under the Community law. European firms were aghast at this. They had been ignoring the provision, whereas the British, not being accustomed to written constitutions, and the laxity with which they are often observed, were saying, "we may not like it but it's the law."

In its second function, maintaining a two-way flow of information and advice with the Government, the FBI operated through its usual Board of Trade channel by means of the small liason group under Sir William Palmer. This contact involved technical details as well as some policy matters. The most important single matter of communication was a confidential survey on potentially hard-hit industries which the FBI presented to HMG in December 1961. The report sought to identify those industries likely to suffer from the effects of Common Market entry, and to work out proposals to aid them. As usual, the FBI was deeply concerned that no comprehensive European settlement take place without the vital interests of industry being fully consulted and accounted for. But while the technical and commercial details of the Common Market

---

[16] May 6, 1962, quoted in Robert L. Pfaltzgraff Jr., "The Common Market Debate in Britain," *Orbis*, 7, no. 2 (Summer, 1963); 280.

[17] FBI, *Restrictive Trade Practices* (August, 1962).

subject made extensive industrial consultation appropriate, few specific items merited being raised to the level of the national interest. Thus, although civil servants alluded to lesser modifications having been arranged to accommodate specific business interests, there is no evidence that any substantial changes were made.

The FBI's third function consisted of contacts at the international level. These took place through the European integration committee of the Council of European Industrial Federations (CEIF), the International Chamber of Commerce, the Council of Industrial Federations of EFTA, the EEC Commission, and bilateral exchanges with German and other industrial federations among the Six. These contacts were not of great consequence, although a month after the Common Market negotiations came to a halt, the FBI suggested that British industry had possibly been in a stronger position than HMG to obtain information and influence developments through its contacts with the EEC Commission.[18]

With the onset of the negotiation period, other British business and industrial groups also took on a more active role. Those which represented cross-sections of industry, such as the ABCC, NUM, and CIA emphasized the importance of close consultation with HMG. The ABCC was surprisingly receptive to Common Market entry, and to a poll asking "Do you consider that the U.K. should join the Common Market?" 75 percent of its members responding answered yes.[19] The NUM maintained a somewhat more cautious position, but nonetheless found Common Market accession acceptable provided basic safeguards and consultation existed. What is worthy of notice is that the overwhelming bulk of individual industrial and trade associations had come to support entry with only minor reservations.

One of the more unusual examples of wholehearted backing

---

[18] FBI, Minutes of the Second Trade Association Liaison Meeting, S. 7A. 63, February 14, 1963.

[19] *The Guardian,* June 23, 1962.

for membership came from the cotton textile industry—traditionally highly protectionist in outlook. The industry adopted this surprising position in the belief that only by joining the Common Market, under the terms of the Rome Treaty, could it survive against the massive free entry of Commonwealth and other cheap textile imports. Whereas these imports made up 36 percent of Britain's home textile consumption, they constituted only 5 percent in the Common Market countries. The head of one of Britain's largest cotton textile firms expressed confidence that Common Market producers would insist that Britain enter the Common Market only on the existing terms, thus eliminating the massive free imports from Hong Kong, India, and Pakistan.[20] Indeed the industry's Textile Action Group even exploited a transnational community of interest by meeting with Common Market textile leaders and advising them to oppose British entry unless HMG agreed to full protective textile tariffs.[21]

This instance of an unfavorable attitude toward the Commonwealth based on tangible economic interest found its converse in the passionate Commonwealth attachment of the Commonwealth Industries Association. Virtually the only general business group opposed to Common Market entry, the Association maintained a steady fire of criticism throughout the negotiations. What is interesting about this campaign is the way in which it centered upon political objections to Britain's entry. The Association argued that Common Market membership would destroy the political and economic cohesion of the Commonwealth and damage Britain's sovereignty by decreasing the power and prestige of Parliament and the Crown. The depth of the organization's sovereignty objection was great enough to lead it to state that "It is not necessary to approve of socialism to claim that it is the right of the British

---

[20] Arnold Ogden, Chairman of Townhead Mill Company Ltd., letter to the *Daily Telegraph* (London), December 6, 1961.

[21] *Financial Times,* June 21, 1962.

people to make the decision."[22] The CIA asserted that the Government's motives were not economic, but political; moreover, it maintained that those in favor of entry were obsessed with anti-communism and with a blind admiration for size. Instead of entering the Common Market, Britain could best serve Europe as the center of the Commonwealth, to which Britain and Europe's debt was "written in blood from Flanders to Gallipoli."[23]

The methods used by the CIA in putting forward its views on the Common Market question included features typical of both promotional and sectional pressure groups. It supplied speakers to nearly 300 various private and public meetings, yet also invoked the concurrent majority doctrine by asserting that the great majority of those in U.K. industry—both employers and employed—must clearly be seen to be in favor of such a move before Britain could enter the Common Market.[24] At the same time, the Association directed special efforts at the Conservative Party, where the traditional Commonwealth and sovereignty position could be expected to have the greatest appeal (the CIA's executive body already included ten Conservative MP's). The organization sent leaflets advocating the Commonwealth alternative to all MP's and Conservative constituency association officers. The emotive power of this approach is typified by the warning of John Biggs-Davison, a Conservative MP and CIA member: "the betrayal of British agriculture and Colonial Preference destroyed the Party of Peel. The betrayal of British agriculture and Commonwealth Preference will destroy the Party of Macmillan."[25]

---

[22] Commonwealth Industries Association, *Monthly Bulletin* (June, 1961), p. 2.

[23] *Ibid.* (July, 1962), pp. 3-5; and (February, 1962), p. 6.

[24] *Ibid.* (June, 1961), p. 2.

[25] *Ibid.* (September, 1962), p. 11.

CONCLUSION — THE ROLE OF BUSINESS

What importance did the business sector in general and the FBI in particular possess? It is safe to say that while the FBI played a small initial role in the formative policy stages, a hostile FBI would quite definitely have prevented HMG from going ahead with a decision to seek access to the Common Market. The innate importance of the business sector was reinforced here by the heavily commercial treatment (analyzed below in Chapter 7) which the Government gave to the Common Market issue in public. At least the support given first by individual major industrial leaders, and later by major organizations such as the FBI, gave assurance to HMG that its European policy was likely to be viable within the U.K. The basic role of the FBI, as far as the Government was concerned, was in bringing along the amorphous mass of British business through its intermingled education and persuasion efforts, and, during 1962, in being one of the most important sectors of the British political community actively promoting the European cause.

The events in this period shed considerable light on the nature and limitations of the FBI as a pressure group. A relative lack of discipline and resources at times weakened the Federation's role, and numerous major firms and associations had the capacity to by-pass the FBI and communicate directly with the Government. FBI leaders were always sensitive to avoid describing the role of the Federation as one of pressuring anybody: rather they preferred to speak of consultations. Indeed the organization displayed a striking unwillingness to touch what it considered to be political issues. In the words of the *FBI Review:*

But faced with the question of whether Britain should come to terms with the Six, the economic judgment of many is coloured, or even over-ridden by political considerations. If only for that reason, the function of the FBI *vis-à-vis* the Government could hardly be that of a pressure group, urging a definite line of policy: it was bound to remain largely confined to those of sounding board of opinion and adviser on technical problems.[26]

In fact, the writer of these words went so far in disclaiming political involvement for organized industry that he asserted the industrialist had in the last resort to determine his stand only as a voter. This remarkable sensitivity to avoid involvement with political issues was more verbal than actual. Despite a certain difficulty in reconciling divergent opinions, and a stress on technical matters, the implications of the Federation's positions were inherently political. It is self-evident that the involvement of industrial leaders in the policy-making process was not merely as humble and individual voters in the party government channel of political communication between society and government; rather, it was as major spokesmen utilizing the functional representation pathway between organized interest groups and government.

Of course it is true that communication between government and industry is a two-way process and that on the Common Market issue business was as much the object as the manipulator of pressures. The FBI as an organization occupied something of a middle ground in this channel, since it maintained a mutual flow of information and advice not only with the Government above it, but with the industrial membership below it. The reality of this position can be observed by reference to criticisms made of the FBI by its own membership. In replying to assertions that the FBI was in the Government's pocket, the FBI Director-General observed that the organization was "half-way between Government and industry," and that once HMG had adopted a policy affecting industry, the FBI's task became one of explaining to its members what implications this would have for them. The act of expounding Government policy did not necessarily mean that the FBI endorsed it.[27]

[26] *FBI Review* (February, 1961), p. 33.
[27] Sir Norman Kipping, *FBI Review* (January, 1962), p. 22.

THE TUC AND APPROVAL OF
GOVERNMENT POLICY

ATTITUDES AND POLICY

TUC policy toward the Common Market rested on the same basis which underlay its previous European views. That is, its interest and attitude were determined by calculations of how the European proposals would affect full employment and economic expansion.

A basic change in attitude began to take place about April and May 1960. Formerly the TUC had not welcomed the idea of Britain joining the Common Market, but TUC leaders such as Harry Douglass and Frank Cousins[28] became more concerned about the consequences for the British economy of an EFTA/EEC split. They made it known to HMG that they favored Government efforts at bridge-building between the Six and the Seven. The first major labor endorsement for Common Market membership came in an August 1960 report by the executive of the Confederation of Shipbuilding and Engineering Unions, which proposed that the Government be urged to seek entry "without delay" and before "irreparable damage" was done to British automobile export prospects.[29] This viewpoint closely paralleled that of the automobile manufacturers.

The TUC reacted sympathetically to Macmillan's July 1961 announcement. A General Council statement agreed in principle with the decision to open negotiations, adding the commonplace reservation that "satisfactory arrangements" should be made for the needs of the U.K., Commonwealth, and EFTA. The General Council noted that it would refrain from judging whether Britain should actually enter the Community until the conditions of membership had be-

---

[28] Frank Cousins subsequently became an opponent of entry in the spring of 1961 on basically political grounds.

[29] *Financial Times,* August 11, 1960.

come clearer, and it affirmed that, rather than taking a theoretical view of supranationalism, it would "judge any agreement by the test of how it would affect the well-being of working people. . . ."[30] The statement also showed some concern for problems involving the balance of payments, labor mobility, equal representation on the Economic and Social Committee, effective planning, and protection of poorer sections of the Community against rises in domestic food prices. On the vital questions of full employment, economic growth, and improved living standards, the General Council observed that the Rome Treaty was inadequate in that it failed to define aims and methods; however it recognized that the practical record of the Europeans had nonetheless been good. What is striking about the TUC's response is the absence of any kind of political assessment. Neither as threat nor opportunity did non-economic factors emerge as the criteria for judgment.

In September 1961, the Annual TUC Conference endorsed the General Council's policy statement. The main opposition came from the left, which (in contrast to its position inside the Labour Party) then possessed very little voice within the leadership. Led by three of the small unions (National Society of Operative Printers and Assistants; Draughtsmen's and Allied Technicians Association; Association of Supervisory Staffs, Executives and Technicians), the opposition found fault with the EEC largely on political grounds, such as damage to Commonwealth ties and British sovereignty, and exacerbation of the division between Eastern and Western Europe. Due to the flexibility of the General Council and the choice of phrasing in its report, the opposition motions were heavily defeated, with even the otherwise skeptical Agricultural Workers and the Transport and General Workers voting against the Draughtsmen's resolution.

Comparative unemployment and earnings figures con-

---

[30] TUC, *Report* (1961), pp. 468-470. Also see TUC, *Industrial News,* no. 15 (August 25, 1961).

tributed to the unions' favorable attitude toward the Common Market. By the middle of 1961, only Italy and Belgium had higher unemployment rates than Britain[31] and even in total wage rates Britain lagged behind Germany.[32] Equally important, the prospect of social harmonization was not threatening to the unions. With the exception of the National Health Service, the U.K. was no longer the leader in any one Social Welfare field, and only Italy possessed a system seriously inferior to that of the U.K. In any event, the harmonization was only to be in an upward direction.

Before the end of 1961, the TUC had established lines of communication with the unions of the Six and with Edward Heath, the Lord Privy Seal and leader of the British negotiating team. In early November the European trade unionists met in London, where those of the Six welcomed the TUC's acceptance of social policy harmonization and agreed with the TUC view on improving full employment provisions. The Common Market unions especially approved the prospect of U.K. entry because of their expectation that this would strengthen union solidarity and influence within the EEC. Meanwhile, and more importantly, the Lord Privy Seal had proposed to the TUC in December that he meet with its representatives after each round of Ministerial talks (approximately monthly). The TUC leaders were delighted to accept Heath's offer; this contact with the Government enabled them to receive information about the progress of negotiations and to keep the Government informed of their own views.

By far the most significant contacts between the TUC and Heath were a series of written exchanges. The first of these

---

[31] Source: Common Market Campaign, *Forward Britain Into Europe: the case for Britain joining the Common Market* (London, 1962), pp. 22-23.

[32] Source: U.K. Council of the European Movement, *Common Market Plain Facts* (October, 1962). Calculations based on average cash earnings plus employer social security payments.

was a long and detailed memo sent by the TUC in June 1962 and made public in July. Having been briefed several times by Heath, the General Council had drawn up a statement at his request in which it developed the position approved by the 1961 Congress and set out a list of its main concerns. Chiefly the statement cited planned economic expansion as the test of the merits of the case for U.K. entry. The TUC made it clear that EEC policies ought to be directed toward this, and that HMG must suffer no loss of its own planning power over such things as price control, aid to nationalized industries, and control of capital issues. The memo also observed that the Treaty of Rome provisions on employment policies were a serious weakness, and raised points about the need for limitations on free labor movement and strengthening of the Economic and Social Committee.

Significantly, the memo concentrated almost entirely on the economic facets of the EEC and put forward fairly detailed points. On matters less immediately relevant to union concerns it displayed reasonable flexibility. Thus, on agriculture, the TUC spoke of arranging matters within the framework of the EEC's long-term agricultural policy and did not demand that Britain retain her existing support system. On Commonwealth trade, it spoke of safeguarding the existing volume of trade with Britain and Europe and of allowing for its growth, but made no stipulation that the old arrangement must remain. Even on the issue of political integration, the TUC position was shaped largely by economic criteria. The unions had limited interest in the subject *per se,* and where there were potential benefits attached they were willing to seek increased integration. Hence the General Council argued for strengthening of the EEC's Economic and Social Committee, and (perhaps under the influence of the Six's unions) issued an impressively supra-national statement concerning the EEC Social Fund: "The General Council considers that the European Social Fund should be strengthened by increasing the funds available to it, and by amending its terms of reference to reduce its dependence on the prior action of governments and to extend its operations beyond the transitional period."[33]

Nowhere in the memorandum was there the inflexibility of means and righteous posturing which characterized numerous other groups and individuals criticizing entry or officially reserving judgment. The contrast with positions then being taken in the Labour Party and by the NFU is striking.

The sequel to this memo was a meeting between Heath and representatives of the General Council on July 23. Some weeks later, the Privy Seal sent the TUC a long written reply. This dialogue calmed a number of fears among labor leaders, leaving many of them with the general view that while specific TUC demands were not likely to be satisfied, the overall result would be acceptable. In his reply, Heath welcomed TUC support for closer European economic association, offered reassurances that Governmental assistance to nationalized industries seemed compatible with EEC membership, and replied to the main TUC point that a general obligation to full employment be written into the Rome Treaty. He cited Articles 2 and 104 of the Treaty, which committed the EEC to economic expansion and high employment, and pledged that "If the U.K. becomes a member of the Community, HMG would naturally use their influence, if necessary, to ensure that the policies of the Community paid proper regard to the need to maintain a high and stable level of employment."[34]

Basically, Heath dealt with each of the unions' items of concern by offering reassurances or pointing to the words of the Rome Treaty or the actual operation of the EEC. The impression left by his reply was that the TUC's words had been carefully listened to, but that no modifications in HMG's bargaining position were really necessary or desirable.

---

[33] Memorandum to the Lord Privy Seal, Edward Heath, TUC, *Report* (1962), pp. 261-267.

[34] TUC, *Report* (1962), p. 474.

In turn, the Economic Committee prepared a report for the General Council which indicated that, with the exception of full employment, it had been reassured on most points. It observed that Heath had given such assurances as he could, and—possibly most significant of all for the TUC leaders— he had taken the General Council's proposals seriously. Although the unanimous report of the General Council to the Annual Congress stated that it was still too early to commit the TUC to approval of or opposition to Britain's entry, the sentiment of the General Council rested with the Common Market; its policy of reserving judgment was less attributable to lack of knowledge of the exact terms than to a concern not to embarrass the Labour Party. There was also some fear that a more positive statement would meet with difficulty at the Annual Congress.

The September 1962 Congress adopted the General Council report by nearly a 3 to 1 margin. In the words of the resolution, "In present circumstances, and while the Government is still engaged in negotiations, it is too early for the Congress to commit itself to approval of or opposition to Britain's entry into the EEC."[35] What is most revealing about the standard of judgment within the TUC is the split inside the organization between those who were pro- and anti-Common Market. Basically, those who decided on economic grounds were pro, with opposition coming from unions in the few industries obviously likely to suffer as a result of EEC membership. However, the basic criticism within the TUC ranks originated mainly on political and personal lines. Many who were anti on political grounds, also added an economic rationale in an effort to carry their unions. The left, with important exceptions such as Robert Edwards of the Chemical Workers, invoked arguments about a narrow, Catholic and capitalist Europe, the dangers of being tied to Germany, and the need to preserve the multiracial and third-force Com-

---

[35] *Ibid.,* p. 480.

monwealth.[36] Apart from Frank Cousins (T&GWU) and Ted Hill (Boilermakers), the General Council members were pro-Common Market, with the opposition coming from leaders of smaller unions, and from rank-and-file activists.

Despite the dramatic hardening in the position of the Labour Party a month later, and the increased politicization of the Common Market issue, the TUC maintained its "wait and see" policy. Indeed General Council members seemed on the verge of approving entry if the final terms were no worse than those already negotiated, though it is not wholly certain they could have carried the TUC with them.[37]

DIFFERENCES WITH THE LABOUR PARTY

What stands out most prominently about the TUC's position is the contrast with that of the Labour Party. This divergence reveals some of the differences and tensions between the economic and political wings of the British labor movement.

Despite assertions to the contrary by some members of both organizations, the differences were of major importance. First, the TUC was far more thorough in analyzing the Rome Treaty and the operation of the EEC. Its major policy statements of August 1961 and June 1962 were impressive in their detail. By contrast, the Labour Party positions were more vague, even on specifically economic points such as Commonwealth trade and agricultural support. Secondly, the TUC

---

[36] The first union to declare itself against entry was the National Union of Railwaymen. Critics in the union described the Common Market as the enemy of Socialism and a threat to working-class standards. The rebuttal by the Union General Secretary was that if the NUR opposed joining everything unless it were socialist, it could not approve the UN, the TUC, or the Commonwealth. *Daily Telegraph*, July 5, 1962.

[37] The majority of TUC leaders were pro-entry, but faced the difficulty that—although the rank and file were approximately divided on the question—local union activists tended to be anti-EEC. Colin Beever, "Trade Union Re-Thinking," *Journal of Common Market Studies*, 2, no. 2 (November, 1963): 150.

imposed fewer and mostly different conditions from those of Labour. (The Party's celebrated five conditions comprised safeguards for the Commonwealth, agriculture, and EFTA, and independence in foreign policy and economic planning.) This contrast is underlined by the fact that at the September 1962 TUC Congress, a resolution essentially taking the Labour Party position was put forward but failed to be adopted. Third, the TUC was more flexible; rather than insisting on an immutable set of prerequisites, the General Council spoke of the need to decide on probabilities. Finally, while the TUC remained on the fence, it continued to face in the pro-Common Market direction. Whereas the debate in Labour's NEC was over outright rejection versus just barely keeping the Common Market option open through the five conditions, the General Council was debating whether to recommend entry or maintain its wait-and-see position. Indeed, at the October 1962 Labour Party Conference, following Gaitskell's passionately critical address, two of the most powerful General Council members (William Carron of the Amalgamated Engineering Union and Jack Cooper of the General and Municipal Workers) spoke in favor of entry. In November 1962, the TUC General Council conspicuously refused to follow the lead of Gaitskell and the Labour Party. Then, following the de Gaulle veto in January 1963, at a time when Labour was criticizing the Government for having negotiated on its knees, representatives of the TUC and unions of the Six signed a declaration unanimously agreeing that "the governments concerned should continue their negotiations with a view to the U.K. becoming a full member of the Community."[38] According to one trade union source, the signing led to an argument between Harold Wilson (then on the verge of becoming Labour Party leader) and George Woodcock (General Secretary of the TUC). Woodcock is supposed

---

[38] *Ibid.*

to have said, "Well, Harold, the bomb is yours, but bread and butter for eight and a half million members is ours."[39]

Whether apocryphal or not, the above comment reflects the major reason for the difference in approach between the TUC and Labour; the former judged Europe on basically economic criteria, while for the latter the issue was unquestionably political. This difference was both inherent and logical. For the Labour Party, the truism applied that "the opposition opposes." Hugh Gaitskell's major speech to the Labour Party Conference in September 1962 contained the judgment that the economic aspects of Common Market entry were evenly balanced, pro and con, and that Labour must make up its mind on political grounds. For the TUC, the European subject was dealt with not by the International Committee of the General Council but by the Economic Committee. Because their standards of judgment were economic growth and full employment, the unions tended to look upon Common Market entry from the viewpoint of their individual industries. Given the increasing sentiment by industrial leaders that the balance of economic argument favored Common Market entry, it was not surprising that union leaders should begin to adopt a similar outlook.[40]

If the major explanation for the differences between Labour and the TUC rests on the complexities of a political versus economic approach, there were nonetheless additional factors determining the TUC attitude. For one thing, the General Council simply had better information about the subject. The TUC secretariat had prepared excellent briefings for the leadership and, especially in mid-1961, the TUC knew more about the Common Market than did the Labour Party. In addition, there was a personal aspect. Sir Alan

---

[39] Quoted in a confidential conversation with a trade union leader, April 24, 1967.

[40] For example, chemical union leaders tended to share the favorable Common Market view of their industries, while printing unions sided with their employers in opposition.

Birch, who headed the Economic Committee, had long been a partisan of Europe; during the years when not many others had been interested in Europe, he and a few General Council members helped to establish pro-European precedents for the TUC. Another important personal factor involved TUC relations with Edward Heath. These were generally very good, dating from Heath's earlier days as Minister of Labour, and Heath obviously took pains to keep the TUC well briefed on the Common Market negotiations. Finally, there was the fact that the TUC's international ties were strongest with the European trade union movement, while the Labour Party had closer ties with the Commonwealth. Years of TUC meetings and informal contacts with the European unions, all of which, with the exception of the Italian CGIL and French CGT, were strongly pro-EEC, had dispelled many potential worries. By contrast, Labour (and Hugh Gaitskell) had strong affinities with the Commonwealth Socialist parties and with the Scandinavian Socialist governments, but less so with the Continent.

THE TUC AND HMG

As a pressure group, the TUC was neither in advance of nor much behind the Government's policy, but rather willing to go along provided it received reasonable assurances on full employment. Despite regular communication with Edward Heath, the unions had little impact on the Government's position or the negotiations themselves. By contrast, the roles of the FBI and of the NFU were more significant. What explains this relative weakness of the TUC?

For one thing, the Government was unlikely to join or not join Europe on the basis of TUC views. HMG was determined to go into the Common Market and the TUC could really only shape its policy with the expectation that Britain would become a member. Furthermore, the crucial bargaining issues, on which HMG found it advisable to work closely with the relevant groups, did not involve labor. Unlike the

EFTA negotiations, it was not the case that the details of association were unimportant to the TUC, but that the principal items of inherent national significance under negotiation at Brussels involved industrial, agricultural and Commonwealth matters, rather than full employment or mobility of labor. Finally, the TUC was without the ultimate power resources of the NFU and FBI. In contrast to the NFU, the TUC lacked the political power involved in having a bloc of votes to withhold from the Conservative Government. (That in many respects the NFU's voting power was rather illusory is less important than the fact that some Conservatives feared the loss of up to forty-six seats, and that agriculture still had strong emotional appeal within the Party.) Agriculture was also of national consequence because of the balance of payments problem, long-term trade balances, and cost of living. Nor did the TUC leaders have the importance of the main business and industrial leaders. Whatever its political implications, the Common Market was substantially a trading arrangement, and the FBI represented the people who had immense resources of information and who would be among the main decision-makers. Since Britain must "export or die," the voices of these individuals had weighty importance. It is therefore readily understandable that the Government-TUC consultation was basically a process of explanation and reassurance rather than bargaining. As part of a campaign to win over the bulk of British opinion and interests, HMG was eager to woo the TUC to the European cause, but at the same time, the TUC neither inherently possessed nor was accorded any significance as a veto power.

THE NFU AND THE TERMS OF ENTRY

Of the three major interest groups, the NFU had the most to lose by any British move toward Europe. Furthermore, agriculture represented the most difficult domestic problem for Britain in coming to terms with the Six. This basic importance reinforced the position of the National Farmers' Union and made it the group with the most impact on Britain's position at Brussels.

NFU POLICIES AND GOVERNMENT PLEDGES

Agriculture was the one sector of the British economy basically critical of Common Market membership. NFU fears were due mainly to the prospect that the postwar British agricultural support system, based on the Agriculture Acts of 1947 and 1957, would come to an end. In this system, the Government annually reviewed the state of the agricultural sector in extremely close consultation with the NFU, then set levels of support for the year. It fixed guaranteed prices for the main products (e.g., beef, lamb, pork, eggs, wool, milk, cereals, potatoes, and sugar beets) and also made direct grants to encourage certain types of farming. Usually the guaranteed prices were maintained by deficiency payments to farmers because large amounts of basic foods were imported (especially from the Commonwealth) at low world price levels, and hence the price the housewife paid for food was relatively low. Horticulture (fruit and vegetables) constituted the major exception to this system and was supported by protective tariffs and grants to improve its competitiveness.[41]

The support system provided considerable advantages for Britain as a whole and for the farmers in particular. Basically it maximized three things: high domestic production by a stable and prosperous agricultural sector, cheap Commonwealth food imports, and low food prices for the consumer. Under the system, Britain produced about two-thirds of all her temperate-zone food products and about one-half of all the food she consumed.

The Common Market system was quite different from the British one. It involved a managed market in agriculture,

---

[41] *Britain and the EEC, the Economic Background* (HMSO, May, 1967), p. 24.

protected by tariffs on imports, and the cost of support fell mainly on the consumer rather than on the taxpayer. Most of the tariffs collected went to the EEC's Agricultural Guidance and Guarantee Fund, which the Commission used to finance and improve agriculture within the Community. The NFU had numerous objections to this system. The most important of these were that its stability would be less than that provided under the Agricultural Acts, many guaranteed prices would be abandoned for looser target prices, horticulture would be seriously hit by competition from within the Common Market, and production costs, especially for food grains, would rise.[42] Most important of all, the NFU feared the removal of control of agricultural policy from the British Government to the European Commission. Under the existing U.K. system, the NFU was the supreme and unchallenged spokesman for agriculture. Of all the quasi-corporate relationships between the Government and interest groups, the NFU's, under the Agricultural Acts and the experience of many years, was the most intimate and powerful. In no circumstances could the NFU expect to exercise such a role if agricultural policy-making were removed to Brussels.

Although the fact was later generally obscured, there were, in addition to the substantial disadvantages, certain real benefits for British agriculture in Common Market membership. From a competitive standpoint, British farmers were far more efficient and were organized in larger units than their European counterparts. For example, Britain's average net output per man in agriculture was more than double that for the EEC as a whole. With the U.K. figure set equal to an index of 100, the most efficient of the Six were the Netherlands and Belgium with 89. Germany had a figure of 57, and the most important agricultural producer, France, a level of 49. Counting Italy, the EEC average was 42.[43] With Britain in the Com-

---

[42] NFU, "Agriculture in the Community," *Information Service*, 16, no. 2 (1961), 68.

[43] D. T. Healey, "The Common Market and British Agriculture,"

mon Market, British farmers could avoid the dumping of European surpluses on the British market, would have the benefit of higher prices for their products, and would not even have to bear the costs of the new system since these would fall mainly on the consumer. In addition, there were potential gains in political weight. Whereas those in agriculture comprised only 4 to 5 percent of the U.K. population, the figure for the Six as a whole was a potent 25 percent. Thus the NFU might benefit by cooperating with European farm organizations.

As far as HMG was concerned, there was a different set of agricultural considerations surrounding Common Market membership. The cost of the British system had become so great (about £270 million on the Exchequer in 1960, representing three-quarters of the agricultural industry's net income)[44] that changes were becoming necessary. Although adoption of the EEC's Common Agricultural Policy would present problems, some of the money which the Exchequer was likely to save could be used for family allowances to ease the burden on the poorer sections of the public. There was, however, a prospect of a rise in the cost of living. Various estimates placed the increased food cost to the consumer at 9-10 percent over a six-year transition period, which meant a total rise in the cost of living of 3 percent (or ½ of 1 percent per year).[45] Given that prices for manufactured goods might fall slightly, and that membership was expected to bring increased prosperity, this prospect was not very threatening. HMG's greatest concern was that Commonwealth temperate-zone food

---

London and Cambridge Economic Bulletin, No. 40, in *The Times Review of Industry,* 15, no. 179 (December, 1961), vii.

[44] *The United Kingdom and the EEC.* Text of the statement made by the Lord Privy Seal at the meeting with Ministers of Member States of the EEC at Paris on October 10, 1961 (Cmnd. 1565, HMSO, November, 1961), p. 14.

[45] *The Guardian,* May 24, 1961. Also Conservative Research Department, "Cost of Living" (2), *Common Market Topics,* no. 5 (December 12, 1962).

suppliers (such as producers of New Zealand lamb and butter and Australian wool) would lose their privileged place in the U.K. market and face instead a tariff barrier, while agricultural products from the Common Market countries would enter freely.

In May 1959, the NFU circulated a somewhat pro-European statement to its branches, but this was submerged by their isolationist response.[46] Some months later, in January 1960, the retiring President, Lord Netherthorpe, urged rapprochement with the Six.[47] However his successor, Harold Woolley, took a more uncompromisingly critical approach.

During 1960, HMG began searching for a means to resolve the split between the Six and Seven and, beginning in May, held talks with the NFU. These included meetings between farm leaders and the then Minister of Agriculture, John Hare, and a tête-à-tête at 10 Downing Street between Woolley and Prime Minister Macmillan. The outcome of these talks was a Government White Paper issued in December, and designed to reassure agriculture. Although Macmillan was then only on the verge of deciding to seek Common Market entry, the outlines of NFU attitudes and Government pledges were already clear.

The essence of the White Paper was the statement that: "the Government and the Unions agree that the British system of agricultural support is the one best suited to the interests of this country."[48] The NFU made it clear that any steps toward closer integration between the Six and Seven must not prejudice the objectives and procedure of the Agricultural Acts and the tariff protection for horticulture. However, HMG stopped short of adopting this position. Instead, it had only "taken note" of these views, pledged that it "would not favor

---

[46] *Farmers Weekly* (May 22, 1959), cited in Graham Hallet, "British Agriculture and Europe," supplement to *Crossbow* (Spring, 1961), p. 13.

[47] NFU, *News,* January 25, 1960, cited in Hallet, *op. cit.*

[48] (Cmnd. 1249, HMSO, December 19, 1960), paragraph 37, cited in *British Farmer,* no. 163 (January 7, 1961).

unconditional entry" and assured the farmers that in considering any arrangements, it would be concerned "to see whether means can be found of achieving closer European unity without sacrificing the vital interests of U.K. farmers and horticulturists."[49]

The NFU expressed jubilation at the White Paper, though perhaps overrated the guarantees it had just received. A guarantee against unconditional entry was something of a moot point since the Government was certain to attach at least some conditions to its application. The "vital interests" of agriculture, which HMG would seek not to sacrifice, were defined by the NFU as the Agricultural Acts and tariff protection of horticulture, but nowhere did HMG specifically accept this definition. However, the statement that the U.K. support system was best suited to the interests of the country was significant and became part of the entangling system of pledges which later encumbered the Government's freedom of maneuver.

In the next several months, the NFU position emerged in greater detail. The phrase which appeared again and again in NFU statements was that the organization would maintain "an open mind" to consider any agricultural proposals emerging from negotiations between Britain and the Six. At the same time, NFU leaders insisted that the existing system was best suited to British interests, and that they preferred a solution whereby there would be a wider European agreement on objectives of national policies, but each country would pursue methods appropriate to its own national needs. The NFU developed its position comprehensively in a pamphlet entitled *Agriculture in the Community*, issued in May 1961.[50] What this publication and other NFU statements did was to link the interest of British farming with the national interest. By doing so, the Union sought to broaden the base of support for

---

[49] *Ibid.*

[50] NFU, *Information Service*, Vol. 16, no. 2.

its position. Its statements pointed to the rise in consumer food prices which a changed agricultural system would entail. This in turn would bear heavily on the lower income groups of the population, resulting in demands for higher wages and ultimately in increased manufacturing costs for the goods upon which Britain depended for her export trade.[51] Nor did the link with other national concerns stop at merely economic or commercial issues. The NFU sought to play upon generalized public sentiments about the value of agriculture as a thing in itself, and Harold Woolley also made a number of passionate declarations in support of the Commonwealth.[52]

In late July, the NFU Council approved a comprehensive policy statement which again described the vital interests of British agriculture as being embodied in the 1947 Agricultural Act and its system of guarantees, and in tariff protection of horticulture as cited in the December 1960 White Paper. However the most significant part of the statement was the warning that, "unless the Six are disposed to acknowledge these facts, negotiations could have no prospect of success."[53]

The NFU thus held an ostensibly open-minded, but actually hostile, position when Macmillan made his July announcement that Britain would seek to negotiate Common Market entry. In the Prime Minister's statement to the House of Commons, agriculture constituted one of the three British conditions (the other two being the Commonwealth and EFTA). However in safeguarding the special needs of British farming, he spoke only of a prosperous and efficient agriculture and a good life for those engaged in it. Nowhere did he commit Britain to maintenance of the existing support system, which the NFU had defined as agriculture's vital interest.

---

[51] Harold Woolley, cited in *Financial Times,* January 24, 1961. Also James Reedy, Head of NFU Information Division, letter to *Daily Telegraph,* June 29, 1961.

[52] *Daily Express* (London), January 20, 1961.

[53] Statement of July 20, 1961. Quoted in *British Farmer,* no. 193 (August 5, 1961), p. 21; italics in original.

For all the NFU's threats implied in the assertion that only maintenance of the existing system could meet the needs of agriculture, and for all the invocation of previous Governmental pledges, there was at this point a great vagueness in the guarantees for agriculture. The *British Farmer* uneasily observed that Macmillan's assurances of maintaining a prosperous agriculture organized to provide a good life for those in the industry could in the end be reduced to no more than matters of opinion.[54]

Ironically enough, agriculture received its most substantial pledge in the speech made by Edward Heath in putting forward Britain's application to the Ministers of the Six at Paris on October 10, 1961. The speech was widely regarded as one of wholehearted commitment to Europe, going well beyond Macmillan's parliamentary statement in both detail and spirit. Nonetheless, Heath mortgaged the terms of entry to domestic agriculture in a way which seriously complicated the Government's position at Brussels and later at home. He affirmed that the agricultural objectives of the Treaty of Rome (stable, efficient, and prosperous agriculture, fair standard of living for agricultural populations, etc.) were in line with those of Britain, and that Britain was now ready to take the major step of participating in a common agricultural policy and moving toward the Community's method of support.[55] Following this, he stated three fundamental points necessary to safeguard the essential interests of British farmers: first, a transition period of between twelve and fifteen years; second, the retention by Britain (which was "of the utmost importance") of the ability "to use such means as are necessary to safeguard our farmers' standard of living"; and third, special arrangements for horticulture to enable HMG to implement its pledge on a measure of support equivalent to that for the agricultural industry generally. The problem was that the Six would eventually

---

[54] *British Farmer,* No. 194 (August 12, 1961), pp. 1-2.
[55] Cmnd. 1565, pp. 12-14.

find each of these three elements largely unacceptable, and that the British would have to retreat from these demands if they wished to reach agreement.

These then were the basic positions. Throughout the next fifteen months of negotiations the NFU continued to insist on its terms. It refrained from formally opposing Common Market entry, but asserted that the arrangements being negotiated were unacceptable. Most ominously for HMG, the NFU began to call attention to what it saw to be the failure of the negotiations to satisfy Macmillan's pledge for arrangements to assure the well-being of agriculture, and criticized the receding of British representatives from Heath's position that the right to safeguard the living standards of British farmers must rest essentially with HMG.[56] Finally, at its Annual Meeting in January 1963, the NFU unanimously rejected the EEC's agricultural terms as unacceptable in both the short and long run.[57]

Organizational Considerations

To understand why the NFU took such an unfavorable view of the Common Market, it is necessary to examine a few of the circumstances surrounding the organization itself. It was never inevitable that the Union take the position it did. Interest groups conceive of their interests as a result of various factors, and in this case the inherent nature of the Common Market was only one of these. Certainly, the NFU could have been more flexible than it was. No less a figure than Lord Netherthorpe, President of the NFU from 1946-60 (and regarded as the "sacred bull" of British agriculture)[58] stated in September 1961 that the Common Market presented a challenge and an opportunity to U.K. farmers.[59] Throughout 1961

---

[56] *British Farmer,* no. 268 (January 12, 1963), p. 12.

[57] *The Times,* January 22, 1963.

[58] Peter Self and Herbert J. Storing, *The State and the Farmer* (London: Allen & Unwin, 1962).

[59] *Daily Telegraph,* September 12, 1961.

and 1962, a succession of newspaper editorials and articles by agricultural correspondents and economists argued that British agriculture could live with the Community's Common Agricultural Policy.[60] Indeed, the Union actually did adopt a far more flexible attitude in the subsequent 1966-67 approach to the Common Market.

There are several reasons why the NFU identified its vital interests so closely with the status quo that it could not approve any arrangement with the Six. First, the hostility toward the Common Market was based on a fear for the prospects of the small farmers and horticulturists. The Union's "muscle" as a whole was used to protect what on strictly economic grounds might have been sacrificed. In fact, many large farmers seem to have favored Common Market entry, with smaller farmers and dairymen being opposed. A survey taken among 120 farmers in the East Midlands by the Nottingham University Department of Agricultural Economics showed 42 percent for Common Market entry, 39 percent against, and the remainder abstaining or uncertain.[61] These results were roughly parallel with those of the Gallup Poll for the British public as a whole. The second reason for the NFU's attitude was the issue of national government control over agricultural policy. As already noted, the NFU held a position of uniquely intimate and corporate status vis-à-vis the Government and was reluctant to see this situation changed by the removal of agricultural policy determination to Brussels. Thirdly, there was the person of the NFU President himself, a man possessed of strong traditional Empire and Commonwealth sentiments. The difference from his predecessor was partly one of method and manner, but in Whitehall and Cabinet circles he seems to have been regarded as unhelpful and unyielding. The somewhat more flexible attitude of the NFU before and after his

---

[60] E. g., Hallet, *op. cit.*, and Political and Economic Planning, "Agriculture, the Commonwealth and EEC" (London, July, 1961).

[61] *The Guardian*, October 18, 1962.

presidency lends substance to the belief that Sir Harold Woolley had much to do with taking the NFU into its critical
posture.

CHANNELS OF INFLUENCE AND COMMUNICATION

To secure its objectives, the NFU directed its influence at
three targets: the Government (mainly the Minister of Agriculture and the Brussels negotiating team), Members of Parliament (especially Conservatives), and public opinion. Concentration on the first of these objectives was typical of pressure
group activity since it involved attention to the administrative
departments of government via the process of functional representation. Less characteristic was the attention to MP's and
public opinion in that this implied an effort to influence policy
along channels of the party government process.

First, the NFU attempted to exercise influence directly
upon the Government with the aim of affecting developments
at Brussels. Although the NFU did not succeed in gaining
official consultative status at the talks, it did maintain regular
contact with the Government. This took the form of intimate
consultations between NFU Leaders (especially Sir Harold
Woolley and the NFU's Chief Economist, Asher Winegarten)
and Government Ministers (notably Edward Heath and the
Minister of Agriculture, Christopher Soames). The Ministers
were willing to make a special effort to consult with the NFU
because they felt the desirability of seeking to bring along the
Union behind the Government's Common Market policy. The
NFU, on the other hand, had the objectives of stiffening the
Government's position in order that it concede as little as possible at Brussels. Despite the good relations between the two
sides, their first priorities were fundamentally contradictory.
The Government's objective was to enter the Common Market and, if possible, secure favorable terms for agriculture. For
the NFU the implicit hope was that Britain would not enter
the Common Market, but that if it did this should be on as

favorable terms for agriculture as possible. This meant that in its consultations with the Government the NFU was unconcerned that the terms it sought might be unacceptable to the Six. While this problem might trouble governmental negotiators, the NFU leaders would deserve the approbation of their membership as "good chaps" for having fought resolutely for the farmers' interests.

Second, the NFU directed its efforts at creating a favorable hearing for agriculture in all three Parliamentary parties. Ultimately Common Market entry would be subject to approval by the House of Commons, and the more concern MP's showed for agriculture the more likely the Government would be to take heed in its negotiating position. One method the NFU used was to interview all Parliamentary candidates from non-urban constituencies. These interviews were carried out at the local level but were not always too successful, for what sometimes happened was that the local NFU branch leaders asked questions based on a Union headquarters memorandum, and the candidates in turn answered these with the standard replies they had been given from Conservative or Labour Party headquarters in Smith Square. Despite this limitation, the questioning did at least make MP's and candidates sensitive to agricultural fears, and also had the effect of calling attention to the reputed strength of the agricultural vote and the importance that a 1 or 2 percent national shift could have. While the significance of this farm vote has always been overstated (as is discussed in Chapter 7), some Conservatives nonetheless feared the loss of scores of Tory-held agricultural seats. The dramatic case of the Dorset South by-election in November 1962, where a seemingly safe Conservative seat was lost to Labour as the result of the intervention of an independent anti-Common Market Conservative candidate, gave reinforcement to these fears. Coupled with this electoral threat, agriculture benefited from its special place in the Conservative Party ethos. Back-bench Tory ranks (as well as the constituency organizations) included many individuals having emotional or occupational ties to the soil.[62]

The third object of the National Farmers' Union's attentions, and the one least characteristic of the functional representation process was public opinion in general, and here the Union directed its efforts predominantly at elements of the mass media. The NFU furnished information to those requesting it, issued pamphlets and statements, and tried to influence the content of the more than fifty radio and TV programs each week which featured agriculture in some way. The Union claimed that the press quoted NFU views more than those of any other organization. These views also received special attention from the *Daily Express*. Opinion elites were a target of the NFU, and the Union held numerous dinners for opinion leaders and politicians at Agriculture House. In commenting upon the popular impact of its publicity campaign, the NFU observed, "Although it is virtually impossible to measure the success of the effort, the fact that the people of Britain had a vague idea that British agriculture might be hurt by the Common Market can be attributed in large part to the influence of the NFU."[63]

EFFECTIVENESS OF THE NFU

The NFU never flatly opposed Britain's accession to the Common Market because it recognized the traditional limits within which it needed to operate. Since Government policy was to negotiate for membership, the NFU had a better chance of influencing developments by concentrating upon the terms involved rather than by outright opposition. In

---

[62] The House of Commons elected in October 1964 contained 47 MP's whose occupation was farmer or landowner; 43 of these were Conservatives. Source: *The Times' Guide to the House of Commons, 1964* (London: The Times Publishing Co., 1965), cited in S. E. Finer, *Anonymous Empire* (2nd ed. rev.; London: Pall Mall Press, 1966), p. 146.

[63] Quoted in R. A. Holmes, "The National Farmers Union and the British Negotiations for Membership in the EEC," *Res Publica,* Vol. 5, no. 3 (1963), p. 48.

recognizing this situation, the NFU informed its membership that it was dealing with the European question "on the traditional principles of the NFU that to the best of our ability we make our views known clearly to Government and as far as possible endeavor to work within decisions made by Government."[64]

The role of the NFU consisted in articulating agricultural demands in a manner based on organizational considerations. By shrewdly playing upon inherent difficulties and assimilating these to the national interest, the Union translated basically technical issues into political ones, thereby making pressure on the Government more acute.

Certainly the existing agricultural problem was already substantial. Regardless of the political efficacy of the NFU, any British Government would have needed to be concerned, and indeed the attention of the Labour Government in 1966-67 testified to the persistent nature of the problem. A further factor complicating the situation for the Macmillan Government was the need to negotiate with a "moving escalator," since the Six were hammering out their own agricultural arrangements as the negotiations went on. (An agreement among the Six in January 1962 was reached entirely without U.K. participation.) However the significance of the NFU was enhanced by HMG's technical approach to the Common Market negotiations and by Macmillan's unwillingness or inability to appeal to the public on a Churchillian basis. This had a great deal to do with allowing pressure groups to make their positions felt through functional representation and even—as in the case of the NFU—via party government. Finally, the Government's political position worsened throughout 1962. As it became more "accident-prone," the relative importance of a group such as the NFU climbed.

Bearing these factors in mind, what major effects did the NFU have upon the Government and the fate of Britain's EEC

---

[64] *British Farmer*, no. 270 (January 26, 1963), p. 2.

application? First, and most important, the NFU succeeded in eliciting pledges of safeguards for British agriculture. While it is true that any British Government would have needed to ensure the well-being of the agricultural sector, HMG went so far as to make pledges which were incompatible with Common Market entry. To a considerable extent these were due to NFU pressures, either directly or as the result of the operation of the law of anticipated reactions (policy-makers adopting certain positions because they feared the reaction of the agricultural community were they to do otherwise). Edward Heath set out the most entangling of these safeguards in his October 1961 speech to the Six at Paris. The first of his requirements, a 12 to 15-year transitional period, was much longer than the Six were willing to grant; the second, national means of safeguarding agriculture, was inconsistent with the integration required by the Community; and the third, protection of horticulture, failed to admit the fact that by the nature of climate, efficiency, and marketing structure that sector of British agriculture would necessarily have to face serious retrenchment. The Common Agricultural Policy stood as one of the key aspects of the Community, especially for France, and by initially setting out what some regarded as excessive demands, Britain made her task at Brussels the more difficult.[65]

The second major impact of the NFU was in delaying the Government's retreat from its initial position. Through its various communication channels, the NFU privately and publicly urged the Government to stand firm. Although the NFU naturally found it advantageous to make claims of its own importance, there was at least a kernel of truth in this assertion: "It is not too much to say that the Union counsels . . . are moulding the climate of opinion in regard to common agricultural policy as it is now being shaped in Paris and Brussels."[66]

---

[65] The Six, as Miriam Camp notes, did not help matters by their lack of generosity. *Britain and the European Community, 1955-63* (Princeton: Princeton University Press, 1964), p. 453.

[66] *British Farmer*, no. 268 (January 12, 1963), p. 9.

Agriculture became the main sticking point in the Common Market negotiations. The Six were already highly sensitive about the agricultural arrangements they had been threshing out among themselves and tended to be rigid even on the question of the transition period. France especially was adamant and in no way disposed to enable the U.K. to retreat from its exposed positions under cover of face-saving agreements. As British negotiators began to accept agricultural terms falling short of the Government's initial pledges, this could be presented at home, by the NFU and others critical of entry, as the acceptance of terms which were harmful to Britain's vital interests and a betrayal of Governmental commitments. An agricultural dispute erupted within the Cabinet in the fall of 1962. Ministers such as R. A. Butler, who held the tomato growers of his Saffron/Walden constituency close to his heart, were willing to accept Common Market entry, but not on what they felt were harmful agricultural terms. Within the Conservative Party in Parliament, Government whips reported increased concern on the part of rural MP's. In an attempt to stiffen Britain's position, Iain Macleod, the Party Chairman, announced in early November that there was a price Britain could not afford to pay for entry. He suggested the U.K. retain her agricultural payment system until the end of a lengthy transition period. The Six rejected Macleod's efforts to strengthen Britain's bargaining position. In turn, Sir Anthony Hurd, Chairman of the Tory Agricultural Committee, strongly opposed the Six's farm proposals.

The third significant NFU impact was in contributing to a situation where HMG became boxed in between the demands of the Six and the requirements of domestic politics. At Brussels, HMG found it difficult to accept the Six's agricultural terms because of growing pressure at home. Within Britain, the Government was unable to explain that once inside the Common Market, it might then make use of the veto power as a bargaining tool. Because the Europeans could overhear, it was simply not politic for Mr. Heath to reassure the tomato growers of Saffron/Walden that Britain later could maneuver for improved agricultural arrangements by threatening to use her veto over the French desire for higher steel tariffs or the Italian wish for a nuclear reactor.

These points having been made as to the NFU's impact on Government policy and the negotiations, what can be said about the potential outcome had de Gaulle not vetoed British membership and had the U.K. somehow managed successfully to conclude negotiations at Brussels? Despite opposing such an agreement, the NFU would not by itself have been in a position to do a great deal to prevent its political acceptance within the U.K. The importance of the farm vote is not likely to have been substantial, since farmers, as Peter Self notes, are like other people in that they tend to vote their past allegiances. Furthermore, the organization would have been unlikely to campaign so vehemently as to compromise its close relations with the Government or its non-political status ("non-political" meaning, in the mixed metaphor of Samuel Finer, that "an organization reserves the right to look a gift horse in the mouth and bite the hand of the party that feeds it").[67] No doubt the NFU might have influenced a few more MP's, but even here reliable estimates were that no more than forty Tory MP's would oppose Common Market entry, of whom less than half would do so on agricultural grounds. The NFU would certainly have launched publicity efforts in opposition to the terms of entry; nonetheless the Union's impact in itself would have been limited. Its real strength lay more in the relatively private bargaining processes of functional representation than in the overt political processes of party government.

CONCLUSION

Although the major interest groups played a rather limited

---

[67] Finer, *op. cit.* (1st ed., 1958), p. 44.

role in the Common Market decision, the Government did take care to ascertain their positions. Obviously the decision could not have been made without assurances of its political feasibility. Had the business sector been opposed, it is scarcely conceivable that Britain could have sought entry. On the other hand, had business been more enthusiastic or the NFU actually in favor of entry, Macmillan's decision could have come sooner and more easily.

It is a fundamental of pressure group politics that the Government sets the terms of reference and the major groups find it necessary to work within these. Appropriately the groups played their principal roles during the negotiation period, especially in establishing the terms of entry to be sought by Britain. This substantial group influence, via the functional representation process, was due largely to Macmillan's choosing to treat the Common Market on an economic basis. The relatively economic treatment and emphasis on detail were enhanced by several factors. First, the Government erroneously believed it could negotiate details *à sept,* that is, as though it were a participant at the point of initial bargaining, dealing on equal terms with six other individual countries, rather than as one separate applicant facing a unified group. Second, it felt obliged to negotiate on behalf of the Commonwealth, which involved elaborate arrangements further complicated by the unhelpful attitude of many Commonwealth countries. Third, the Government conducted its negotiations fairly openly, involving Heath in an at times embarrassing public dialogue with the groups.[68]

Because the groups foreclosed certain alternatives or obtained various pledges, they encumbered the Government's position at Brussels. Indeed, in the case of agriculture, the pledges elicited were incompatible with Common Market entry. Had the application not been so hedged with conditions, it is at least conceivable that Britain could have gained an

---

[68] For these observations I am indebted to Professor S. E. Finer.

agreement before the negotiations recessed in early August 1962. However the talks dragged on, and President de Gaulle's position became strengthened enough by the results of the French November legislative elections that he could feasibly veto the British application.

Each of the sectional pressure groups had interests applying only to a specific portion of policy and not to the EEC issue as a whole. The FBI was concerned with terms of trade, the TUC with full employment questions, and the NFU with the agricultural support system, but none of them could claim a vital involvement in the central political issue of whether Britain should merge her destiny with that of the Europeans. It is therefore significant that after HMG made the decision to enter negotiations for Common Market entry, a decision based on calculations of broad national significance rather than on cost-benefit considerations involving the effect of membership on individual interests, these groups still managed to exercise a highly important role during the formulation of Britain's negotiating policy. The explanation for the persistence of their corporatist or concurrent majority power lies in the absence of effective politicization of the Common Market issue. Consequently, we must now turn to the sphere of party government in order to analyze the reasons for this treatment.

PART III

PARTY GOVERNMENT AND
EUROPEAN UNITY

Chapter 6

The Politics of European Unity:
FTA and EFTA

The purpose of this chapter is to examine basic party attitudes during the 1956-60 period, then to analyze the nature of and reasons for the relative non-politicization of the European issue. Then, drawing upon the previous discussion of the relationship of the pressure groups to the FTA and EFTA this chapter will treat some of the broader implications of non-politicization for the relationship between functional representation and party government.

BASIC PARTY ATTITUDES

The sequence of events and of Governmental policies toward European unity has already been outlined in Chapters 3 and 4. Thus it will here suffice to note that the elements of European policy remained broadly similar from late 1956 until 1960. The initial British idea of the form the Free Trade Area should take was ultimately embodied in the EFTA, which came into being in 1960. This conception involved free trade in industrial products only, the isolation of agriculture in a separate and limited arrangement, a minimum of institutions, no infringement upon Britain's relations with the Commonwealth, and no political or economic integration. While the idea and practice of European policy in this manner strongly conflicted with that of the six Common Market countries, it reflected a basic agreement of Conservative and Labour Party attitudes.

THE CONSERVATIVE PARTY

Conservative (and Government) priorities were much the same in 1956 as they had been for the previous decade. That is, Britain should play her part in European arrangements, but these must not entangle her to the extent of infringing upon her Commonwealth role or endangering her relationship with the U.S. Actually, Europe constituted the least important of the "three circles" in which Britain included herself, and Conservative and Governmental leaders spoke consistently of how Britain was "with" but not "of" Europe.

Beyond foreign policy considerations, certain internal factors shaped the Conservatives' European policy. Chief among these was agriculture, which occupied an entrenched position in the Tory ethos. This consideration was even more important than the actual farm vote. British sovereignty also evoked considerable sentiment. Many Conservatives would look with disfavor upon any derogation of sovereignty to a supranational European authority. Indeed the concept of European political federation elicited as negative an emotional response as Empire and Commonwealth evoked a positive one. Finally, historic Conservative protectionism played a residual role in shaping Party attitudes.

The Common Market itself provoked little attention at first. The issue was not raised in Parliament until more than a year after the Six foreign ministers' June 1955 Messina meeting, and only then on the initiative of two Tory backbenchers, Robert Boothby and Sir Geoffrey Rippon, who feared Britain's exclusion from Europe. In July 1956, Harold Macmillan (then Chancellor of the Exchequer) announced that Britain might associate with the Six in a Free Trade Area. At the time, this was regarded as a major step. The October 1956 Party conference endorsed the idea of an economic association with the Six, but insisted that Imperial Preference remain unscathed. The following month, Macmillan formally presented the FTA proposal to the House of Commons, carefully stipulating that Britain's association with Europe must not damage her relations with the Commonwealth and Atlantic Community, and that unless foodstuffs, drink, and tobacco were excluded, Britain could not proceed with negotiations. The most important part of his speech invoked Commonwealth trade as the reason why Britain could not enter the Common Market, and contained words with which he would be confronted again and again within a few years time:

> I do not believe that this House would ever agree to our entering arrangements which, as a matter of principle, would prevent our treating the great range of imports from the Commonwealth at least as favourably as those from European countries.
>
> *So this objection, even if there were no other, would be quite fatal to any proposal that the U.K. should seek to take part in a European common market. . . . I think that we are all agreed there.*[1]

The main opposition to a tri-partisan consensus on the FTA came from a Commonwealth-minded and protectionist element within the Conservative Party. Major Legge-Bourke and John Biggs-Davison, back-bench MP's, supported an amendment opposing the European efforts and reaching back to Disraeli and a chauvinistic distrust of foreigners to justify its point:

> . . . this House regrets the repeated attempts made since 1940 to federate Europe by economic means, and so to tie the U.K. to a system as alien as it would be dangerous to the individual traditions of the states concerned; and calls to mind the words of Benjamin Disraeli, to the effect that . . . the ancient communities like

---

[1] *Hansard, Parliamentary Debates* (Commons), Vol. 561 (November 26, 1956), c. 36-38, italics added.

the European must be governed either by traditionary [*sic*] influence or by military force.... [2]

Throughout 1957, the Government offered reassurances that the FTA would cause no harm to the Commonwealth and that the exclusion of agriculture from the arrangement would protect that sector from any danger. Nonetheless, a number of Tory MP's were concerned at signs of a weakening in the Government's conditions, especially on agriculture, and this worry increased as it became more apparent that HMG would have to modify the terms set out in its February 1957 White Paper.[3]

The Prime Minister sought to assuage some of these fears, and in August he appointed Reginald Maudling to supervise and coordinate the FTA negotiations for Britain. This appointment was smart politics but not good Europeanism. By appointing Maudling, who was regarded as R. A. Butler's "favorite son," Macmillan neutralized an important part of the Party leadership, hitherto rather cool toward Europe, by involving it in the negotiations. However competent a job Maudling performed, he lacked the European enthusiasm which could have hastened the bargaining process. Furthermore, as Paymaster General, he did not possess the necessary political authority to return to London from the Paris negotiations and persuade the Cabinet that certain concessions or changes of position were essential. Another result of the restiveness within the Party was that Macmillan found it tactically advisable to offer Canada a kind of Anglo-Canadian free trade area.[4] The proposal was soon buried (Canada would have suffered an import imbalance from it) after having served the purpose of embarrassing the Diefenbaker Government and of demonstrating to the October 1957 Tory Con-

---

2 *Hansard*, Vol. 557 (July 23, 1956), c. 74.

3 *Financial Times*, August 8, 1957.

4 The Canadian Prime Minister had campaigned on the need for closer Commonwealth ties. This made Macmillan's proposal desirable from an international standpoint.

ference HMG's eagerness to expand trade with the Commonwealth as well as with Europe. However at the Party Conference there were still some very critical speeches. A few weeks
later, Macmillan again found it necessary to assure the faithful that although HMG had suggested the FTA in order to
avoid an economic split and ultimately a political division in
Europe, Britain's deepest ties remained with the Commonwealth.[5] Throughout 1958, as the FTA talks dragged on toward their weary conclusion, there was little sense of urgency
within the Party; though, as the negotiations deteriorated,
there were certain increases in both intraparty debate and
support for HMG. At the time of the FTA collapse in November 1958, Government and Party priorities remained
much the same as they had been two years earlier. Since Common Market entry was out of the question, the subsequent
EFTA proposal received general acceptance. While there
was thus a continuity of policy, the establishment of the
EFTA was rather more of an effort to vindicate HMG's (and
Maulding's) original FTA conception than an effective bridge-
building device between two European groups.

When Parliament gave formal approval to the EFTA in
December 1959, some critics on the Conservative back-
benches argued that Britain had become too preoccupied with
Europe. R. H. Turton worried that for the country to become
so engrossed in Europe as to neglect the Commonwealth
would see Britain "sink back and become a small, insignificant, over-populated little island."[6] In general, there was little enthusiasm and a common feeling that "our club is not as
good as the other one,"[7] yet no willingness existed to reexamine the basic suppositions of Britain's policy. Summing
up the Government's case, Reginald Maudling admitted the
EFTA arrangement was second best in comparison to a free
trade area for all Europe; however, because of Britain's world

<hr />

[5] *Financial Times,* November 11, 1957.
[6] *Hansard,* Vol. 615 (December 14, 1959), c. 1095.
[7] Maurice Macmillan, *ibid.,* c. 1138.

responsibilities, her agriculture policies and her Commonwealth trade, joining the Common Market would be third best.

Although an influential pro-European element existed within the Conservative Party (e.g., Robert Boothby, Duncan Sandys, Peter Thorneycroft), almost no Conservatives were ready to advocate outright Common Market membership before 1960, and Prime Minister Macmillan and other Cabinet Ministers spoke publicly of the impossibility of Britain joining the Common Market. Throughout 1960, high-level thinking was in ferment, but as yet there was no attempt to swing the party away from its deeply held beliefs. As late as the October 1960 Party Conference, only nine months prior to Macmillan's Common Market announcement, Edward Heath paid homage to the traditional attitude toward Europe by addressing himself to the Six and stating what they faced if they wanted Britain to "continue" to take part in the unity of Europe, as she had done for nearly fifteen years: "We are here with our Commonwealth, with our agriculture, with our well known Parliamentary system and our known attitude to supranational institutions. If you want us to take part in the unity, we are here."[8] Remarkably enough, in a one-hour speech to the 1960 Conference, Prime Minister Macmillan devoted only thirty seconds to Europe.[9] The basic political commitment was as yet unmade.

LABOUR PARTY ATTITUDES

Throughout the FTA negotiation period, and to a slightly lesser extent during the setting up of the EFTA, Labour's European policies paralleled those of the Conservatives, though for a variety of reasons. Whereas the Tories had

---

[8] National Union of Conservative and Unionist Associations, *79th Annual Conservative Conference* (October 12-15, 1960), p. 62.

[9] *The Guardian, October* 17, 1960.

strong emotional links to the old white dominions and the memory of Empire, Labour's attachment to the Commonwealth owed its strength to a view of a new-emerging multi-racial and independent grouping which included a number of nominally socialist governments. Whereas many Conservatives distrusted the Common Market for its planning or infringement of sovereignty, many Labourites, especially on the left, viewed the Six suspiciously as a neo-liberal, Catholic and anti-Socialist grouping. Finally, Labour's European precedents had already been established by the 1945–51 Labour Government, with its policies of limiting arrangements to inter-governmental cooperation, of refraining from supranational involvement, and of viewing Europe as the least important of the "three circles."

The FTA issue involved Labour in little political controversy with the Conservatives. The Tory Governments of the 1950's maintained the same attitude toward Europe which Labour had shown while in power. When HMG first put forward the FTA proposal, the Parliamentary Labour Party offered its conditional endorsement. Speaking for Labour in the November 1956 debate, Harold Wilson mildly criticized the Government's reasoning but noted that economically and politically Britain could not afford to stay out. He also raised the theme (much used in the following years) that Labour, not the Tories, was now the Commonwealth party, and by implication suggested that the Conservatives were turning their backs on the Commonwealth. Wilson then listed the safeguards which Labour required: exception of foodstuffs, retention of powers to deal with any balance of payments crisis, full employment policies, improved labor conditions, prevention of cartels, safeguards on re-exports, and no limitations on double pricing. These were not incompatible with the FTA conception and, except for employment and labor conditions, mirrored the Governmental position. Finally, he grandly announced: "I say to the Chancellor [Macmillan],

'Enter the negotiations with our encouragement and support.' "[10]

Throughout the FTA negotiations the similarity of Conservative and Labour policy was obvious, and members of both parties took note of this agreement, even to pointing out that a Labour Government would hold the same position on the FTA as the existing Conservative one. It is indicative of the low political temperature that Labour's NEC made no effort to bring any motion on the FTA before the October 1957 Conference (indeed Europe scarcely received mention at the 1956 and 1958 Conferences either).

The one semblance of debate within the Labour movement occurred after Aneurin Bevan had attacked Labour's support for the FTA in the weekly *Tribune* (journal of Labour's left wing). Bevan wrote, "Socialists cannot at one and the same time call for economic planning and accept the verdict of free competition, no matter how extensive the area it covers. The jungle is not made more acceptable just because it is also limitless."[11] In turn, *Socialist Commentary* (a journal more or less of the Labour right) rebuked Bevan with a long article backing the FTA as a means toward increased planning, an opportunity for Socialists to speak with one voice, and a step toward a united Socialist Europe.[12]

Only with the collapse of the FTA talks in November 1958 and the rise of the EFTA conception did the treatment of the European issue begin to become slightly more partisan. Even so, party differences tended to take the form of disputes over method rather than principle. In the subsequent Parliamentary debates, Harold Wilson criticized HMG's judgment in weakening Commonwealth trade links in advance, in failing to seek a "realistic" means of association with the Six when it became evident that the FTA concept was in diffi-

---

[10] *Hansard*, Vol. 561 (November 26, 1956), c. 61-70.
[11] Quoted in *The Times*, October 14, 1957.
[12] See *Observer*, September 1, 1957.

culty, in blundering in the negotiations and in being unwilling to heed Labour's advice that the FTA ought to be a
positive vehicle based on expanding economies and harmonization of social policies.[13] Nonetheless, Wilson's criticisms
applied to the Government's approach rather than its basic
conceptions. The challenging of fundamental policy came
only from a few back-bench MP's on both sides of the House.

While Labour criticized HMG during the establishment
of EFTA, the Party remained divided internally on the preferred course of action. A certain minority was staunchly pro-
European, and included a number of Gaitskellites—most
notably Roy Jenkins and George Brown. Their main criticism of HMG was that it overlooked crucial political issues to
concentrate upon the less important economic ones. They
also believed that the EFTA proposal would be more likely
to divide than bridge European gaps. In the words of John
Hynd, "If the President of the Board of Trade [Maudling] is
given the designation 'Mr. Europe' for his contributions in
this sphere, all I can say is, that Herr Ulbricht deserves the
title 'Mr. Germany.' "[14] Speaking in the December 1959
Parliamentary debate over EFTA approval, Roy Jenkins
stated that while he did not oppose the EFTA, he felt its
form was too negative and that the Stockholm Convention
seemed to have been designed more as compensation for the
loss of self-esteem during the FTA talks than as a bridge to
the Six. Jenkins also argued that EFTA was likely to foster
Britain's own Great Power illusion and that her self-righteous
fault-finding had much to do with her increasing exclusion
from Europe.[15] On the other hand, Harold Wilson's criticisms
appear to have been representative of a larger body of opinion
within the Party. He spoke of the necessity for expansionist

---

[13] *Hansard,* Vol. 599 (February 12, 1959), c. 1471-8; also Vol. 595
(November 17, 1958), c. 846.

[14] *Hansard,* Vol. 615 (December 14, 1959), c. 1147-48.

[15] *Ibid.,* c. 1072-81.

economic measures and urged that Britain strengthen Commonwealth markets and consider creation of a Commonwealth FTA.[16]

Whereas Labour had supported HMG's FTA efforts, it
abstained in the Parliamentary vote over EFTA on the
grounds that the Association was second best in comparison
with a general European free trade area and that HMG was
"labouring under damaging illusions." European unity was
becoming an issue of greater political attention.

THE LIBERALS

While the Conservatives and Labour persevered in their
stale European policies, the Liberals were urging outright
Common Market entry as early as 1958. This commitment
seems to have owed a great deal to the Party's need for new
issues with which to emphasize its differences from the dominant Labour and Conservative parties, and to an understandably lesser attachment to the political status quo. Polls taken
later during the Common Market negotiations provide little
evidence that Liberal voters were any more dynamic in their
Europeanism than their Conservative and Labour counterparts. While the pro-Common Market policy was adopted and
pushed by the Party leadership, there were differences of
opinion there too. Oliver Smedley, a Liberal Party Vice-
President, opposed the FTA because—in contrast to Aneurin
Bevan—he felt it did *not* mean laissez-faire, but instead a vast
international bureaucratic socialism.[17] He later resigned and
became a vocal opponent of Common Market entry.

In Parliament, the Liberals supported the FTA, but spoke
and voted against the EFTA agreement. Jo Grimond, the
Party leader, criticized the bland patronage of Europe by both
Conservative and Labour governments and urged Common

---

[16] *Ibid.*, c. 1151-62. See also The Labour Party, *Report of the 58th
Annual Conference* (November 28 and 29, 1959), p. 71.

[17] Empire Industries Association, *Monthly Bulletin,* no. 199 (November, 1957), pp. 5-6.

Market entry as a step toward better world relations.

The Liberal's early advocacy of EEC entry was not without its perils. Mark Bonham-Carter had spoken in the House of Commons, in February 1959, on the necessity for HMG to state its willingness to consider Common Market entry. He had also criticized the FTA concept and to a certain extent the role played by Reginald Maudling. For his troubles, the Liberal MP lost his seat at the farming constituency of Torrington in the October General Election. His Conservative opponent, aided by Maudling, successfully attacked Bonham-Carter's European position and claimed that EEC entry would have harmful agricultural effects.

EUROPE AS A NON-POLITICIZED ISSUE, 1956-60

THE MEANING OF NON-POLITICIZATION

The European issue, in the form of Britain's policy toward the FTA and EFTA, did not receive political treatment. This non-politicization was reflected by three important indicators: the involvement of basically economic ministries; a relative quiescence of public debate, the press, and special promotional groups; and a low level of party involvement.

First, as we have seen, especially in Chapters 3 and 4, the ministries chiefly responsible for Britain's European policy were economic ones such as the Board of Trade. Reginald Maudling led the negotiating efforts for the FTA and EFTA as Paymaster General and then as President of the Board of Trade. Considerations of trade and technical details tended to predominate and the sectional pressure groups enjoyed a natural access because of their competence or inherent involvement in such matters.

As for the second indicator, Europe was simply not a matter of general public debate, nor a subject for which public opinion was mobilized—again in contrast to 1961 and onward. There were no mass meetings, nor were the results of opinion polls trumpeted or scrutinized. To the extent that members of the British general public paid any attention to the FTA proposal, they appear to have calmly accepted it.[18] Any real argument was confined to the specialized plane of details rather than the overall advisability of the FTA arrangement. Even at the General Election of October 1959, Europe was not yet a salient concern. The subject received mention by less than 1 percent of the Labour candidates, 8 percent of the Conservatives, and about half of the Liberals.[19] This lack of attention is all the more remarkable because by the late 1950's, voter self-interest and self-identification with the parties had relatively weakened. This made issues, party programs, and records all the more important.[20] Therefore, had Europe been a matter of public attention at the time, it is reasonable to expect that this would have been reflected during the election campaign.

Another element in this absence of public controversy was that the British press did not treat Europe as a major political issue. It is true that Europe received substantial—and increasing—attention in the elite press, but there was none of the passionate involvement and campaigning on the part of the mass press *(Daily Mirror, Daily Express, Daily Herald)* which characterized the Suez issue in November 1956 or the Common Market issue from 1961 onward. Indeed, even the elite press was tardy in coming to grips with Europe. It suddenly awoke in September 1956 (Miriam Camps speculates that it did so as a result of Government prodding)[21] to the fact that HMG was already considering the FTA. Much of the press effort was directed against traditional protectionist

---

[18] See the *Financial Times,* April 2 and April 16, 1957.

[19] Uwe Kitzinger, "Britain and Europe: The Multivalence of the British Decision," reprinted from *The European Yearbook,* Vol 9 (1962), Martinus Nijhoff, The Hague, p. 38.

[20] Social Surveys Ltd., *Gallup Political Index,* no. 1 (January, 1960), p. 12.

[21] Miriam Camps, *Britain and the European Community, 1955-63* (Princeton: Princeton University Press, 1964).

sentiment which existed within the Conservative Party. Later it became absorbed with the details of the FTA negotiations, and not until 1960 did any newspapers begin to urge Common Market membership.

Still another aspect of this low level of public debate was the unimportance or virtual absence of the specialized pro- and anti-European promotional groups. Virtually the only active body at this time was the U.K. Council of the European Movement, which had been established some years earlier. This prestigious but somewhat inert group included both Conservative and Labour figures within its leadership,[22] and its Chairman, Sir Edward Beddington-Behrens, had close relations with the top levels in Government and industry. These ties constituted an important aid in fund-raising, but (along with differences among its leaders on the preferable type of European association) kept it from campaigning in favor of Common Market entry until the Government itself seemed favorable to this course. In February 1958, the organization sponsored an important free trade conference in London (discussed in Chapters 3 and 4), which brought together major European business and trade union leaders. The conference took place with the blessings of HMG, and not inconceivably with its encouragement. The Movement's other noteworthy effort was an unsuccessful 1960 campaign to generate enthusiasm within Britain for the newly organized EFTA. The Federal Trust for Education and Research was another group active in this period, though its efforts were limited to such things as preparing a strongly pro-European pamphlet for the Labour movement.[23] What is noteworthy about the promotional efforts of these two bodies is that they

---

[22] E.g. Conservatives: Peter Thorneycroft, Maurice Macmillan, Robert Boothby. Labourites: Roy Jenkins, Fred Mulley. See Arthur Woodburn, *A Common-sense View of the Common Market* (London: UK Council of the European Movement, n.d.), p. 20.

[23] *Britain in Europe: Viewpoint for the Labour Movement* (London, n.d., 1958?).

had virtually no significance for the general public nor any impact in generating political controversy. In the case of the U.K. Council of the European Movement, the efforts were not even directed at the public or at party political targets, but at those groups and individuals involved in the process of functional representation.

The third indicator of non-politicization, a low level of political party involvement, has already been discussed. In Parliament, Europe did not constitute a major area of debate. The subject of the Common Market was first raised only at the initiative of two Conservative back-bench MP's, and the occasional debates were marked by an underlying agreement on priorities and policy. HMG was so reluctant to discuss the issue in the House of Commons that only one debate actually took place during the course of the FTA negotiations, and even this was only because a Tory back-bench MP, Julian Ridsdale, managed to introduce a Motion for closer association with the EEC.[24] To the extent that Europe ever constituted a political issue in Parliament or Party conferences, it was more one of disagreement within each party than of general significance or bipartisan disaccord. Only the Liberals sought to make of Europe a matter of prime political importance, but their position was viewed as unimportant and unrealistic.

THE REASONS FOR NON-POLITICIZATION

What explains the relative absence of politicization for the FTA and EFTA issues? Basically, Europe did not become an object of broad public attention because external events did not compel such treatment and because the parties and their leaders did not choose to make it so. What will concern us here is why the parties did not choose otherwise.

For a long time, the parties, and especially the Government, tended to perceive Europe as in substance an economic

---

[24] *Hansard,* Vol. 585 (March 28, 1958), c. 711-803.

matter—and a fairly low priority one at that. This was so despite occasional and ritualistic references to a long-range political significance. It has already been noted how the FTA and EFTA were handled by the economic ministries and that the aspects of those arrangements at issue were chiefly the technical details. Edward Heath even told the 1960 Conservative Conference that the Government had striven to create the FTA and had brought together the EFTA "for economic reasons."[25] Furthermore, the parties held somewhat ambivalent attitudes toward European unity because they were divided within. This was especially important for the Conservative Party since the time was not long past when the issue between Free Trade and Protection had been, in the words of L. S. Amery, "essentially a conflict between two wholly different philosophies of national life."[26] But perhaps the major reason for the low political saliency of the European issue, was the similarity of Conservative and Labour policies. These policies were based not on calculation but on an instinctive revulsion from European entanglement which politicians and public shared alike.[27] Many Tories rejected Europe because they held illusions about Britain's world role, because they were tied to the Commonwealth and because domestic agriculture was part of the Tory ethos. Labour, in turn, overestimated the moral influence a Labour Government could have in the world (which partly explains the fervor behind the movement for unilateral nuclear disarmament), preferred the multiracial Commonwealth to Europe, and could see social welfare and full employment policies only in the context of the nation-state. Above all, both parties lacked the vision of the European idea that motivated Jean Monnet and his followers.

---

[25] *79th Annual Conservative Conference* (1960), p. 62.

[26] L. S. Amery, *My Political Life*, Vol. 3 of *The Unforgiving Years* (Hutchinson: London, 1955), p. 95, quoted in Leon D. Epstein, *British Politics in the Suez Crisis* (London: Pall Mall Press, 1964), p. 22.

[27] Evan Luard, *Britain and Europe* (Fabian International Bureau, January, 1961), p. 2.

IMPLICATIONS

What were the implications of non-politicization of the European issue? Among other things it meant the predominance of the process of functional representation rather than that of party government. This had important consequences for the role of pressure groups. Foreign policy is normally the prerogative of the executive, but customarily this control is subjected to certain limits by the participation of the parties, press, and public opinion. In the case of European policy during the 1956-1960 period, this usual political constituency was quiescent; any constraints would thus be imposed mainly by the groups, which gained a major role because of their inherent involvement or expertise in what was treated as a technical and commercial matter. It was logical therefore that HMG saw its main task as one of defeating opposition to free trade by winning over business, agriculture, and labor. Indeed (as noted in Chapters 3 and 4) the FBI, NFU, and TUC called attention to the need for HMG to acquire their consent. The situation was one in which the groups claimed— and were accorded—the role they ordinarily played in the domestic politics of the Managed Economy and Welfare State. But a critical difference existed. The issue was not one of agricultural price supports or National Health Service arrangements, affecting a particular sector of the polity; rather it was one of foreign policy, involving the national interest and having potentially broad repercussions for the country as a whole.

Although other factors such as ethos and history are often crucially involved, sectional interest groups calculate their attitudes toward a policy essentially on the basis of the foreseeable balance of commercial gain and loss. An unfavorable, or even doubtful, forecast will cause a group to oppose vociferously any such course of action. (More diffuse considerations of general public advantage rarely obtain such forceful articulation except when expressed by the political parties or vigorous promotional groups.) It has been seen how the FBI, NFU, and TUC were obsessed with safeguards and feared loss of their own consultative status in any supranational arrangements. They therefore adopted a negative attitude toward Europe. Because the European issue was handled through the channels of functional representation rather than those of party government, the groups enjoyed a position of power, and one which acted as a major restraint upon Britain's movement to Europe. In the case of the FTA, the NFU succeeded in obtaining the exclusion of agriculture from HMG's initial European proposals, and the FBI and TUC acted to press for a multitude of safeguards. Only gradually did the Government modify its initial position, which had hampered the reaching of a European agreement, and which had been established in the context of bargaining for the support of domestic sectional groups.

Perhaps Britain would have made the same overall choices in European policy had the process involved been one of party government rather than functional representation. Nonetheless, a major role in this choice was not rightly the prerogative of the sectional interest groups. The consequence of the predominance of functional representation was that those closest to the process of policy determination were nonelective, not responsible to the public, and concerned to maximize values less broad than those of the country as a whole.

Chapter 7

The Common Market I: The Parties

We now come to the subject of the Common Market and party government in the period 1961-63. This chapter deals with the unfolding of the major events and the relationship of the Labour and Conservative parties to the issue of British membership. Chapter 8 treats the broader public in this period and then offers some wider conclusions concerning the subject matter of both chapters.

A CHRONOLOGY OF EVENTS: FEBRUARY 1960 TO JANUARY 1963[1]

1960

Feb 3   Macmillan addresses South African Parliament about "Winds of Change."

Apr 10 The *Observer* sees no political reason not to join EEC.

　　13 HMG announces end of Blue Streak Missile program.

May 17 Paris summit meeting collapses.

Jun 9   Six reject early negotiations to join with EFTA.

Jul 14 British exports fall. Widest trade gap since 1957.

Jul 27 Cabinet changes. Lord Home becomes Foreign Secre-

---

[1] Sources: mainly *The Times* (London), *Financial Times*, *Daily Telegraph* (London), and *Gallup Political Index* (London, Social Surveys Ltd.).

tary, Edward Heath becomes Lord Privy Seal with special responsibility for Europe.

Nov 7   Macmillan calls for European economic unity in speech to U.K. Council of the European Movement.

Dec 1   WEU invites U.K. to negotiations for full Common Market membership.

1961

Jan 1   Common Market takes first action in establishing common external tariff.

Feb 27   Heath tells WEU that U.K. is ready to accept common tariff in principle.

Mar 1   France rejects U.K. proposal for European system in which she would retain her Commonwealth Preference and agricultural arrangements. French Foreign Minister Couve de Murville invites U.K. to join EEC.

Mar 26   Macmillan talks with President Kennedy.

Jun 13   Senior Ministers begin Commonwealth visits to discuss Common Market.

Jul 31   Macmillan announces U.K. will apply to EEC. Seeks conditions for Commonwealth, agriculture, and EFTA.

Aug 3   Commons majority of 313-5. 20 Tories abstain.

Sep 5   TUC supports HMG decision to open negotiations.

Sep 13   Commonwealth Finance Ministers criticize U.K. decision.

Sep 26   Common Market Council of Ministers unanimously agree to open negotiations.

Oct 10   Heath statement at Paris. Accepts Rome Treaty and political consequences but seeks agricultural terms.

Oct 12   Conservative Party approves Macmillan's decision.

Nov 8   Formal negotiations begin in Brussels between Britain and Common Market Council of Ministers.

Dec 30   Common Market countries postpone decision on agriculture.

1962

Jan 20 Common Market talks delayed while Six seek agreement on common agricultural policy approach.

Feb 10 Hugh Gaitskell says U.K. can't enter Common Market if there is a strong outcry from the Commonwealth or British agriculture.

Mar 14 Liberals' surprising victory over Conservatives at Orpington by-election.

Mar 22 25 Tory back-benchers issue warning on Common Market.

May 11 Tory losses in local elections.

May 11 Heath puts forward first practical offers.

May 30 U.K. makes concessions on Commonwealth manufactured goods.

Jun 5   Criticism from Australia, New Zealand, Canada.

Jun 2   Macmillan visits de Gaulle in Paris.

Jun 4   Beaverbrook press announces it would oppose Tories over Common Market issue in a General Election.

Jun 10 Labour, Liberal, and Conservative leaders in Parliament agree that best solution is entry on good terms.

Jun 26 National Opinion Poll shows for the first time that more oppose than favor entry.

Jul 6   Six accept annual agricultural reviews.

Jul 13 Sweeping Cabinet changes.

Jul 20 Gaitskell suggests General Election if entry terms not satisfactory.

Jul 24 Crucial agricultural talks begin.

Jul 31 40 Tory MPs sign motion urging HMG to stand firm.

Aug 5   Marathon session fails to produce agreement. Spaak says U.K. was unable to accept Six's proposal. Talks recess until October.

Sep 19 Commonwealth Prime Ministers sign communique agreeing to Britain's continuing Common Market negotiations.

Sep 21 Macmillan telecast speaks of harm if Britain fails to enter EEC. He now treats entry as of major political importance.

Sep 29 Labour issues critical policy statement on Britain and Common Market.

Oct 3 Gaitskell speech to Labour Party Conference is highly critical of entry.

Oct 26 Deadlock in Brussels over agricultural policies.

Nov 22 Conservatives suffer severe by-election losses.

Nov 28 Individual Ministers state there is a price Britain cannot afford to pay for entry.

Nov 28 Gaullists win absolute majority in French National Assembly.

Dec 3 Gaitskell speech in Paris attacks Brussels terms.

Dec 5 Dean Acheson's speech: England has lost an Empire and not yet found a role.

Dec 14 Macmillan meets with de Gaulle for talks.

Dec 21 Macmillan-JFK talks in Nassau. Cancellation of Skybolt. U.S. to supply Polaris missile to U.K.

1963

Jan 14 President de Gaulle announces at press conference that U.K. not yet ready to join EEC.

Jan 22 De Gaulle and Adenauer sign Franco-German Treaty.

Jan 29 Common Market negotiations end.

TRANSITION: FROM EFTA TO THE COMMON MARKET

To argue that events were pushing Britain toward a change in European policy would be easy and inexact. Such an approach would minimize the important role of Prime Minister Macmillan as well as the significance of various constraints imposed domestically by pressure groups, political parties, the bureaucracy, and public opinion, and internationally by the Commonwealth, EFTA, and the special relationship with America. Instead of being predetermined, Britain's movement toward the EEC was a product of both external events and conscious choices.

Three general sets of circumstances made a change in British policy more likely. First, there was pressure from the Six's own progress. Initially, Britain had been skeptical about the significance of the EEC, regarding it as not much more than another paper scheme of the European integrationists, perhaps analogous with the abortive EDC. However, it soon became evident that the Common Market was functioning very successfully and even possessed an important momentum of its own. The Six's economies were booming, with impressive rates of investment and growth. As this success added to the attractiveness of potential U.K. membership, British industrialists, civil servants, and politicians increasingly perceived entry as technically feasible and assumed that Britain could play a prominent or leading role in Europe. This attitude was supported by the belief that only two good European civil services existed, and that of these, the British could "run circles around the French."

Second, and more importantly, Britain suffered from chronic economic problems. She possessed a low growth rate, encountered repeated balance of payments difficulties, and experienced harmful fluctuations of the "Stop-Go" cycle. While it does seem true, as Samuel Brittan argues, that Britain's application was not due to the Sterling crisis in 1961,[2] the chronic economic problems of Britain did attract incessant concern. To the extent that Common Market membership might offer tangible economic benefits, for example by providing a large market, economies of scale, technological cooperation, and a competitive stimulus to inefficient British industries, the economic problem constituted an important reason for turning toward Europe.

International political problems comprised the third, and perhaps the most important, set of circumstances impelling

---

[2] Samuel Brittan, *The Treasury Under the Tories, 1951-1964* (Harmondsworth, Middlesex; Penguin, 1964), pp. 212-214.

Britain toward the Common Market. In essence, the country faced an absence of attractive alternatives. The disastrous Suez expedition of 1956 had dramatized her inability to act in opposition to the wishes of the U.S. and Britain's April 1960 termination of the Blue Streak missile program underlined her incapacity to go-it-alone in advanced weaponry. The foremost alternative role which Macmillan had seen for Britain was as promoter of a lasting East-West *détente*. The Prime Minister's part in this was as an experienced diplomatic advisor, bringing the Americans together with the Russians in order to alleviate the Cold War and the risk of nuclear disaster. But the U-2 incident and the ensuing collapse of the May 1960 summit conference at Paris dealt a grave blow to two years of his efforts at *détente*. A major role for Britain in promoting world peace seemed to be foreclosed.[3]

Great Britain's role as leader of a large and important Commonwealth, uniting the developed and underdeveloped worlds, also faced increasing limitations. In the opinion of Lord Harlech (the former David Ormsby Gore), Ambassador to the U.S. and later Deputy Leader of the Conservative Party in the House of Lords, the Commonwealth had become a "broken reed," especially after South Africa's departure.[4] Conceptions of expanded Commonwealth trade (for example as later advocated by some left-wing critics of Common Market entry, or as formulated in the idea of a Commonwealth FTA by a few right-wing critics) were illusory. The Commonwealth

---

[3] Lord Harlech strongly emphasized the importance of the summit collapse in pushing the Prime Minister toward Europe. The foreclosure of summitry seemed to leave Europe as the sole outstanding outlet for a meaningful direction of Britain's (and Macmillan's) energies. Interview with the author, April 28, 1966.

[4] According to Lord Harlech, British leaders had believed that South Africa's *apartheid* policies might be subject to greater restraint if it remained within the Commonwealth. Countries such as Ghana and India had agreed not to press for expulsion, but Canadian Prime Minister Diefenbaker's attack on South Africa at the 1960 Commonwealth Prime Ministers' Conference left the Afro-Asians no choice but to join in the condemnation. South Africa was thus edged out of the Commonwealth.

countries were simply not interested in such an arrangement. Britain could neither absorb all the primary products of the members nor meet all their needs for manufactured goods and they increasingly looked to the development of their own industries, which required the kind of protection a Commonwealth Free Trade Area would not provide. Finally, the importance of Commonwealth Preference was declining. For a variety of reasons, including the General Agreement on Tariffs and Trade (GATT), the average general level of preference enjoyed by Britain on all Commonwealth trade fell from 11 percent in 1937 to 7 percent in 1948 to less than 5 percent in 1958.[5]

In addition to failures or weakenings in the possibilities for *détente* and for a cohesive Commonwealth, the special relationship with the U.S., which had constituted the sheet anchor of British policy since World War II, also showed signs of erosion. The election of Kennedy in 1960 to succeed Eisenhower gave further impetus to this drift. The Americans had been encouraging the process of European unity and could be expected to downgrade their special relationship with the U.K. in order to turn to the EEC countries as the leading power grouping in Europe. However, the American conception of the Atlantic Alliance did offer Britain a means toward a revived partnership with the U.S. if she could become the leader of an integrated Europe. Indeed, President Kennedy later indicated America would welcome Britain's entry. Miriam Camps accords this consideration the central role in the British decision.[6]

The events themselves did not necessarily elicit specific choices. Indeed, awareness of the erosion of Britain's position and of the successes of the European Community was slow in coming to both public and elite attention. The year 1959 was still one in which Britain's entering the EEC was regarded as

---

[5] The *Financial Times*, August 22, 1960.
[6] Miriam Camps, *Britain and the European Community, 1955-1963* (Princeton: Princeton University Press, 1964), p. 336.

an extreme move.[7] In the General Election of October 1959, the problem of trade with Europe was mentioned by less than 1 percent of Labour candidates, 8 percent of the Conservatives, and half of the Liberals.[8] Europe was not yet a salient concern.

The year of the most dramatic change was 1960. At the start of the year, advocacy of EEC membership was beyond the pale, but as British leaders increasingly realized that a close association with the EEC would not be acceptable to the Europeans, they began to perceive the choice facing Britain as one of full entry versus complete exclusion. Given the paucity of alternatives, British membership thus assumed a growing likelihood.

With the onset of Common Market entry as a major possibility, Europe appeared to become an increasingly politicized issue within Britain. Specifically, this meant that the European question at last attained substantial consideration by the processes of party government. The three indicators of politicization reflected this shift. First, Europe became less a matter for the Government's economic ministries. Whereas the FTA and EFTA negotiations had been handled by Reginald Maudling, originally as Paymaster General and later as President of the Board of Trade, the Common Market became the responsi-

---

[7] In the February 1959 Parliamentary debate over the collapse of FTA talks, Reginald Maudling listed numerous reasons why the Government could not consider EEC entry. These included the undesirability of allowing an area which accounted for only 13 percent of British trade to determine common commercial policy by majority vote; the existence of a common external tariff which would end free entry of Commonwealth food and raw materials into Britain; EEC agricultural provisions which would cause Britain to violate agreements with the Commonwealth and with her own farmers; the EEC's aim of political federation; problems involved in the free movement of capital and labor, and in the harmonization of social policies; and the need for full renegotiation of the Rome Treaty, which would upset the Six's own delicate balance. See *Hansard, Parliamentary Debates* (Commons), Vol. 599 (February 12, 1959), c. 1489-1494.

[8] Uwe Kitzinger, "Britain and Europe: The Multivalence of the British Decision," reprinted from *The European Yearbook,* Vol. 9 (1962), Martinus Nijihoff, The Hague, p. 38.

bility of Edward Heath, who, as Lord Privy Seal, was second in command at the Foreign Office. Heath, appointed to his position in a July 1960 Cabinet change, became foreign affairs spokesman in the House of Commons due to the fact that the new Foreign Secretary was Lord Home. His responsibility for European unity signified a recognition that the political implications of Europe were now more important than the economic ones. Second, the question of Britain's relationship to Europe entered the arena of public debate for the first time. From early 1961 onward, the British public was inundated by a wave of discussion of Common Market entry involving the mass media, promotional groups, and public lectures and debates. As part of this process, public opinion polls appeared almost monthly and received considerable attention, as did several by-elections in which Europe figured prominently. Numerous promotional pressure groups arose on an *ad hoc* basis, and directed their propaganda efforts at either the general public or Britain's opinion elites. Third, the political parties perceived EEC membership as a major issue, and dealt with it as such. The subject became one of considerable intra-party debate, and the parties found it necessary to formulate public positions. While the establishment of partisan disaccord is not by any means a requisite for politicization, Labour's October 1962 Conference did have the effect of turning the question of Common Market entry into a major partisan controversy.

As for the actual decision of the Prime Minister to enter negotiations for EEC entry, it is neither possible nor necessary to unearth the entire inside story. Nonetheless it is feasible to analyze some of the motives of the Prime Minister in taking what Robert McKenzie has called the most daring initiative by a Conservative Government since the repeal of the Corn Laws.[9]

While divergent impressions exist as to whether Macmil-

---

[9] Robert McKenzie, "Between Two Elections (II)," *Encounter*, 26, no. 2 (February, 1966): 21-29.

lan's aim in taking Britain into Europe was political or economic, the overwhelming preponderance of view by elite respondents interviewed for the present study was that political motivations (both short- and long-run) predominated. To a slightly lesser extent, these respondents also concurred in the observation that Macmillan presented the European choice to the public as though it were primarily an economic matter. Macmillan's European decision, in its political aims, corresponded with the conclusions of an early 1961 report by the Economic Steering Committee under the chairmanship of Sir Frank Lee (then newly appointed as Joint Permanent Secretary to the Treasury). This interdepartmental group of senior civil servants had been brought together to study possible association with the Six, but it concluded that Britain should seek outright membership in the Common Market, and do so for primarily political reasons.[10] Indeed, as one prominent civil servant later commented, "It was a political and not an economic decision. Most of us regarded the economic arguments as at best balanced." British policy-makers clearly expected that Britain could exert leadership within a united Europe, and that this offered a means for restoring the country to a place of world influence. As the foremost nation in a grouping of 220 million people, she might speak as the voice of one of the world's three great industrial superpowers. Furthermore, they felt with good reason that such a move might bring closer transatlantic ties.

On the domestic side, economic concerns unquestionably played a substantial role, but here too there existed political factors of great importance. Throughout the 1950's, the two major parties had drifted toward the political center as factors of ideology and class diminished. Indeed, Robert McKenzie observed in 1958 that "pressure groups, taken together, are a far more important channel of communication than parties for the transmission of ideas from the mass of the

---

[10] Anthony Sampson, *Macmillan: A Study in Ambiguity* (London: Allen Lane, The Penguin Press, 1967), p. 210.

citizenry to their rulers."[11] While it is true that the Tories were not in domestic political difficulty at the time (1960-61), Conservative leaders anticipated the obvious necessity for a new appeal with which to approach the electorate in seeking an unprecedented fourth straight victory in the 1963-64 General Election. Europe offered this novel issue on which to set the Conservatives apart from the Labour Party. In the words of a Senior Tory official "Europe was to be our *deus ex machina;* it was to create a new, contemporary argument with insular Socialism, dish the Liberals by stealing their clothes; give us something new after 12-13 years. . . ."[12] Indeed, this logic best explains the damaging failure of the Government in not making any strenuous effort to seek Labour party support for Common Market entry.

There was still another fundamental domestic motivation in the necessity for shaking up British society and institutions. There existed strong reasons for seeking to shatter the prevalent restrictive habits and techniques in business, labor, and agriculture. Politically however this constituted a hazardous course and the subsequent turmoil over the ending of resale price maintenance highlighted the problem. It would be far easier to carry out such measures as tariff cuts and the abandonment of the agricultural support system if these could be treated as part of the price forced upon Britain by the requisites of an otherwise advantageous Common Market entry.

Finally, there was the person of Macmillan himself. The aging Prime Minister was looking for a lasting contribution with which to cap his public career. He previously had been favorably disposed toward European unity, and had long ago cautioned that Britain must keep in Europe "or be doomed to find ourselves fighting our way back into Europe every

---

[11] McKenzie, *Political Quarterly,* 29, no. 1 (January-March, 1958): 8-10, quoted in Samuel H. Beer, *British Politics in the Collectivist Age* (New York: Knopf, 1965), p. 303.

[12] Quoted in D. E. Butler and Anthony King, *The British General Election of 1964* (London: Macmillan, 1965), p. 79.

twenty years."[13] Though his initial enthusiasm had waned somewhat, he had been an early supporter of Churchill's United Europe Movement. In his memoirs Macmillan later observed, "About Europe, regrets still haunt me,"[14] and he recalled that he had written Churchill in protest when the newly elected Conservative Government of 1951 failed to take action to bring Britain toward the European Coal and Steel Community. Upon becoming Prime Minister in early 1957, Macmillan had faced the urgent tasks of liquidating the Suez enterprise, assuming control of the Conservatives, and then rallying the dispirited Party for an overwhelming victory in the 1959 election. Now, in 1960-61, when the circumstances seemed appropriate, what more enduring accomplishment could there be than to cast Britain's lot with the Continent and thereby create a united Europe?

From the available evidence, it appears that the Prime Minister made his decision in late December 1960, during the Christmas holidays. While he thus led the movement toward Europe, or at least held unique responsibility for consolidating those groups and individuals seeking Common Market entry, he preferred seeming to be pushed toward this option. This operational preference, which his intimates chose to regard as consummate "subtlety" and his opponents as mere "deviousness," had served successfully as his method in terminating the Suez venture and de-colonizing Africa with a minimum of upheaval at home. Lamentably, Macmillan's customary technique of avoiding direct confrontations proved far less successful in Europe. Rather than resort to a Churchillian approach, which would have meant invoking a transcendent national interest and appealing to the British public on the lofty basis of securing the lasting consolidation of the European peoples, Macmillan adopted a far more limited method. In the words of Richard Neustadt, he oper-

---

[13] *Hansard,* Vol. 469 (November 17, 1949), c. 2326-2328.
[14] *Sunday Times* (London), July 31, 1966.

ated "by disguising his strategic choice as a commercial deal."[15] This left considerable scope and legitimacy for the operation of sectional pressure groups and various other interests whose range stopped well short of the national interest.

A key point here is that the July 1961 announcement that Britain would seek EEC entry reflected a political judgment, made by political authorities before pressure groups had strongly articulated their own interests. In particular it meant that considerations of broad national interest, construed in terms of Britain's overall international position, took precedence over cost-benefit calculations as to the effects of Common Market membership on individual economic interests. It also reflected the existence of policy powers held by the Prime Minister and Cabinet which could be exercised relatively free of the constraints that interest groups typically imposed on lesser domestic issues. The fact that Macmillan would not or could not make the case to the British public in grandly political terms, as opposed to less ambitious commercial ones, meant that the subsequent formulation of Britain's negotiating position offered the opportunity for the assertion of a powerful pressure group role. There is thus a crucial distinction to be made between policy-making in the period before the July 1961 decision, which reflects effective politicization and the operation of a party government function insulated from pressure groups, and the post-July 1961 period, when sectional pressure groups managed to reassert their influence.

THE ROLE OF LABOUR

Prior to 1961, the Labour and Conservative front benches shared basic views about European unity; they also increasingly perceived a certain decline in Britain's power and in-

---

15 Richard E. Neustadt, "Whitehouse and Whitehall," Paper delivered at the 1965 Annual Meeting of the American Political Science Association, Washington, D.C., September 8-11, p. 9.

fluence, an erosion of her special relation with the U.S., and the failure of EFTA to emerge as a serious rival to the EEC. But with the emergence and development of the Common Market issue there came a progressive demise of bipartisanship.

LABOUR IN SEARCH OF A POLICY, 1961-62

Initially it seemed logical that the Conservatives, with their traditional attachment to agriculture, the Commonwealth and national sovereignty, would be the party most likely to experience bitter division over the Common Market. However it was the Labour Party, where basic organizational factors combined with differences over the merits of the European issue, which most rapidly divided on the question of Europe. While a multiplicity of views existed within the Labour Party as a whole, the general outlook was one of wariness. Labour had been reluctant to see social welfare, full employment, and planning in a framework other than that of the nation-state. This attitude reflected a latent tendency toward insularity. During the immediate postwar period of tripartism in France and Italy, substantial pro-European feeling had existed within the Party, but this sentiment waned with the rightward drift of those countries. Despite later support for the EEC by the Continental Socialists and the considerable economic planning undertaken by the Community, Labour critics saw the EEC as essentially a device for the preservation of free enterprise and as a "rich-man's club." There were fears about the inhibiting effect of Common Market membership on the socialist policies of a future Labour Government, and some worries were also expressed of harm to individual industries.

Most Labourites opposing Europe did so on largely political grounds. They were concerned over the implications for a neutralist, or at least less Cold War oriented foreign policy and felt membership in the EEC would jeopardize British efforts at "bridge-building" between the Soviet Union and the

U.S., and even between China and the U.S.[16] Thus Labour's defense spokesman, Denis Healey, described the economic arguments as approximately balanced, but voiced concern about the political harm to Britain's Commonwealth role, the possible danger of pushing the European neutrals (Finland, Sweden, Austria) toward the Soviet Union and the effect on relations with neutral African nations.[17] Among all the critics there was an unwillingness to aid the Conservative Government, whose policy the Common Market application was after all.

Most Labour MP's agreed among themselves in criticizing the Government's actual execution of European policy and condemned what they identified as an excessive concern with short-term commercial advantages when the real issue was political. However, even though the bulk of the Party was aloof toward Europe, an important and identifiable group, largely on the Labour right and led by some of the Gaitskellites, took a much more sympathetic view of European unity. George Brown and Roy Jenkins were the most prominent members of this group, and Jenkins actually resigned from the Labour Party front bench in the late spring of 1961 over the Common Market issue. The pro-Common Market group held that entry was desirable provided that the interests of EFTA, British agriculture, and the Commonwealth could somehow be safeguarded. Unlike many Common Market advocates in the Conservative Party, they dwelt heavily on political purposes. George Brown bluntly told Labour that the Commonwealth offered no alternative to Europe[18] and Roy Jenkins sought to persuade the Party that socialism could not be constructed in an autarchic framework and that European entry offered the best remedy against a drab decline away from the world's mainstream.[19]

[16] The Labour Party, *Report of the 59th Annual Conference* (October 3-7, 1960), p. 75.
[17] *Financial Times,* May 19, 1961.
[18] Labour, *60th Annual Conference* (1961), pp. 224-225.
[19] *Hansard,* Vol. 645 (August 2, 1961), c. 1583-1589.

Organizational factors also influenced the line-up within the Labour Party. Unlike the TUC, which experienced a less divisive Common Market debate, the Labour leadership tended to include a wider cross-section of viewpoints. In other words, the TUC elite represented the apex of an organizational pyramid, but Labour leaders came from the top of a truncated pyramid. TUC leaders were usually heads of their own large bureaucratic unions, while prominent Labourites included not only those elected to the NEC to represent constituency party organizations but also individual and highly vocal members of Parliament. Then too, the entire Party had been riven by a right–left split stemming from the 1951 Bevanite rebellion, passing through the struggle over German rearmament, then reaching a peak of intensity at the time of the October 1960 Blackpool Conference where the proponents of unilateral nuclear disarmament carried the day. This deep ideological division within the Party was also reinforced by substantial personal animosity. European policy never evoked the same intensity of feeling as nuclear disarmament and the proposed repeal of the commitment to nationalization in Clause IV of the Party constitution. Yet, while Europe constituted an issue for which tenets of party ideology, whether revisionist or orthodox, did not dictate an immediate and clear-cut choice, the traditional left-right split played a significant part in the differences over Common Market entry.

Virtually the entire left of the Party adopted a reserved or hostile position toward Common Market entry. Only three figures of consequence on the left approved of Europe. These were Robert Edwards, head of the Chemical Workers, Walter Padley, leader of the Union of Shop, Distributive, and Allied Workers (USDAW), and Fenner Brockway, an elderly and respected party figure. Frank Cousins, head of Britain's largest union, the Transport and General Workers Union (T&GWU), briefly favored a European course, but (as noted in Chapter 5) subsequently reversed his position. The main cross-cutting cleavages existed within the normally right-wing sections of the Party, some of whose leaders adopted anti-Common Market positions. These included a few important Gaitskellites, especially Patrick Gordon Walker, Wilson's choice for Foreign Minister in 1964; Denis Healey, later Minister of Defense; and Douglas Jay, President of the Board of Trade from 1964 to 1967. In both numbers and importance, many more members of the right opposed Europe than those of the left supported it. The Labourites in favor of Common Market membership came almost exclusively from the right. The majority of Gaitskellites, who had fought together in opposing unilateral disarmament and in seeking to repeal Clause IV, were the heart of this group, along with a number of important trade union leaders. In addition to Jenkins and Brown, the group included Anthony Crosland, Ray Gunter, Sam Watson, Charles Pannell, and Douglas Houghton. Hugh Gaitskell himself, after an initial period of sympathy for the European cause, deeply stunned his longtime followers by (in essence) opposing Common Market membership.

It was by no means obvious in advance what position the Labour Party would adopt on the Common Market. Rather than force the issue at an early date, Labour assumed a position described as being "on the fence." Thus in the Parliamentary vote on August 3, 1961, which followed Macmillan's announcement, the Parliamentary Labour Party (PLP) abstained. HMG carried the division by a vote of 313 to 5. Those voting "no" included one Conservative (Anthony Fell) and four left-wing Labourites (Michael Foot, Emrys Hughes, Konni Zilliacus, and S. O. Davies). At this point it appeared that the PLP was fairly evenly divided. Roughly one-third of the 258 Labour MP's supported the Common Market, one-third opposed it, and the remaining one-third remained undecided and presumably willing to accept Hugh Gaitskell's direction.[20]

The months between August 1961 and the October 1962

20 See, for example, *The Times,* June 17, 1961. Estimates of this kind for both parties appeared frequently during 1961 and 1962, and fluctu-

Labour Party Conference are largely a record of frustrated efforts by the pro-Common Market forces and an increased movement of Party sentiment away from entry on the terms emerging in the negotiations. The first real test of Party sentiment came at the October 1961 Scarborough Conference. The Conference overwhelmingly rejected a resolution by Roy Jenkins which would have offered unconditional support for membership. A resolution unconditionally opposing entry also failed to win approval. Instead the Party adopted a composite motion, slightly negative in tone, which stated that Labour would not approve entry unless guarantees were obtained for agriculture, horticulture, EFTA, the Commonwealth, and for Britain's right to retain the power of nationalization and economic planning. The room that this formula left for maneuver was evident even in the way the resolution was moved by John Stonehouse, who stressed the negative aspects, and the way the debate was summed up by George Brown, who supported the Resolution but regretted its tone.[21]

By early 1962, the task of pushing Labour off the fence in the direction of Europe had become more difficult. The Gallup Poll indicated that Labour voters, who as recently as December 1961 would have approved a Government decision to enter Europe by a huge margin (52 percent for, versus 20 against), were changing their position. The figures for April-May 1962 had slipped to the ratio of 38 percent to 33 percent[22] and were to worsen during the remainder of the year. Furthermore, the temperature of debate within the Party had risen. The Victory for Socialism group, on the left of the Party, issued a manifesto demanding that Labour oppose the Common Market (as reactionary and capitalist) and that the Party

---

ated widely depending on the European persuasion of the analyst or the newspaper.

[21] Brown also expressed the view that the economic arguments favored entry, and the political obstacles were exaggerated. See Labour, *60th Annual Conference* (1961), pp. 334-338.

[22] *Gallup Political Index*, No. 24 (December, 1961), p. 8; and No. 28-29 (April-May, 1962), p. 68.

should warn HMG that it would refuse to be committed by a
Government decision on the matter. Roy Jenkins in turn told
Gaitskell that severe upheavals within the Party would inevitably occur if it opposed entry.[23] By this time, a majority
of the PLP opposed entry except on terms that appeared
highly unlikely of attainment. Nor did this drift go unnoticed.
In an unusual feature entitled "A Nation in Search of a
Party," the pro-Common Market *Daily Herald* (formerly
owned by the TUC, and only recently placed under control
of the King-Mirror group) accused Labour of trying to dodge
the historic Common Market issue.[24]

There were signs too that Gaitskell might join the opposition to Government policy. His Fulham speech of April 14
castigated HMG for keeping the country in a fog of confusion
and insisted that it should not reach a decision without giving
Parliament and the public an opportunity to discuss fully the
actual conditions of entry.[25] However, his insistence on terms
and his attack on Government handling of Europe still stopped
short of outright opposition. On May 8, Gaitskell spoke
on TV, citing the Commonwealth as the key issue and saying
the best solution still was to enter Europe on good terms. Accordingly, Labour again abstained in a Parliamentary vote on
June 8.

By mid-1962, the chances of the pro-Common Market group
had slipped again. The temper of the Party seemed increasingly anti-Europe, and the list of proposed Conference resolutions offered by the constituency parties contained 38 motions
of unconditional opposition, six of conditional opposition,
and only three of conditional or unconditional support.[26]

THE FIVE CONDITIONS

The Labour Party finally committed itself at its annual

---

23 *Sunday Telegraph* (London), January 14, 1962.
24 *Daily Herald* (London), January 31, 1962.
25 *Sunday Times*, April 15, 1962.
26 *The Times*, July 27, 1962.

Conference in October 1962. A statement by the National Executive Committee (NEC), issued on September 29, expressed official party policy, and Hugh Gaitskell's speech to the Conference on October 3 effectively and emotionally voiced what the NEC had only implied.

The heart of the NEC statement consisted of five broad conditions which would be required for joining the EEC:

1. Strong and binding safeguards for the trade and other interests of our friends and partners in the Commonwealth.
2. Freedom as at present to pursue our own foreign policy.
3. Fulfillment of the Government's pledge to our associates in the EFTA.
4. The right to plan our own economy.
5. Guarantees to safeguard the position of British agriculture.[27]

The statement stipulated that political considerations, not the uncertain balance of economic advantage, constituted the real test of entry: "If . . . our membership were to weaken the Commonwealth and the trade of the underdeveloped nations, lessen the chances of East-West agreement and reduce the influence that Britain could exert in world affairs, then the case against entry would be decisive."[28] It also detailed what it considered to be harmful concessions made by HMG and stated that the August 1962 White Paper on Commonwealth trade provided safeguards which no major Commonwealth

---

[27] *The Guardian* (London), "The Labour Party Conference, 1962." Actually the conditions were not new. As early as January 31, Gaitskell had stated precisely these five points. On March 7, Labour MP's offered a compromise motion in Parliament, containing similar provisions (though without the signature of the Shadow Cabinet). The same points recurred in Gaitskell's April 15 Fulham speech and, more prominently, in his speech to the House of Commons on June 6. For details see *The Times*, February 1 and March 8, 1962; and *Hansard*, Vol. 661 (June 6, 1962), c. 507-527.

[28] Labour, *61st Annual Conference* (1962), pp. 470-475.

Prime Minister found adequate. Finally it argued that HMG must seek new terms, and only the Six's acceptance of these would show them to be outward looking.

There are two possible ways to judge Labour's five conditions. One is to view them as demonstrating a willingness to enter Europe subject to certain essential reservations. The other is as a politically astute manner of *de facto* opposition to entry. The first interpretation was frequently voiced by Labour spokesmen and is perhaps extant in the actual wording of the terms. Those who maintained this interpretation noted that three of the conditions (Commonwealth, EFTA, and agriculture) already had been set out by the Prime Minister himself. Furthermore they could point to the facts that several NEC members who unconditionally opposed entry (Barbara Castle, Tom Driberg, Ian Mikardo, and Anthony Greenwood) had actually abstained from voting on the statement because they felt it too conciliatory, and that a motion expressing unconditional opposition was beaten on the conference floor.

But whatever the formal appearance, the implications were clearly anti-Common Market, and Labour's five conditions provided a means for effectively opposing Common Market entry without appearing to be too negative.[29] This is borne out by the in-fighting within the NEC during the drafting of the statement. After adopting a position based on a paper written by Peter Shore of the Labour Research Department, the NEC had appointed a committee to compose the official statement. The group consisted of two men favorable to Europe (Sam Watson and George Brown) and three anti's (Hugh Gaitskell, Harold Wilson, and R. H. S. Crossman). Brown and Watson argued strenuously for a weakening of

---

[29] A July 1961 research paper, prepared for the Labour Party's Home Policy Committee, had stated that because amendments to the Rome Treaty were not a serious possibility, the Treaty's application to the U.K. must be considered in broadly its existing form.

For an excellent though one-sided rebuttal of the points made in the NEC statement, see the comments by Lord Gladwyn in the *Daily Telegraph,* October 6, 1962.

the proposed statement because the terms appeared impossible of achievement. Eventually they succeeded in obtaining several nominal concessions; these included an acknowledgment that the Common Market was a great conception and that entry would be desirable on better terms.[30]

Hugh Gaitskell was almost alone in believing Labour's five conditions could actually be obtained in negotiations with the Six. R. H. S. Crossman was more realistic, asserting that there was "not the slightest chance" of HMG even trying to write the five conditions into the text of the agreement. Crossman described Labour's terms as a face-saving arrangement so that the pro-Europeans could eventually vote against the Government without in principle opposing Common Market entry.[31]

If the NEC statement invited diverse interpretation, no such difference of opinion was possible over the meaning of Gaitskell's address to the Party. More than any other single factor, the speech marks the point at which the Common Market issue finally became one of distinct partisan contention. In a brilliant eighty-minute address, the Labour Party leader delivered a sweeping attack on the European case. The response to this speech, which had gone well beyond the hopes of even some prominent opponents of entry, was a prolonged standing ovation and a wave of popularity for Gaitskell unprecedented in his prior period of leadership. George Brown followed Gaitskell with a speech seeking to shift the balance of argument back toward the center, but it was clearly anticlimactic.[32]

The person of Hugh Gaitskell thus constituted one of the

---

[30] Something of the political culture of the Labour Party is illustrated by the fact that the two working class members of the drafting committee (Brown and Watson) succeeded in getting one of their three Oxford-educated intellectual antagonists (R. H. S. Crossman) to draft the wording of the modifications for them.

[31] *The Guardian,* October 5, 1962.

[32] The anti-EEC T&GWU actually paid for the printing of two million copies of the speech in pamphlet form. As an afterthought, Brown's speech was also included.

most important elements in the establishment of Labour's opposition to EEC entry. His position seems in part to have been determined by the difference in his outlook toward the Commonwealth as opposed to Europe. The Labour Party leader had childhood ties to India and made no secret of his deep attachment to the Commonwealth. Although during 1960-61 he held a somewhat sympathetic attitude toward possible Common Market membership, he made it clear that his main object of concern in the Brussels negotiations would be that Britain obtain suitable terms for the Commonwealth.[33] The underlying tension between European and Commonwealth priorities became evident when Gaitskell attended a meeting of the EEC Socialist Parties at Brussels on July 16, 1962. While he was nominally the head of European Social Democracy (as leader of the Labour Party), he never relished the role, and at Brussels he clashed with the Belgian leader, Paul-Henri Spaak. Gaitskell felt the Europeans were pushing too hard and that they failed to understand the importance of the Commonwealth. The Europeans came away from the meeting with the view that the British were more concerned with safeguards than with the necessity for European unity. The clash did nothing to increase Gaitskell's affection for Europe.

Gaitskell's relations with his Commonwealth counterparts betrayed no such strains. Prior to the Commonwealth Prime Ministers' Conference in London, he led a meeting of Commonwealth Socialist leaders on September 9. Until this time, and despite his enunciated reservations, Gaitskell had viewed the economic case for Common Market entry as balanced, but the political one (especially the value of Western unity) as advantageous. The Commonwealth meeting proved to be a turning point, with the Indian representative playing the key role. Labour's Indian tie was actually through the small Praja Socialist Party, whose leader, Ashoka Metha, was not only a

---

[33] *Observer* (London), December 10, 1961.

personal friend of Gaitskell's, but sympathetic to European unity as well. Because he was unable to attend, Gaitskell reluctantly agreed to invite an observer from the Indian Government (and Congress Party), B. K. Lal, the Ambassador to Brussels. Lal made an outstanding contribution to the conference in voicing India's deep anxiety about finding outlets for her manufactured goods. Gaitskell came away from the meeting profoundly convinced of the harmful effects upon India and deeply moved by the fears expressed by other Commonwealth Socialist leaders.[34]

While personal experiences and relationships had always strongly influenced Gaitskell, and were important in the Spaak and Lal contacts, the situation within the Labour Party itself also operated to push Gaitskell in the same anti-Common Market direction. He had already undergone a series of exhausting fights with the left, in which he had shown his ability to master it. There would be a kind of symmetrical justice, as well as a strengthening of his own position, if he now sided with the left on a major issue. Respondents involved in these events differ sharply over whether such a factor really constituted an important motivation for him, but it is true that the balance of power situation within the Party had at least to be taken into consideration in any effort to arrive at a decision. Gaitskell admitted as much in December 1961: "I don't mind telling you that although I think it is right and common sense to take the attitude that I have taken, I do not want another party row about this."[35]

Indeed, there is some question whether, under the circumstances, Gaitskell could have succeeded in carrying the Party in favor of EEC entry. Despite his anti-unilateralist success in

---

[34] *The Times'* political correspondent, David Wood, later related how Gaitskell had sharply criticized him when he mentioned what he thought to be the opposition leader's position, based on an earlier conversation prior to the meeting. See William T. Rodgers (ed.), *Hugh Gaitskell, 1906-1963* (London: Thames and Hudson, 1964), pp. 155-156.

[35] *Observer,* December 10, 1961.

1961, he had been beaten in the battle over Clause IV. Certainly he could not carry the Party into Europe without seriously dividing it again. Indeed, by adopting the policy for Labour of "Yes, if . . . " and later shifting toward "No, unless . . . , " Gaitskell succeeded in preserving Party unity because the conditions could be interpreted loosely enough to cover a wide range of views. This policy also had the effect of directing the focus of attention to the actions of the Conservative Government rather than to the desirability of membership *per se.* The consummate logic of Labour's position became more evident as the talks wore on, since Labour could maintain that while it favored entry in principle, it could not support the present unsatisfactory arrangement being negotiated by the Conservatives.

Significantly, Gaitskell's handling of the issue enhanced his political stature. Following the 1962 Conference, Harold Wilson observed that Labour was now more united than at any time in the previous ten years.[36] While the Gaitskellites remained intensely unhappy, they constituted a definite minority and also had at least the face-saving cover of the NEC statement's five conditions with which to hide their nakedness. R. H. S. Crossman wrote that Gaitskell's opposition to entry had won him "unprecedented popularity with his own party, and for the first time compelled the general public to accept him as a genuine alternative to Mr. Macmillan."[37] Not since Suez, as Crossman noted, had the Opposition leader been so hated outside the Party and so popular inside it, and the reason was that, as in 1956, he had attacked the Government at a critical moment when it was counting on his tacit support.

LABOUR AND MACMILLAN

It is not possible to explain the deepening of Labour antagonism to the EEC without considering the matter from

---

[36] *The Guardian,* October 6, 1962.
[37] Crossman, *loc. cit.,* pp. 735-736.

the viewpoint of domestic party politics. Unlike the situation of the previous European unity issues, there was an unusual absence of bipartisanship over Common Market policy. Major foreign policy issues normally receive bipartisan support, but this key element was lacking from consideration of British membership in the EEC. The major postwar exception to this bipartisan tradition had been Suez, the experience of which still colored the political environment. In the words of one Labour junior minister, looking back over the 1961-62 period: "The Tories hated Hugh Gaitskell as a traitor over Suez, and the channels of communication had silted up."[38] Lack of communication only partially accounted for the absence of bipartisanship. The crucial element was that the Conservatives consciously chose not to make the issue bipartisan. At the time of the October 1960 Conference, Labour seemed so deeply divided over unilateralism, Clause IV and the question of whether Conference decisions could be binding upon the PLP that the Party appeared to present little potential electoral threat to the Tories.[39] Thus in making his December 1960 decision, Macmillan could understandably have minimized the importance of actually seeking to carry the Opposition with him. While Edward Heath apparently did offer to give Gaitskell information on the negotiations (which Gaitskell refused in order to maintain freedom to criticize), HMG made no major effort to win Labour support. According to Miriam Camps, Conservative Party Chairman Iain Macleod decided in mid-1962 that the Common Market offered popular election appeal, and at this point the issue began to become a definite party question.[40] Whatever the sequence of events, Labour was prone to regard Macmillan's motives with skepti-

---

[38] Confidential interview with the writer, April, 1967. This antagonism produced a lack of communication greater than that between Prime Minister Wilson and Edward Heath in the 1966-67 period.

[39] Labour trailed the Conservatives in the Gallup Poll of voting intentions until July 1961. *Gallup Political Index,* no. 37 (January, 1963).

[40] Camps, *op cit.,* p. 450.

cism. In the eyes of the Opposition, the Prime Minister had been forced to adopt Common Market entry as a last resort following economic and financial crises and a series of diplomatic and military failures.[41] In Labour's view, the Common Market constituted not a statesmanlike act but a purely political gimmick, "an attempt by a most adroit and ingenious politician to extricate himself from his domestic difficulties and manoeuvre himself into a situation where, having successfully negotiated terms of entry, he could appeal to the country posing as the greatest statesman since Disraeli."[42]

The rare bipartisan efforts in support of the Common Market that did exist came via promotional pressure groups, and with limited impact. Indeed, there may have been as much bipartisan cooperation directed against Europe as for it.

In addition to the lack of bipartisanship, another domestic political factor affected Labour's EEC policy. This was the question of whether to demand that HMG hold a General Election on the Common Market issue. Gaitskell resisted the pressures on him to make such a demand; instead he defined his position in a more complex fashion which only admitted the possibility of calling for an election on the issue after the terms of entry had been decided upon and not beforehand:

> If . . . the final terms produced by the government on which it is proposed that Britain should enter the Common Market do not in our view fulfill the conditions we have laid down so that the Labour Party feels bound to oppose entry on these terms and there is a clear division of opinion between the two major parties, then Britain should not be compelled to enter until the British people have been allowed the opportunity to decide for themselves.[43]

In the same vein, the NEC rejected by a vote of 17-7 a demand that it call for an immediate election, and the 1962 Annual

---

[41] For example, see the comments of Peter Shore in *Twelve Wasted Years* (London: Labour Party Research Department, 1963), p. 319.

[42] R. H. S. Crossman, "British Labour Looks at Europe," *Foreign Affairs*, 41, no. 4 (July, 1963): 735.

[43] *The Guardian*, October 1, 1962.

Conference defeated a related proposal by a vote of 4.5 to 1.9 million.

This decision reflected some sophisticated political calculation. For one thing, in the aftermath of the 1962 Party Conferences, Labour was still less unified than the Conservatives. The pro-Common Market members of the NEC: William Boyd of the AEU, Walter Padley of USDAW, and Fred Mulley of the clerical workers, along with Sam Watson and George Brown all were trade unionists who had supported Gaitskell in opposition to unilateral nuclear disarmament and now opposed him on Europe. They, together with men such as Roy Jenkins and Ray Gunter were far more formidable antagonists for Gaitskell than were the Tory die-hards Macmillan faced. Furthermore, the British electorate normally voted on the basis of domestic issues;[44] and on these Labour was running well ahead of the Tories. Since July 1961, Labour had led the Conservatives in polls of public voting intentions, and the percentage net swing of votes away from the Conservatives to Labour had been running in Labour's direction since March 1961. By the fall of 1962, by-election results for the year were showing average swings to Labour of 5-10 percent (and occasionally more).[45]

Although Common Market enthusiasm can hardly be said to have been sweeping the country, the electorate did view entry more favorably than it did the Conservative Party. For example, in September 1962, 46 percent of Gallup Poll respondents indicated they would approve of a Government decision to enter Europe, and only 30 percent disapproved

---

[44] Kenneth Younger notes that opinion polls in recent years indicate a two to one majority giving priority to domestic issues. "The relative remoteness of the ordinary citizen from international issues, coupled with the intense interest of . . . pressure groups may be responsible for the oligarchic flavour which still attaches to foreign policy." See "Public Opinion and British Foreign Policy," *International Affairs*, 40, no. 1 (January, 1964): 22-25.

[45] *Gallup Political Index*, no. 37 (January, 1963); and no. 47 (December, 1963).

(24 percent were undecided). Furthermore, Labour voters were less strong in their opposition to the EEC than Tory voters were in their support. The poll showed the Labourites disapproving by a fairly narrow margin of 37 percent to 32 percent.[46] Jean Blondel finds that the British electorate has tended to vote on the basis of parties rather than issues, and he gives evidence that there is little sign of partisanship over foreign policy issues as compared to economic and social ones. What is more, he notes how the parties even molded public opinion to some extent after July 1961, Conservative voters becoming more pro-Common Market and Labour voters more anti. Even though large majorities of voters indicated that they would still continue to support their party if they eventually disagreed with it on the Common Market, as many as 13 percent of Tory voters and 16 percent of Labour voters would have changed their votes on the basis of the Common Market question.[47] Given the highly marginal nature of British electoral contests, it is no wonder that Hugh Gaitskell rejected a strategy which would have divided his party and allowed the Conservatives to fight an election on an issue which favored their position.

Meanwhile there also existed a constitutional question as to whether the Government should be required to hold an election to legitimate its dramatic European initiative. A traditional view, for example that of H. R. G. Greaves, held that it was a convention of the constitution that "governments do not impose legislation of a keenly controversial nature unless they have a mandate from the electorate."[48] The Common Market question was obviously controversial, and since it had not been part of the program on which the Macmillan Government fought the 1959 election, this would seem to have indicated the necessity of seeking a mandate by means of an

---

[46] *Ibid.*, no. 33 (September, 1962), p. 160.

[47] Jean Blondel, *Voters, Parties and Leaders* (Harmondsworth, Middlesex: Penguin, 1966), pp. 78-87.

[48] Quoted by Robert McKenzie in the *Observer*, June 18, 1961.

election. However, the British constitutional authority, Sir Ivor Jennings, rejected this conception in his book, *Parliament,* and it did not in practice carry much weight. The concept of an election mandate was constitutionally uncertain and traditionally forced only on the party of the left by the Conservatives and House of Lords. Thus, despite the importance of the Common Market, the Government was under no constitutional obligation to hold an election. Robert McKenzie even implied that the process of functional representation, with interest group consultation, was providing a thoroughly satisfactory substitute for the party government channel and its electoral methods:

... [the] public is being 'consulted' in what is by far the most appropriate method: through the 'interest group' system and even, in a sense, through public opinion polls. The Government itself must make the decision; but it should do so in full knowledge of the attitude of every organized group which cares to express an opinion and also in full awareness of the state of public opinion generally.[49]

Finally, there was no way in which a General Election could operate as a valid single issue contest. For example, a vote for Labour would not be just a vote against the Common Market, but also one in favor of renationalization of the steel industry.

Given the partisan controversy, Labour constituted a substantial constraint on Macmillan's freedom of maneuver. This presented one advantage for Macmillan in that increased politicization nearly silenced anti-Common Market sentiment within his own Party. Furthermore, because the Common Market issue was a matter of policy initiation and international negotiation (clearly areas of Government prerogative), rather than one of legislation and administration, Labour had some difficulty in bringing pressures to bear or in playing as great a role as it might otherwise have done. Nonetheless, Labour significantly added to the constraints upon Government action in three ways.

---

[49] *Ibid.*

First, the Labour Party's position had the effect of reinforcing group pressures. When Gaitskell stated that he did not think the British Government would take the country into the Common Market "if there were the most unholy row in the Commonwealth or if there were a massive outcry from the farmers,"[50] he was strengthening the legitimacy of Commonwealth and agricultural demands.

Secondly, by its position, Labour provided the only significant formal vehicle for the effective expression of opposition to the Common Market. Because it existed as the alternative Government, Labour's threats had to be taken seriously. Macmillan thus committed a critical error in failing to seek bipartisan support. By contrast, the opposition to Wilson's 1966-67 Common Market initiative could be virtually ignored because, given bi- (or tri-) partisan unity, it lacked a point of leverage upon the Government.

Thirdly, Labour's position had a harmful, if not devastating, effect upon the Brussels negotiations. Following Labour's October 1962 Conference, *The Guardian* observed editorially that because the Macmillan Government was weak and the country now severely divided, the Europeans could judge that the British Government was not a reliable partner and might well doubt whether any purpose was to be served by continuing the negotiations.[51] A Government which had received only 49 percent of the vote in 1959 without the Common Market in its program, currently getting only 30 percent of the vote in by-elections and opinion polls, and now opposed by a vigorous anti-Common Market Opposition party, could hardly be expected to commit the U.K. for all time to entry.[52] Though the threat was never formally voiced by the Labour Party, prominent Labourites did warn that a future Labour Government would not be bound by a Rome Treaty signed

---

[50] *New York Herald Tribune,* European Edition, February 10-11, 1962.

[51] October 4, 1962.

[52] The phrase is McKenzie's. *Observer,* September 9, 1962.

under such conditions.[53] Hugh Gaitskell himself may have administered the *coup de grâce* when he travelled to Paris in early December. There, in conversations with Foreign Minister Couve de Murville, Prime Minister George Pompidou, and Socialist Party leader Guy Mollet, and in a speech to the Anglo-American Press association, Gaitskell made it clear that the provisional agreements of July and August were "profoundly unsatisfactory," and stated that "there is no overriding necessity for Britain's entry into the Common Market."[54]

MACMILLAN AND THE CONSERVATIVE PARTY

Converting the Conservative Party appeared to be Macmillan's most difficult task, for this was where his power base lay and where his policy faced the greatest danger of defeat. Conservative Prime Ministers have tended to encounter greater threats to their office from within the party than from the voting public; thus to preserve harmony and carry the Party required a great deal of care.

The Prime Minister's European policy faced serious obstacles. Macmillan had gone on record as saying that because of harmful consequences for the Commonwealth, Britain should not enter the Common Market; other Conservative leaders had made similar statements.[55] Opponents of Common Market entry frequently threw these words back at Macmillan. Far more seriously, the proposed policy shift threatened three of the most sensitive aspects of Conservative faith: the Commonwealth, agriculture, and British sovereignty. As Robert McKenzie observed, Macmillan had a definite preoccupa-

---

[53] However Hugh Gaitskell and the PLP refused to repudiate in advance any agreement the Conservative Government might make. See *The Guardian,* November 1, 1962.

[54] *The Times,* December 4, 1962.

[55] See, for example, the collection in Evan Luard, *Britain and Europe* (London: Fabian International Bureau, January, 1961), p. 7; and Forward Britain Movement, *The Case Now Against Britain's Entry into the Common Market* (London, 1962), pp. 3-4.

tion with historical parallels such as the harmful intraparty disputes over Peel's rescinding of the Corn Laws in the 1840's, Tariff Reform in 1905, and Baldwin's tariff proposals of 1923.[56] He was therefore intensely concerned with the necessity for converting the Tories and maintaining their unity on an issue which was, if anything, potentially even more far-reaching and divisive in its implications than the tariff controversies.

Macmillan moved extremely skillfully in working with the Party membership and activists, the 1922 Committee, and the Cabinet—so skillfully in fact that he lost not a single Parliamentary Secretary or Junior Whip in the August 3, 1961 Parliamentary vote (which contrasts strikingly with Harold Wilson's May 1967 loss of a half-dozen). However, he maneuvered at the cost of being less than candid about the basic implications of Common Market membership. This strategy not only required damaging compromises but also forced the Government to face in one direction at Brussels and another within the U.K. Macmillan gambled successfully on the development of sentiment within his Party but at considerable cost to his freedom of maneuver.

HOW MACMILLAN CARRIED THE PARTY: THE ADVANTAGE OF LEADERSHIP

How then did the Prime Minister carry the Conservative Party in the European direction? To begin with, he had on his side two extremely important aspects of Party tradition: the absence of any definite ideology and the acceptance of strong leadership. The former element implied that a reversal of policy on even such an important issue as European unity could be fought through largely on its own merits rather than facing obstacles intrinsic to the Party's nature. The latter aspect meant that the members might accept a policy at the urging of their leaders, which—as in their 1947 acceptance of

---

[56] *Observer,* June 18, 1961.

the Industrial Charter and the July 1961 imposition of economic planning—they would otherwise have been expected to contest heatedly.

Added to these factors, Macmillan benefited from the circumstance that the leadership of a party in power is in a stronger position *vis-à-vis* its own membership than when it is in opposition. The Conservative Party does not normally display fissiparous tendencies, and is accustomed to being managed.[57] The Party organization lacked a decisive role in policy formulation, and as a body could only endorse or reject. Given Party tradition and Macmillan's skillful method of phrasing the European question, the Prime Minister held a considerable advantage.

Accordingly, the Conservative Central Office softened up the Party activists by running a series of invitational meetings in the early part of 1962 for all major area and constituency office holders. Speakers such as Peter Thorneycroft, Edward Heath, Christopher Soames, Sir Edward Boyle, and Iain Macleod gave well-prepared speeches, and produced a major impact on the key opinion formers within the constituencies. In keeping with the general tone of Macmillan's approach, these speakers presented the European argument in a negative fashion, dwelling on the consequences of failure to enter the EEC coupled with reassurances on the Commonwealth and agriculture. There was no effort to lift attention to a great New Design, as a Churchill might have done.

The Parliamentary Party presented more of a problem in that considerable pressure existed there to prevent European entry or at least modify the terms involved. However, once European policy became a matter of partisan disagreement,

---

[57] For example, whereas Labour holds frequent and sometimes closely contested votes on various resolutions at its annual conference, the Conservative Party rarely takes a formal vote. In addition, until 1965 the Conservatives selected their leader in a consensual process whereby one man emerged as the choice of the Party and not from a formal voting process.

Conservative opponents of entry found themselves in an almost impossible position. They could only oppose EEC membership by siding with the Opposition Labourites, and rebellion of this sort has always been exceedingly difficult to sustain. This constraint became especially evident at the Party's 1962 Llandudno Conference which took place soon after the Labour Conference, and which produced not a deep rift but a solidarity demonstration at which no more than 40 of the delegates expressed public disapproval of Macmillan's policy.

In addition to advantages of position, Macmillan relied on a process of gradually edging toward Europe. At no time did he formally confront the Party with the question: "Shall Britain seek to become a member of the Common Market?" At first, Party leaders emphasized that the autumn 1960 preliminary talks with the Europeans were only for the purpose of deciding whether to enter negotiations. When Macmillan made his July 31, 1961 announcement, the Motion placed before Parliament provided only for negotiations to see whether satisfactory arrangements could be made to meet the special interests of Britain, the Commonwealth, and EFTA; and stipulated that no agreement effecting these interests or British sovereignty would be entered into until approved by Parliament after full Commonwealth consultation.[58]

At the October 1961 Conservative Party Conference, the opponents of Europe again found themselves at a severe disadvantage because of the way the European question was put. Speaking for the Government, Duncan Sandys made the issue a test of confidence and stated that HMG had given solemn undertakings to Parliament that Britain would not join the Common Market without special arrangements to protect Commonwealth interests. Sandys opposed an amendment calling on HMG to refuse any proposals which would involve surrender of sovereignty or which were inconsistent

---

[58] *Hansard*, Vol. 645 (July 31, 1961), c. 1480-1484.

with pledges to British agriculture and the continuance of Britain's traditional Commonwealth and world role. He told the delegates that if they approved the amendment they would be tying the Government's hands. ". . . . [This] would be interpreted as a vote of censure on the Government and rejection by the party of the whole of our policy towards Europe."[59] Thus alternatively cajoled and threatened, the delegates passed by an overwhelming majority a resolution stating that Britain "should lose no time in negotiating a form of closer association with the Six compatible with our Commonwealth and EFTA responsibilities, economic and political, and our pledges to British agriculture."[60]

A year later, opponents were thwarted because of the suddenly partisan nature of the debate. This effectively killed the Common Market as an issue within the Party. An Amendment recalling Britain's pledges to agriculture, EFTA, and Commonwealth, and stating that Britain would not sign the Rome Treaty unless these were fulfilled, was defeated heavily. Instead, the Conference passed overwhelmingly a resolution expressing confidence in the Government's determination to find safeguards (but not insisting that these be met) and stressing the importance of a successful outcome to the negotiations.[61] In effect the Conservative Government had been handed an unconditional endorsement of its policy without the opponents ever having an opportune moment to achieve rejection of it within the Party as a whole.

HOW MACMILLAN CARRIED THE PARTY: PLEDGES

The Conservative Government made various assurances of safeguards. These included the three seemingly obvious concerns of EFTA, the Commonwealth, and agriculture, plus reassurances on sovereignty. Why did these areas possess

---

59 *The Times,* October 13, 1961.

60 National Union of Conservative and Unionist Associations, *80th Annual Conference* (October 11-14, 1961), pp. 46-47.

61 *Idem, 81st Annual Conference* (October 10-13, 1962), pp. 46-48.

enough significance to be incorporated into Britain's terms for membership, and what pledges did they elicit?

EFTA.—The EFTA constituted a fairly obvious encumbrance to HMG's efforts at EEC entry. Diplomatically, the Conservative Government could not afford to drop into the dirt the Association it had constructed; and personally, British leaders had generally closer ties with the Scandinavians than with the French, Italians, and Germans. The position of the EFTA neutrals, Sweden, Switzerland, and Austria, merited some concern, and there were also Labour Party sensitivities.

Pledges to EFTA took two forms. First, in late June 1961, the EFTA Ministerial Council met in London and formulated what became known as the "London Agreement." This provided that the Seven should coordinate their actions throughout the negotiations and especially that the Association "would be maintained at least until satisfactory arrangements have been worked out in negotiations to meet the various legitimate interests of all members of EFTA, and thus enable them to participate from the same date in an integrated European market."[62] This constituted an exceptionally strong pledge by Britain, but no one in the U.K. questioned the country's moral obligation to the Seven, even though the London Agreement virtually committed Britain not to join the EEC unless the Six agreed to become a market of thirteen.[63]

The other guarantees came in Parliament. On July 31, Macmillan's announcement contained the stipulation that negotiations would be with a view to joining the EEC, "if satisfactory arrangements can be made to meet the special needs of the U.K., of the Commonwealth and of the EFTA."[64] The Government's Motion incorporated this wording, and in the subsequent debate, Reginald Maudling stated, "We have

[62] Quoted in *Hansard,* Vol. 644 (June 28, 1961), c. 191.
[63] Camps, *op. cit.,* p. 356.
[64] *Hansard,* Vol. 645 (July 31, 1961), c. 929-930.

given the same undertaking to our Commonwealth partners and to the other EFTA countries, namely, that we will not join the Community unless special arrangements have been worked out in negotiations to protect their essential interests."[65] The Association which Britain had constructed under the prodding of the FBI now constituted a major formal diplomatic commitment.

The Commonwealth.—HMG's concern here was far greater than that for EFTA because the Commonwealth had powerful support within the British public and its maintenance was an article of faith for the Tories, especially the party militants. The key elements in the Tory conception of Commonwealth were the old (white) dominions. Britons held the notion that they could genuinely communicate with and influence the Australians, New Zealanders, and Canadians. This special tie to the ANZACS was reinforced by a latent sense of Anglo-Saxondom, explicitly embodied in the writings of an historian and Common Market opponent, Arthur Bryant. In his view, Britain would be cutting herself off from nearly all of the "British race" for the sake of a possibly illusory commercial advantage. Citing common blood, faith, and allegiance, Bryant wrote that the Common Market proposal would mean:

to discriminate against our own kind and children . . . to distinguish between those nation-members of the Commonwealth whose peoples derive from the same stock as ourselves and are every whit as much as we are the heirs of Alfred, Shakespeare, Hampden and Livingstone, and those other nation-members of different blood, faith and history who became associated with us through the temporary accident of conquest . . . . The peoples of Canada, Australia and New Zealand are by birth and inalienable descent as much British as the peoples of England, Scotland and Wales.[66]

Another factor reinforcing the powerful Commonwealth

---

[65] *Hansard,* Vol. 645 (August 2, 1961), c. 1601-1602, quoted in Camps, *op. cit.,* p. 358.

[66] Arthur Bryant, *A Choice for Destiny: Commonwealth and Common Market* (London: Collins, 1962), pp. 60-63.

sentiment within the Conservative Party was that many Tory activists were retired from previous Commonwealth service. They figured prominently in the intraparty opposition to the Common Market. The general strength of sentiment was such that even the mover of the Government's Resolution at the 1961 Party Conference was compelled to observe, "There is not a single person in this audience this morning who, if told that the choice in front of us was the Commonwealth or Europe, would not immediately go for the Commonwealth."[67]

In addition to sentiment, which rested on both the remnants of Empire feeling and the comradeship with the Old Dominions, the Commonwealth evoked diplomatic concerns. It had a certain value for Britain inasmuch as it gave her the opportunity to lead a vast international grouping. Britain without this configuration seemed unnaturally small and insignificant. She derived considerable diplomatic support from the independent Commonwealth countries, and the results of turning her back on them would be even more of a diplomatic loss than ditching the EFTA. Finally, for those to whom sentiment and diplomacy did not matter, there were economic implications. While most people had long since ceased to argue, with Cecil Rhodes, that the alternative to Empire was unemployment riots in Lancashire, the Commonwealth did have a considerable trading importance. This involved cheap agricultural and raw material imports, and export outlets for manufactured products.

The Commonwealth picture was not, however, wholly one-sided. Britain's closest emotional ties were not with the poor third-world countries but with the ANZACS whose standards of living were among the highest in the world. For another thing there was a considerable amount of selective perception involved in seeing the Six as "inward-looking." In comparison

---

[67] The speaker also observed that Britain fortunately need not make this choice. National Union of Conservative and Unionist Associations, *80th Annual Conference* (1961), p. 47.

to the British, the Germans were already investing more in India and the French directing a greater percentage of their resources to the underdeveloped world. Even in terms of external tariff levels, Britain was more protectionist than the so-called "inward-looking" Six. What is more, trade patterns were shifting rapidly. Whereas the Sterling area had taken 47 percent of Britain's total exports in 1953 and Western Europe only 27.4 percent, by 1959 the Sterling area had dropped to 40.3 percent as compared to 27.6 percent for Western Europe, and by 1963 had fallen to 35.6 percent, where it was now surpassed by the European figure of 37.3 percent.[68]

British elites also displayed a certain willingness to sacrifice Commonwealth interests to promote Britain's European ones. A 1961 study revealed that the margin here was 52 percent in favor and 38 percent opposed.[69] Even so, the results of the same study confirm the observation that British elites still believed the European link to be the least important of the three circles. They judged Britain's single most important relationship to be that with the Commonwealth (33 percent). The Anglo-American connection came next (19 percent), followed by the Atlantic Alliance (10 percent). The EEC was even less favored than the UN in the respondents' eyes (9 percent for the Six versus 10 percent for the world organization).[70]

While British allegiance to the Commonwealth was not unqualified, it is thus not surprising that the Government

---

[68] Source: EFTA, *EFTA Trade: 1959-64* (Geneva, 1966) p. 104, quoted in Kenneth Waltz, *Foreign Policy and Democratic Politics: The American and British Experience* (Boston: Little Brown, 1967), p. 245. Exports to Western Europe first surpassed those to the Commonwealth during 1962. For more detailed figures see Uwe Kitzinger, *The Second Try: Labour and the EEC* (Oxford: Pergamon Press, 1968), p. 335.

[69] Daniel Lerner and Morton Gorden, *A Decade of Challenge: The Responses of European Leaders* (Cambridge, Massachusetts: MIT, Center for International Studies, August, 1967), Chap. IV, p. 14 (Mimeographed).

[70] *Ibid.*, Chap. VI, p. 4.

found it necessary to offer major safeguards. It has already been noted above how Macmillan's July 31 speech and the ensuing Parliamentary debate committed HMG not to join the EEC unless special arrangements could be worked out for Commonwealth interests. Similarly, the 1961 Party Conference carried a resolution supporting entry "compatible with our Commonwealth . . . responsibilities."[71] The Conservative Government made other kinds of pledges too. One was the repeated assurance of consultation and another a flow of statements that should a choice be necessary, Britain would always favor the Commonwealth over Europe. Perhaps the most important of the Government's operational pledges came in Edward Heath's October 10, 1961, speech to the EEC Ministers at Paris. The key point was that the Commonwealth must receive "comparable outlets" for its products.[72] This constituted a retreat from an earlier Government position that Britain would never accept tariff discrimination against the Commonwealth, and it too underwent erosion as bargaining continued. In fact, all these statements were susceptible to flexible interpretation; the question was how the Government would seek to implement them in the negotiations.

One repeated tactic of HMG was to frame its proposals as window-dressing in order to placate the Commonwealth. When the U.K. offered these proposals at Brussels, it did not press them if it felt them too extreme. However, this meant that HMG faced increased discontent from the Six, who felt Britain was asking too much, and from the Commonwealth countries (with their numerous supporters in Britain), who felt the pledges were not being met. The Government thus succeeded in pleasing no one.

---

[71] NUCUA, *80th Annual Conference* (1961), p. 6.

[72] *The United Kingdom and the EEC:* Text of the statement made by the Lord Privy Seal at the meeting with Ministers of Member States of the EEC at Paris on October 10, 1961 (Cmnd. 1565, HMSO, November, 1961), p. 12.

Even the consultation process consisted more in the exchange of information, via regular meetings between British representatives and Commonwealth officials accredited to Brussels,[73] than in a two-way process of give and take. Indeed, Britain abandoned this consultation on two occasions (July and November 1962) in order to seek rapid progress at Brussels. By September, the Commonwealth Prime Ministers' Conference at London revealed pervasive anxiety about the negotiations, but on October 8, Heath told the Six that the Commonwealth recognized the decision was Britain's alone and that she was determined to press ahead.

In addition to taking advantage of flexible interpretation, Government spokesmen were careful to claim that there really was no choice necessary between Europe and the Commonwealth, and that EEC entry would help the Commonwealth in the long run by strengthening Britain. The Conservatives' Llandudno Conference of October 1962 reflected this easing off of pledges, in that the resolution approved by the delegates merely stressed confidence in the Government's determination to find adequate safeguards.

Why, if HMG was going to retreat from its assurances, did it initially offer them? One answer is that Macmillan expected extreme difficulty in getting the Conservatives to accept the Common Market. He therefore sought to negotiate for the Commonwealth in order to meet anticipated criticisms from within the Party. Five years later, Harold Wilson could virtually ignore the Commonwealth issue, but in 1961–62 disillusionment with the Commonwealth was not yet widespread.

Agriculture.—The subject of British agriculture and the Common Market has already been treated in depth in Chapter 5, but it is appropriate here to discuss further some of the political dimensions of this problem. Agriculture constituted one of the foremost complexities for Britain in its dealings

---

[73] Other channels existed, for example the meetings of a Commonwealth Liaison Committee in London, and also via the usual diplomatic procedures.

with the Six, and probably made up the Government's single greatest domestic problem. Not only did the NFU prominently articulate the interests of British agriculture, but so did a large number of back-bench Conservative MP's, as well as certain Cabinet Ministers. As we have already seen, this pressure, coupled with the inherent national importance of agriculture, constituted a definite limitation on HMG's freedom of movement.

While the agricultural problem was thus one of substantial political importance, the Conservative concern over the possible General Election loss of up to eighty seats was greatly exaggerated. A 1958 study by J. Roland Pennock concluded that much of the political power of agriculture rested on myth.[74] Basing his calculations on seats where a majority of less than 8 percent existed at the previous election and the presence of males in agricultural occupations totalled more than 8 percent of the electorate, Pennock observed that only twelve to sixteen Parliamentary constituencies could be classified as genuinely marginal agricultural seats.[75] However, the likely loss to the Conservatives was even less than that. After the 1959 General Election, Labour already held four of the sixteen seats. Of the other twelve, the Tories ultimately lost only three in 1964 (two to Labour and one to the Liberals) while capturing a Labour seat themselves. In 1966, the Tories lost two more seats (one Labour and one Liberal) for a net loss since 1959 of only four marginal agricultural seats.[76] Another study by V. H. Beynon and J. E. Harrison identified only fourteen agricultural marginal seats.[77] These estimates

---

[74] J. Roland Pennock, "The Political Power of British Agriculture," *Political Studies,* 7, no. 3 (October, 1959), pp. 291-296.

[75] *Ibid.,* p. 295.

[76] These calculations are my own, using Pennock's list of seats and election statistics from B. R. Mitchell and Klaus Boehm, *British Parliamentary Election Results, 1950-1964* (Cambridge, England: Cambridge University Press, 1966), and *Election '66, Gallup Analysis of the Voting Results* (London: Daily Telegraph Limited, 1966).

[77] V. H. Beynon and J. E. Harrison, *The Political Significance of the*

contrast with widely held guesses by political professionals of from thirty to fifty seats and occasionally, during the Common Market debate, of sixty to eighty agricultural seats being in jeopardy. While it is true that there were 110 seats where agriculture accounted for more than 15 percent of male employment and that ninety-five of these were Tory, most of the Tory seats were safe ones.[78]

The fact is that most agricultural seats are solidly Conservative because farmers tend to vote Tory with unrelenting consistency. The highly favorable agricultural policies pursued by the 1945 Labour Government brought it no more farm votes in 1950 and 1951 than in 1945. Indeed, R.H.S. Crossman once complained that Labour's efforts to woo the agricultural vote in the period from 1947 to 1958 had amounted to selling the Party's birthright for a mess of pottage, and that then the Party had not even gotten the pottage.[79]

The relative handful of agricultural seats actually at stake did, however, remain important. Given the incontestable fact that British politics are highly marginal (for example, since 1935 no winning party has received over 50 percent of the total popular vote in a General Election), a hypothetical Conservative loss to Labour of even the twelve seats which Pennock cites would have constituted a net swing of twenty-four in Parliamentary calculations. A margin of this size was greater than that achieved by Labour in 1950 (and eventually in 1964) and by the Tories in 1951. Even taking the figure of Tory agricultural seats actually lost in the 1964 General Election, the stakes were still possibly enough to determine the outcome (by making it impossible for Labour to organize a majority Government in Parliament). Thus while the number of seats at stake was certainly greatly exaggerated,

---

British Agricultural Vote (Newton Abbot, Devon: University of Exeter, Report No. 134, July, 1962).

[78] Peter Self and Herbert J. Storing, *The State and the Farmer* (London: Allen & Unwin, 1962), pp. 193-196.

[79] Cited *Ibid.*, p. 201.

the importance of the agricultural vote was considerable.

The agricultural problem facing Macmillan did not merely consist of a potential loss of Conservative votes. Agriculture existed as a political problem because of its place within the Conservative ethos. Pressures emanated from the back-bench Tory squirearchy and, more importantly, from within the Cabinet, where sentiment and political pressure converged and where any real political changes would be made.

How then did Macmillan meet the problem of quieting fears about agriculture? In the preliminary period, agriculture acted as a major restraint on an earlier decision to seek entry. Macmillan seems to have had little choice in incorporating agriculture as one of the three conditions in the July 31, 1961, announcement and in the October 1961 Conservative Conference resolution. Heath's October 10, 1961, Paris speech specified the commitment.

During 1962, HMG began to "fudge" its agricultural pledge, as it had done to the Commonwealth one. In part, this consisted of some straight-talking, for example by the Minister of Agriculture, Christopher Soames, who told the farmers they would be better off in the long run within the Common Market.[80] The limit, ultimately, to HMG's agricultural concessions to the Six was as much concrete financial concerns as political pressures. The requirement of levy payments on imports of Commonwealth agricultural products would have placed a massive burden on the British balance of payments and the issue reappeared in 1966–67 when the Wilson Government had little need to worry about political pressures from agriculture. Furthermore, HMG could not neglect the fact that Common Market entry would result in a domestic food price increase of about 10 percent with a corresponding 3½ percent increase in the cost of living.

---

[80] Certainly agriculture could have managed successfully. One prominent political journalist commented privately that if he had the money he would mortgage his grandmother in order to invest in wheatland in Norfolk.

The failure of Britain and the Six to reach agreement during the marathon bargaining session which ended on the morning of August 5, owed much to the question of safeguards for temperate zone Commonwealth agriculture, particularly the products of Australia, New Zealand, and Canada. French intransigence, though a factor, did not constitute an insuperable obstacle. The Conservatives' Llandudno Conference which followed in October gave evidence that HMG finally found it necessary to abandon any specific content for its agricultural pledges. Thus R. A. Butler vaguely assured the Party faithful that the Government would never break faith with the farmers and the Minister of Agriculture, Christopher Soames, announced that while HMG accepted the Six's Common Agricultural Policy, it would take care of agriculture within the broad national interest.

Although the Llandudno Conference had produced an overwhelming show of support for HMG's Common Market policy (to the extent that the delegates even wore buttons proclaiming the word "yes"), the Government encountered increasing restlessness within the Party during the remainder of the year, along with protracted difficulties at Brussels. During this period, agriculture replaced the Commonwealth as the center of attention in Parliament, and the Party displayed mounting fears of election losses due to the issue. While Edward Heath refused (despite back-bench pressure) to commit HMG to maintain the existing agricultural support system during any transition period, Tory back-bench agricultural specialists were busy visiting Brussels to counter the impression that the U.K. would accept any terms available.[81] Macmillan had succeeded in offsetting initial agricultural pressures by making pledges on agricultural safeguards, then replacing these with more generalized expressions of intent. But HMG now seemed to be too weak vis-à-vis British farmers, and the Six appeared increasingly ungenerous on the

---

[81] *The Guardian,* November 6, 1962.

agricultural transition question, which had become the main issue at Brussels.

Sovereignty.—Although the subject of British sovereignty did not receive recognition as one of the three conditions, it certainly possessed great importance, more so, for example, than the pledge to EFTA. To begin with, Macmillan sought to evade the political implications of Common Market membership by insisting that the EEC was an economic, not a defense, foreign policy, or cultural community.[82] But, while he was denying to Parliament that political union was involved, Heath was endorsing the Bonn Declaration which implied just the opposite.

Opponents of EEC entry stressed the dangers to Britain's political independence, citing threats to the role of the Queen, the British legal system, and the supremacy of Parliament. While the Conservative Central Office produced pamphlets dealing with some of the more emotionally exaggerated fears,[83] Cabinet members told the 1962 Annual Conference of the political advantages of Common Market membership, though (in the manner of Macmillan) minimizing the political implications. Thus R. A. Butler reassured the Conservatives that the Government would never agree to anything undermining British institutions, and called attention to the safeguard that unanimous agreement would be required for political union.[84] Indeed, Edward Heath went even further, stating, "We are not going into a federation."[85]

Heath and Macmillan were thus caught once again between the demands of the Six (in this case for a commitment to a

---

[82] *Hansard,* Vol. 645 (July 31, 1961), c. 1490-1491.

[83] A series of nine one-page leaflets dealt with such issues as the monarchy, Parliament, religious freedom, European domination, and the influx of European workers. "Common Market Common Sense" (September, 1962), in *European Unity—Conservative Publications, 1950-1963,* a bound volume of pamphlets (London: Conservative Research Department).

[84] *Daily Telegraph,* October 12, 1962.

[85] *The Times,* October 11, 1962.

supranational Europe) and the requirements of Tory politics (for reassurances that there would be no infringement of sovereignty).

HOW MACMILLAN CARRIED THE PARTY: THE CABINET

Of all the political obstacles facing Macmillan, the Cabinet was unquestionably the most critical. Given the resources of a Conservative Prime Minister, the Parliamentary and constituency parties, as well as the annual conference, could be managed. But in the Cabinet, the Prime Minister could not so easily disarm the European opposition by skillful wording of resolutions and by the careful arrangement of conflict situations so as to minimize the chances for favorable opportunities of dissident expression. Worries over all major substantive issues also focused in the Cabinet, and the relative privacy of Cabinet meetings was well suited to the Conservatives' customary practice of fighting out their disputes away from the public eye.

Prior to 1960, the Cabinet, along with the Civil Service, was broadly opposed to EEC membership. The report of Sir Frank Lee's interdepartmental committee helped to shift attitudes within Whitehall, and it seems to have influenced Macmillan and some of his Ministers. The Prime Minister sought to carry the Cabinet with a low key, basically economic, approach and by qualifying the Common Market bid with safeguards. In this he was aided by the general movement of opinion within British elite circles. He also undertook a decisive Cabinet shuffle on July 27, 1960, which elevated a number of key pro-Europeans: Peter Thorneycroft, as Minister of Aviation; Christopher Soames, as Minister of Agriculture; Duncan Sandys, as Commonwealth Secretary; and Edward Heath, as Lord Privy Seal.[86] Heath's appointment was especially important because he was given responsibility for Eu-

---

[86] For additional details see the *Financial Times,* July 28, 1960; and Camps, *op. cit.,* Chapter Eleven.

rope and was made foreign affairs spokesman in the House of Commons. Macmillan also neutralized the remaining Cabinet opposition by placing the most important of the doubters, R. A. Butler, in charge of the Ministerial committee directing preliminary negotiations.

Following the July 1961 announcement, the major Cabinet figures remaining skeptical toward Common Market entry were Butler, then the Home Secretary; Lord Hailsham, the Lord President of the Council; and Reginald Maudling, President of the Board of Trade. These three were certain to oppose any effort at entry on unfavorable terms and had strong reservations about agriculture, the Commonwealth, and British sovereignty.

While the EEC negotiations were in their exploratory phase and the Prime Minister's public standing remained high, the Cabinet problem lay dormant. However, by the spring of 1962, Cabinet unrest became more apparent. Although the anti-EEC Tories lacked a publicly committed figure of Cabinet rank, or even of major importance, Cabinet members did express serious reservations about the terms emerging at Brussels.

In response to a variety of problems and the worsening situation in polls and by-elections, Macmillan "slaughtered" one-third of his Cabinet on July 13. Though certain of the departing Ministers (e.g., Selwyn Lloyd) were pro-Europeans, the rearrangement generally strengthened the pro-EEC group within the Cabinet. The respite was only temporary, however, and considerable concern arose within the Cabinet over agricultural terms. According to Neustadt, it required from October until December to convince two senior ministers of the necessity for agricultural concessions which everyone knew to be necessary.[87] While this version of the events is somewhat problematic (for one thing, the fact that it took so

---

[87] One of the two ministers cited is almost certainly R. A. Butler. See Neustadt, *op. cit.*

long to convince the recalcitrant Ministers hardly indicates the concessions were obvious), and there is an equally compelling explanation which argues that the British team at Brussels had to "stall" because of an intra-Cabinet power struggle involving the prerogatives of would-be successors to Macmillan, the fact remains that it was a Cabinet dispute which impeded Macmillan and Heath's freedom of maneuver and delayed the negotiations.

The Cabinet rebellion began to take on a more public appearance when Iain Macleod, who was also Party Chairman, stated on November 3 that Britain must not pay too high a price for membership, and that she must keep her agricultural system until the end of the transition period.[88] Then, Frederick Erroll, President of the Board of Trade, asserted, on December 10, that it would be no disaster if Britain remained out of the Common Market. Reginald Maudling also backed up the statement. This may have been meant as an effort to strengthen the U.K.'s bargaining position at Brussels by showing the Europeans that there was a limit to British concessions, but it reflected hostility to EEC entry as well. On the same day, Lord Beaverbrook's heatedly anti-EEC *Daily Express* reported, under the headline "Britain May Call Off Six Talks," that Cabinet opposition had increased substantially, and that those opposing the continuation of negotiations unless better terms could be obtained now included Butler, Macleod, Maudling, Hailsham, and Frederick Erroll. Though possibly exaggerated, this division of opinion within the Cabinet illustrated the difficulties of Macmillan's domestic political situation.

THE CONSERVATIVE OPPOSITION

Intraparty opposition to the Common Market policy existed throughout the 1961-1963 period. As noted, this opposition suffered the disadvantages inherent in any minority effort

---

[88] *The Times,* December 11, 1962.

against the policies of a Tory Prime Minister. It was further handicapped when the Common Market became a partisan political issue. Additionally, the anti-EEC forces were hurt by the need for mostly private expression of their differences and by the lack of prominent leadership. While certain Cabinet Ministers were hesitant toward the Common Market policy, none of them desired to lead an organized anti-EEC movement. The rule of collective responsibility made such opposition exceedingly unlikely, and no Minister chose to follow the examples of Eden in 1938 and Bevan in 1951 and resign in order to express publicly his hostility to Government policy. Accordingly, the leaders of the anti-Common Market bloc within the Party were two ex-Ministers of only moderate stature, Sir Derek Walker Smith and Robert Turton. Yet despite various limitations, the opposition represented something of a threat to Party unity, and hence had the effect of forcing HMG to reassure its back-benchers that sovereignty, Commonwealth Preference, and the existing agricultural support system were sacred objects.

Throughout the EEC debate, the anti-Common Market Tories voiced substantial concern over agriculture, but they tended to concentrate on revealing what they considered to be the concealed political price of membership, especially the cost to national sovereignty and the Commonwealth. Sir Derek Walker Smith's comments at the Llandudno Conference typify this attitude: "Little by little the political cat has eased his way out of the economic bag. He is not just a soft, fluffy, friendly little kitten; he is a full grown political cat with his full complement of claws."[89] While much of the anti-EEC sentiment came from the right wing of the Party, not all the right was hostile. A substantial portion of this feeling was based on age differentials, younger members of the Party being much more pro-European than older ones.

The most prominent method of public expression for the

---

[89] *81st Annual Conference* (1962).

anti-Europeans was the offering of motions or amendments in Parliament and in Conservative Party Conferences. Thus on July 28, 1961, 47 Tory MP's put forward a motion which opposed any surrender of British sovereignty. The anti-EEC group offered a similar amendment on the occasion of the 1961 Party Conference, and their position also included reference to agriculture and the Commonwealth. On March 22, 1962, 25 Tory MP's signed an amendment warning of harm to the Commonwealth, and Derek Walker Smith claimed 68 additional sympathizers. On July 31, 40 MP's presented a motion reminding the Prime Minister of his pledges and urging that he stand firm. At the October 1962 Conference, the anti-European forces produced an amendment citing past pledges and opposing any loss of sovereignty. Finally, on December 31, 47 MP's presented an anti-EEC resolution calling on HMG to stand firm though this might cause the breaking off of negotiations. What links every one of these efforts is their rejection by the Party and their inability to draw substantially increased support as time went by.

The ultimate voting strength of the Tory opposition within the House of Commons was no more than 47, though it was often less, as typified by the 25 who abstained on the August 3, 1961, Parliamentary vote approving Macmillan's EEC approach. Though perhaps 100 Tory MP's in all were reserved in one way or another, most were unwilling or unable to express this rebellion in Conference or Parliamentary votes.

Before passing on to discuss the relationship of the broader public to the Common Market issue, a few observations are in order. The conclusion to be drawn from the situation of the parties during the 1961-63 period is that they presented a potentially unpromising sphere of operation for Macmillan's Common Market venture. This situation heightened the desirability, for the Prime Minister, of seeking to sidestep the grand political implications of his policy. Instead he emphasized the important economic and trade dimensions in order to lessen somewhat the need for confronting the Common Market issue exclusively in the realm of the parties and party government. Because of the need for the sectional pressure groups' expertise and cooperation, this required that Macmillan bargain with the groups through the channels of functional representation. Indeed, the climate within the Conservative Party, and the opposition of Labour, also facilitated the preservation of group access via the dominant channel of party government. Politicization, though it existed, was incomplete.

Chapter 8

The Common Market II:
The Broader Public

Until 1961 the European issue remained very much out of the public eye. As we have seen, the subject possessed a limited constituency which consisted mainly of Governmental officials and sectional pressure groups. The British public enjoyed little knowledge of European developments; as late as September 1961, more than two-thirds (69 percent) did not know, or gave incorrect answers, when asked whether or not Britain belonged to the EFTA and/or to the EEC.[1] The mass media devoted relatively little attention to Europe, and only after Macmillan's July 1961 announcement did the panoply of public opinion channels come into noticeable operation.

This chapter will examine such major public phenomena as the promotional pressure groups, press, polls, and by-elections, then seek to pull together the diverse strands of party and public involvement (which began with Chapter 7) in order to draw conclusions about the operation of party government and functional representation during the 1961-63 period.

---

[1] Source: Social Surveys (Gallup Poll) Ltd., summarized in "British Attitudes to the EEC, 1961-63," *Journal of Common Market Studies*, 5, no. 1 (September, 1966), p. 53.

PROMOTIONAL PRESSURE GROUPS

The most prominent characteristic of the Common Market debate in Britain was the presence of promotional pressure groups which advocated or opposed EEC membership. Some of their activity did take place prior to Macmillan's announcement, especially on the pro-entry side, but broadly speaking the initial decisions of whether to negotiate and on what terms were made before these groups entered the political debate in any meaningful fashion. A few of the organizations had existed prior to 1961, but most sprang up in response to the suddenly increased salience of the European issue. Since the sequence of events leaves them outside the causal framework, the question to be raised is what subsequent impact did they have upon the Government, and upon public and elite opinion, during the negotiation period.

THE ANTI-ENTRY GROUPS

Among the more conspicuous of the bodies on the anti-entry side were the following:

The Anti-Common Market League (ACML), formed August 1961 and led by a former Conservative candidate for Parliament, John Paul. Operating at first as a focus for Conservative opposition, but later becoming a non-party organization, it mounted the most energetic of the mass campaigns.

The Forward Britain Movement (FBM), formed in mid-1961 and headed by Richard Briginshaw (General Secretary of the National Society of Operative Printers and Assistants). It was an active Labour-oriented organization holding scores of meetings and issuing pamphlets.

Britain and the Common Market, a small but important body working within the Parliamentary Labour Party and commanding the support of about one-third of the Labour MP's. The organization was led by John Stonehouse and William Blyton, and included such prominent Labourites as Emanuel Shinwell, Barbara Castle, Douglas Jay and Richard Marsh.

Keep Britain Out Campaign, a less important organization,

headed by Oliver Smedley, a former Liberal Party vice-chairman
and a free-trade advocate.

The True Tories, an obscure group headed by Major-General
Richard Hilton, an old Empire Loyalist prone to refer to Government actions as treasonable.

Anti-Common Market Union, led by Norman Smyth (a former
Henry Wallace activist in the U.S.), it operated as a coordinating
body for some of the anti-Common Market groups.

Unlike sectional pressure groups, such as the NFU, which
were concerned at least to modify the terms of membership if
they could not successfully prevent it, the major promotional
groups critical of Europe spent their efforts almost exclusively
on resisting Common Market entry. Another characteristic of
these organizations was the extent to which they found it
necessary to act outside the corridors of power. As we shall see
below, the pro-Common Market groups obtained elite access
despite their lack of a sectional base because they operated in
agreement with or as reinforcement of governmental policy.
While a group such as the Anti-Common Market League
sought to influence parliamentary and public opinion in every
way possible, its position of antagonism to governmental
policy placed it toward a party extreme and forced it to aim
at recruiting a mass clientele.

The ACML began by catering primarily to Conservatives,
but quickly ran into the problem of a lack of prominent leadership. Tory MP's feared to lend their names to an external
campaign which opposed a central item of Party policy.[2] Leaders of the anti-Common Market forces within the Conservative
Parliamentary Party, such as R. H. Turton and Sir Derek
Walker Smith, occasionally addressed mass meetings organized
by the ACML but resisted a formal tie with the organization.
Excepting the Britain and the Common Market Group
(which functioned as a lobby within the PLP), the anti-
Common Market promotional groups were initially regarded

---

[2] Lord Windlesham (G. R. J. Hennessy), *Communication and Political Power* (London: Jonathan Cape, 1966), pp. 171-174.

with some skepticism and their leaders, John Paul, R. W. Briginshaw and Oliver Smedley, were viewed as colorful and irrelevant characters. The anti-entry movement did gain a certain increased respectability during 1962 as more influential political figures, such as Anthony Eden, Clement Attlee, and ultimately Hugh Gaitskell voiced their own criticisms of Common Market entry.

The groups not only suffered from a lack of respectability due to the absence of well-known leaders and their position on the political extremes, but also because of the nature and flavor of their arguments. The major objections to Europe did not rest on carefully compiled statistical evidence of economic harm but on broader and more emotional concerns involving the Commonwealth, national sovereignty, prejudices against German, Italian, and French interests, and a definite insularity. For example, Viscount Hinchingbrooke,[3] who was then a Conservative MP and soon to become President of the ACML, told an American television audience, "those of us in Britain who oppose the Common Market don't want to subject ourselves to lot of frogs and huns."[4] On another occasion, at a conference of scholars and politicians organized by the Forward Britain Movement at Westminster in July 1962, Hinchingbrooke uttered the reassurance, "the world is still our oyster,"[5] and Konnie Zilliacus, a stalwart of the Labour left, told those assembled, "We would in the Common Market be tied to the chariot wheels of de Gaulle and Adenauer, and in the very delightful phrase used by the Earl of Sandwich . . . we shall be one of the horses attached to the chariot of NATO, driven by the President of the U.S.!"[6]

Nonetheless the anti-Common Market groups did provide

---

[3] He later became the Earl of Sandwich and ultimately (having renounced his peerage) Victor Montagu.

[4] *Daily Express* (London), April 26, 1962.

[5] Forward Britain Movement, *Britain Should Stay Out*. Report of the Britain, Commonwealth, EFTA Conference held at the House of Commons, Westminster, on July 16-19, 1962, p. 84.

[6] *Ibid.*, p. 144.

a certain amount of reasoned criticism. One basic assumption of opponents (for example that of the July 1962 FBM Conference) was that the Six were unprepared to accept the conditions regarded as essential by both Labour and the Conservatives, and that Britain was therefore faced with a choice between the Common Market and the Commonwealth. As an alternative to the EEC, the FBM proposed "active and substained cooperation between the Commonwealth and EFTA countries, enlisting the support of other nations through the UN. . . ."[7] One of the most prominent cases against EEC entry was made by William Pickles in a pamphlet for the Fabian Society entitled, *Not with Europe: the political case for staying out.*[8] Pickles, a Senior Lecturer at the LSE and a Labourite, opposed entry on the politics of the issue, seeing the EEC as an unholy alliance of federalists and exponents of laissez-faire who tacitly agreed that laissez-faire be the method and federalism the goal. He contended that the Rome Treaty made national planning impossible and that since the European Commission could only be controlled by creating a European Parliament, there was a necessity for choice between federalism and an uncontrolled bureaucracy. According to Pickles, the EEC also presented a threat to Parliamentary sovereignty, a commercial policy incompatible with the flexible spirit of the Commonwealth, and a hardening of the gap between rich and poor nations. In turn, the Oxford Historian Max Beloff castigated Pickles' Commonwealth romanticism (Pickles had pictured the Commonwealth reforming itself without the U.K. around a Montreal–Delhi axis) and caustically observed that he had "provided exactly the element of apparently scholarly argument that the leaders of the Labour Party feel they need in order to follow the dictates

---

[7] *Ibid.,* p. 156.

[8] (London: Fabian International Bureau, Fabian Tract No. 336, April, 1962). It should also be noted that the Fabian Society was divided on the European question and did not act as a pressure group on either side of the issue but instead as a forum for debate.

of their own instinctive response—at once isolationist and reactionary."[9]

Broadly speaking, critics on the left distrusted the Common Market as an autarchic cold-war alliance and Tory pro-business trick.[10] They leaned toward the kind of Commonwealth–EFTA–UN ties favored by the July 1962 Conference of the FBM. The Conservative opponents of Europe also favored a Commonwealth alternative, but disliked the Common Market for reasons having to do more with sovereignty and nationalism. Both sides tended to share anti-European (especially anti-German) sentiments.

How then did these groups operate? They oriented their efforts toward the public at large and thus indirectly sought to pressure important governmental and political leaders. For example, the ACML undertook a vast effort to educate the public on the disadvantages of EEC entry. It held a large number of public meetings throughout the country, many of them with MP's as speakers;[11] sold 30,000 copies of its booklet, *Britain, not Europe,* took out newspaper advertisements; distributed nearly two million leaflets (just a few thousand shy of the total put out by the Conservative Central Office); and claimed to have a membership of well over 30,000 people.[12] Near the peak of its efforts, the ACML joined four other organizations in an Albert Hall rally on July 26, 1962. The meeting drew between two and three thousand people to hear a wide range of anti-Common Market speakers, including the

---

[9] Max Beloff, "Labour and Europe: Unreal Romanticism," *Time and Tide* (May 3, 1962).

Uwe Kitzinger figured more prominently in a kind of traveling debate with Pickles over the Common Market issue. They appeared together in print, on the BBC and in public meetings.

[10] See, for example, Perry Anderson and Stuart Hall, "Politics of the Common Market," *New Left Review,* no. 10 (July-August, 1961), pp. 1-14.

[11] In 1962, ACML speakers addressed 237 such meetings. Windlesham, *op. cit.,* pp. 174-177.

[12] Anti-Common Market League, "Press Information," (London, March 31, 1964).

omnipresent Lord Sandwich (whose speech displayed a distinct xenophobia).[13]

While the ACML devoted most of its effort to the broader
public it did not entirely abandon the attempt at directly
influencing the Conservative Party. John Paul spoke to the
1961 Annual Conference as Chairman of the South Kensing-
ton Conservative Association, and to the 1962 Conference
(which hissed his speech) as a representative of the Primrose
League. More threatening to the Party, anti-EEC forces ran
candidates in several by-elections. The first of these was at
Lincoln, a Labour-held seat, in March 1962 and drew just 1.1
percent of the vote.[14] Other anti-Common Market candidates
drew only slightly better at Derbyshire West in June (4.2 percent) and Norfolk Central in November (2.6 percent). However, one November 1962 contest did attract national attention when the Tories lost a seat to Labour at Dorset South by
a mere 704 votes (1.4 percent of the total poll). Here, the intervention of an anti-Common Market candidate, Sir Piers Debenham, drew a decisive 12.3 percent of the voters, almost
exclusively former Tory supporters. The dramatic returns at
Dorset seemed to lend force to the threats by anti-Common
Market Conservatives (such as Lord Beaverbrook), that they
would oppose the Tories in a General Election on the Common Market issue. However the results made only a limited
impact among Tory professionals. Because of purely local
factors, the Dorset by-election overstated the anti-EEC threat
to the Conservatives. The *Gallup Political Index* contended
that the Tories lost not because of the Common Market but
because of voter confusion. This was accounted for by the fact

---

[13] Lord Sandwich castigated the pro-Common Market merchants of
the City whose origins were "in Hamburg and Frankfurt." *The Times*
(London), July 27, 1962.

[14] These and the following figures are drawn from D. E. Butler and
Anthony King, *The British General Election of 1964* (London: Macmillan, 1965), pp. 333-334 and B. R. Mitchell and Klaus Boehm, *British
Parliamentary Election Results, 1950-64* (Cambridge: Cambridge University Press, 1966), p. 38.

that Sir Piers Debenham, the ACML choice, was the more
familiar of the two Tories on the ballot. Long a leading figure
in the constituency, former Chairman of the local party, he
was backed by the previous Tory MP, Lord Sandwich, who
(as Viscount Hinchingbrooke) had held the seat for several
terms. The official Conservative candidate, Angus Maude, was
a newcomer to South Dorset and suffered the additional dis-
ability that his name followed that of Sir Piers Debenham in
the alphabetical listing of candidates on the ballot. The anti-
EEC candidate received nearly 3 percent more votes in the
actual election than had been predicted in the polling forecast,
and Gallup attributes this margin to the above factors rather
than to sampling error, last-minute changes of mind, or a
difference between anticipated and actual turn-out.

SOUTH DORSET: ACTUAL RESULTS VERSUS FORECASTS[15]
(in Percent)

	By-election Nov. 1962	General Election 1959	Gain + Loss −	Net Swing Cons. to Labour	Gallup Forecast	N.O.P. Forecast
Cons.	31.8	49.8	− 18.0	8.4	37	37.5
Lab.	33.5	34.7	− 1.2		28.5	29.4
Lib.	21.7	15.5	+ 6.2		24.5	21.8
ACM	12.3				9.5	11.3
Other	.7				.5	

With reference to the political impact of the anti-entry
campaign, the ACML fondly cited polling results which
showed public support for Common Market entry having
fallen from 43 percent in July 1961 to 29 percent in December 1962, and opposition having increased from 20 percent to
37 percent in the same period.[16] While it would be implau-
sible to argue that the ACML and other groups wrought this
change by themselves, they, along with the *Daily Express*, at

---

[15] Source: Social Surveys Ltd., *Gallup Political Index*, No. 35 (November, 1962), pp. 186-192. Since the British ballot paper lists candidates
without their party label, a slight confusion over the identity of the official Conservative nominees at South Dorset is understandable.

[16] Anti-Common Market League, *op. cit.*, p. 1.

least provided a rallying point for diffuse public discontent, especially in the period prior to the Labour Party's assumption of hostility in October 1962, and thus had the indirect effect of reinforcing pressures upon HMG to secure the most favorable terms possible.

THE PRO-ENTRY GROUPS

On the pro-entry side there were the following major organizations:

The Common Market Campaign (CMC), an all-party group formed in May 1961, including among its leaders Lord Gladwyn (Liberal), Roy Jenkins (Labour), and Peter Kirk (Conservative). It was the most important of the pro-Common Market groups, and operated on an elite basis to influence informed opinion.

The Labour Common Market Committee, established in September 1961 as an outgrowth of the Common Market Campaign aimed specifically at the Labour Party, trades unions and the Cooperative movement. Headed by Roy Jenkins, it directed its efforts at MP's and union leaders rather than the rank and file.

U.K. Council of the European Movement, a prestigious all-party grouping established a decade earlier and closely identified with Governmental and business circles. It had difficulty in operating a single-issue campaign because of the broadness of its purpose (a vague commitment to some form of European association) and the presence of several leaders actually reserved or hostile toward EEC entry (e.g., Denis Healey, John Biggs-Davison).

Federal Trust for Education and Research, established in 1938 to promote world government. It functioned in an active information-oriented capacity though with some of the limitations of the U.K. Council of the European Movement.

These organizations operated to sustain and encourage an existing governmental policy. As such, they occupied the political center and reaped the advantages of respectability[17] and access to the closely woven opinion elites of Great Britain.

The earliest positive gesture toward Common Market entry

---

[17] One might add fashionability, which is a feature Lord Windlesham finds worthy of special attention.

was made by the Federal Trust in April 1959,[18] but for the most part there was little organized promotional group pressure for entry before 1961. The well-known and respected U.K. Council of the European Movement maintained an almost excessive intimacy with HMG, such that it did not exert pressures for any European association beyond the extent to which HMG was willing to go in the pre-July 1961 period. The early pro-Common Market pressures upon the Prime Minister came from individual business and political leaders and not from organized attitudinal groups.

Even the most important of the organizations, the Common Market Campaign, which unleashed its elite-targeted promotional movement two months before Macmillan's announcement,[19] operated only to reinforce a decision the Prime Minister had already made. The group's organizers had planned to concentrate on the prominent opinion leadership of the country in Parliament, government, business, labour, and the public media, gradually building support for Common Market entry and thereby pressuring HMG. To this end, they had released a statement on Europe signed by 140 prominent individuals at their May launching and press conference. Macmillan's announcement, coming with unexpected rapidity, caused them to reexamine the thrust of their efforts, which had already evoked a surprisingly enthusiastic response among members of Parliament. The CMC then sought to demonstrate to the Europeans that Britain was genuinely interested in the Common Market and to stimulate public opinion, which was less favorable than elite sentiment, by showing Europe to be a long-range balance of advantages over disadvantages. However, after an abortive effort or two aimed at establishing a mass audience, the organization chose to remain content with supplying speakers, making statements, issuing publications, meeting with MP's, and contacting Common-

---

[18] *Financial Times* (London), April 10, 1959.
[19] This campaign began with a press conference on May 25, 1961. Windlesham, *op. cit.*, pp. 163-167.

wealth Prime Ministers in order to get their sympathetic understanding for Britain's EEC entry. Although the organization maintained broad all-party backing, it did find it advisable to organize the partisan Labour Common Market Committee in September 1961 in order to concentrate on persuasion within the Labour movement. The new organization employed the same office space and much of the staff of the parent body (R. J. Jarrett was secretary of both groups). These efforts within the Labour Party were largely unavailing, partly because of a concentration upon the elite rather than rank and file, and partly because the pro-Common Market forces came almost entirely from the right of the Party.

For the most part the pro-EEC groups usually functioned under self-appointed officers and were not broad membership organizations. As one of their opponents observed following an anti-Europe rally at Trafalgar Square, no one ever marched pro-entry.[20] However the groups did have the advantage of appealing on a non-partisan middle ground, and also, in certain cases, of obtaining encouragement from HMG and *sub rosa* assistance from the Conservative Party. While less vocal than the opposition groups, they provided a prestigious focus and reinforcement for pro-European sentiment.

SIGNIFICANCE OF THE PROMOTIONAL GROUPS

One major characteristic of these promotional pressure groups, despite their prominence during the July 1961–January 1963 period, was their relative weakness politically. They lacked the inherent strength of the sectional groups because they did not possess the resource of representing identifiable social or economic interests and hence were without the corresponding ability to withhold important services or invoke serious political threats. It is only necessary to recall the intimate relationships of the FBI, NFU, and TUC with

---

[20] Ron Leighton, *What Next For Britain?* (London: Forward Britain Movement, 1963), p. 1.

the various ministries to realize how different was the approach whch the promotional groups needed to take.

Promotional groups acted as rallying points for the committed and sought to pressure HMG by pointing to the demands of public opinion as they interpreted them to be.[21] Yet, substantial differences existed between the approaches used by those on opposite sides. The necessity for an unwieldy mass approach[22] was forced upon the anti-Common Market organizations (with the exception of the Britain and the Common Market group), while the pro-EEC bodies mounted elite-oriented campaigns. Although many party leaders later observed that the promotional groups merely cancelled out each other, the anti-Common Market organizations definitely had the effect of galvanizing certain vague (and often parochial) public sentiments and focusing these doubts in opposition to membership. Together with the *Daily Express,* they prevented these doubts from being dissipated by elite reassurances. In turn, the pro-entry groups, in conjunction with the pro-Common Market press campaign, may have helped to assure HMG of a solid and powerful response in favor of the European policy.

THE PRESS

The role of the press in the Common Market issue requires assessment for two different periods and purposes. First, in the time prior to Macmillan's announcement, what effect did the press have upon the Prime Minister's actual decision? Second, in the following eighteen months, what impact did it have on public opinion?

---

[21] Windlesham, *op. cit.,* pp. 163-164.

[22] James B. Christoph treats the problems of the mass campaign at considerable length in his study. He also employs the term "attitude groups" rather than "promotional groups." *Capital Punishment and British Politics* (London: Allen & Unwin, 1962).

The basic role of the press before July 1961 consisted in contributing to the feasibility of Common Market entry as a viable policy alternative. That is, the major newspapers and periodicals helped to create a setting in which Europe became politically practical. They did this by their circulation first among opinion elites and later the mass public. Macmillan's decision is sufficiently explainable by political and economic factors (cited in Chapters 5 and 7) so that there is no reason to believe the arguments presented by the press acted to sway him directly. Since papers such as the *Daily Mirror* and *Daily Herald* were potentially pro-Common Market but did not find it practical to launch their own campaigns until HMG seemed ready to move, it appears that the predominance in any casual relationship was the Prime Minister's. Insofar as the European decision was concerned, he influenced the press more than they did him. The press then reinforced Macmillan in his policy via a feedback process, since its strong support helped convince him that the public would accept the shift.

During the spring of 1960, the conversion to the European cause of the *Observer* (April), *The Guardian* (May), and *The Economist* (June) guaranteed Macmillan a sympathetic hearing from Britain's liberal humanitarian subestablishment. The bulk of the Tory press weighed in somewhat later (and mostly after the Prime Minister's December 1960 personal decision), with the *Financial Times* leading the way in the latter part of 1960, and the *Sunday Times, Daily Mail, Daily Telegraph,* and *The Times* swinging over (albeit with reservations in the case of *The Times*) during the first half of 1961. The major absentee from this broad journalistic endorsement was the Conservatively oriented Beaverbrook press, notably the *Daily Express* with its 4.3 million circulation.[23] This defection was balanced however by the fact that the pro-Labour (Cecil

---

[23] Circulation figures cited by Raymond Williams in *Britain in the Sixties: Communications* (Baltimore: Penguin, 1962), p. 28.

King) mass press asserted itself enthusiastically pro-European. This support from the *Daily Herald* (circulation 1.4 million) and *Daily Mirror* (circulation 4.6 million) assured the Prime Minister a substantial bipartisan backing. One (non-authoritative) source even described the *Daily Mirror's* strident pro-Common Market campaign of June 1961 as the "tip-over factor" which caused the Government to stop vacillating and actually commence negotiation because it now had sufficient public support.[24] Although of questionable accuracy, the comment is useful in focusing attention upon the importance of press support in its public implications.

THE PRESS AND PUBLIC OPINION

While the pro-EEC press initially was hesitant in taking its stand and then somewhat oversimplified the European problem,[25] it at least had the public function of launching the European issue into the forefront of public attention. Typical of its efforts was a campaign launched on June 21, 1961, by the TUC organ (then controlled by the *Mirror* group), the *Daily Herald*. The series of articles, entitled "Why We Should Join the Common Market," began with the observation that the U.K. was held back by an absence of informed public opinion, that Common Market entry was not an ordinary party issue, and that opposition within the U.K. was mainly the product of ignorance and a reluctance to face reality. This material ultimately found its way into pamphlet form for additional broad circulation. *The Times, Daily Telegraph,* and

---

[24] Woodrow Wyatt, a newspaper publisher and prominent right-wing Labour MP explained that he had been told this by two members of the Government. "Challenge to the Editor," ITV, London, February 20, 1962, cited in Windlesham, *op. cit.,* p. 157. Windlesham also treats the contention as somewhat exaggerated.

[25] On the former point see, for example, the comments of Uwe Kitzinger, "Britain and Europe: The Multivalence of the British Decision," reprinted from *The European Yearbook,* Vol. 9 (1962), Martinus Nijhoff, The Hague: and on the latter, Miriam Camps, *Britain and the European Community, 1955-63* (Princeton: Princeton University Press, 1964), p. 290.

Daily Express also produced Common Market pamphlets.

As mentioned, Beaverbrook's *Daily Express* (together with its companion *Evening Standard)* was the only major national daily to oppose Common Market entry. In this course, it was joined by a smattering of other weeklies and regional papers. These journalistic allies included the *Daily Worker, Sunday Citizen, City Press, New Statesman, Tribune, Time and Tide, Inverness Courier, Ayrshire Post,* and *Shetland News.*[26] What it lacked in media companionship, the *Daily Express* made up in intensity and persistence; no newspaper on the pro-EEC side engaged in the whole-hearted effort of Lord Beaverbrook's paper. In tacit alliance with groups such as the ACML, the *Daily Express* launched an effective and frequently emotional campaign against membership. A daily item on the front page, under the caption, "Common Market Facts," "If We Go In," or "Europe and You," played upon latent English suspicions of Europeans as Catholic, undemocratic, and unclean. No less a personage than the historian A. J. P. Taylor contributed to this by identifying the Common Market with Hitler and Napoleon.[27] At one point, Lord Beaverbrook handed down the edict that World Wars I and II would henceforth be referred to in the pages of his newspaper as the "First German War" and "Second German War."[28] The paper also gave voice to exaggerations involving such potentially emotional matters as pensions, Italian immigrant labor, unemployment, anti-Communism, anti-Americanism, and the Monarchy. The tone of the *Daily Express* was, however, restrained in comparison to that of one provincial spokesman, Michael Mason, whose virulent anti-European speech was printed in the *Witney Gazette.* This old Etonian and former High Sheriff of Oxfordshire characterized France as "the whorehouse of the world," Italians as "scum of the earth," and saw

[26] See, for example, *Daily Express,* January 30, 1963.
[27] *Daily Express,* July 24, 1961.
[28] Cited in the *Observer* (London), March 25, 1962. The directive was withdrawn a week later, *Financial Times,* April 3, 1962.

England governed in the future by "some damned ex-Nazi Prussian Gauleiter." He finished by expressing his wish that "the Atlantic Ocean was 10,000 miles wide and England in the middle of it."[29]

As the focal point for an *ad hoc* anti-Common Market coalition, the *Daily Express* self-consciously drew together groups and individuals from across the political spectrum. It frequently flaunted lists of those siding with it, which on one typical occasion included a reference to 60 Tory MP's, 75 Labourites, and the names of a dozen trade union leaders together with those of Kwame Nkrumah, A. J. P. Taylor, and Clement Attlee.[30] On a number of occasions, Beaverbrook sponsored large advertisements in the other major newspapers carrying the cautionary warnings of Field Marshall Viscount Montgomery ("[the Commonwealth] the greatest stabilizing factor in international affairs since the Roman Empire would be wantonly cast away")[31] and Clement Attlee ("I say 'Halt!' Britain must not become a part of Europe.")[32] Whatever the effect of the *Daily Express's* efforts, its own public opinion poll ("Are you for or against Britain joining the Common Market?") indicated by late June that for the first time a plurality of the public opposed joining, by a margin of 33.5 percent to 28.5 percent, after having steadily favored the Common Market by as much as 40 percent to 24 percent in late February.[33] The paper gloated over this triumph, claiming it as a victory for the *Daily Express* over the rest of the press plus radio and television.

The *Daily Express* did not merely concentrate upon public opinion, but also kept as much pressure as possible upon the Prime Minister via the Conservative Party. In December, it

---

[29] "Mr. Michael Mason Attacks Common Market Entry Plan," *Witney Gazette*, December 28, 1962.

[30] *Daily Express*, May 4, 1962.

[31] *The Times*, June 4, 1962.

[32] *The Guardian* (London), August 15, 1962.

[33] *Daily Express*, March 3 and July 4, 1962.

exhorted British farmers to speak up, noting past successes in detouring undesirable policies: "They have seen how a change of policy over the bombs for Katanga was forced on the Government by rebellion not only in Parliament but throughout the country. Now then, farmers of Britain! Make a similar protest and you will get rid of the Common Market!"[34] Lord Beaverbrook urged in June 1962 that Australian Prime Minister Sir Robert Menzies appeal to the British people over the heads of their governmental leaders, and indicated that if the Conservatives persisted upon their Common Market course, he would oppose them even at the cost of wrecking Macmillan's Government.[35] Since the editors of the *Daily Mirror* and *Daily Herald* had made it clear that absolutely nothing could cause them to abandon their Common Market policies, a General Election on the Common Market issue would have found two left-wing papers supporting the Conservatives and one right-wing paper backing Labour.

Just as the anti-EEC promotional groups found themselves no longer isolated in making their case as the British position at Brussels worsened, so other voices joined those sections of the press already critical of Europe. By October 1962, *The Times* was expressing concern over the price of membership,[36] the *Observer* had become critical of entry on grounds similar to Gaitskell's Commonwealth criteria, and *The Guardian* became troubled over British concessions as well as the serious divisions within the country.[37]

IMPACT OF THE PRESS

On January 30, 1963, immediately following the official termination of the Brussels negotiations, the *Daily Express* displayed the effusive headline, "Glory, Glory Hallelujah! It's all over. Britain's Europe bid is dead. Now—Forward." The

[34] *Daily Express*, December 14, 1961.
[35] *Daily Express*, June 4, 1962.
[36] *The Times*, October 1, 1962.
[37] *The Guardian*, October 4 and November 16, 1962.

next day, the paper asserted that it had "fought almost alone against the sell-out of Britain to the Common Market," and had "triumphed." Was it justified in claiming such an impact? Certainly the *Express* did provide a focus for vague discontent and did prevent the dissipation of doubts. The daily "Common Market Facts" were aimed at those among the paper's twelve million readers with weak opinions. As Lord Windlesham observes, those who might have been impressed by a balanced assessment of facts would be largely set in their opinions already and hence could be ignored. The paper sought to exercise influence on governmental decision-makers by confronting them with evidence that popular opposition was so great that they could not carry the country into Europe.[38]

Yet any direct influence in changing public views appears limited. A Gallup poll taken in the first half of 1962 showed the readership of the *Express* to be more favorable to Common Market entry than that of the *Herald,* and almost as pro-European as that of the *Mirror.* This despite the year of pro-EEC campaigning by the *Herald* and *Mirror* and the anti-Common Market efforts of the *Express.* In addition, more than one-third of the readership of all three papers gave "don't know" responses.[39]

Response of Readers	Daily Herald	Daily Mirror	Daily Express
		(Percent)	
For	38	46	45
Against	25	15	29
Don't Know	37	39	26

The better predictive indicator is not newspaper readership but socio-economic status.[40] Lower positions on the economic

---

[38] Windlesham, *op. cit.,* pp. 160-163.

[39] Gallup Poll figures, quoted in Jean Beavan, *The Press and the Public* (London: Fabian Society, Tract No. 338, July 1962), pp. 12-13.

[40] *Ibid.,* p. 13. A 1959 study also showed upper social economic groups more favorably disposed toward Europe than the general public. See U.S. Information Agency, *Public Opinion in Western Europe. Atti-*

ladder correlate with less favorable views toward the Common Market and a greater prevalence of "don't knows." The lesser

Response of Readers	Well-to-do and middle class	Lower middle	Very Poor
	(Percent)		
For	61	43	26
Against	19	21	18
Don't Know	20	36	56

socio-economic position of the *Herald* readership vis-à-vis that of the *Express* more than offsets the forceful policy positions adopted by the papers.

There are obvious similarities between the roles played by the press and the promotional groups. Both sides of the press functioned to rally those in agreement with them and thereby indicate to the Government that the demands of public opinion made their course of action preferable.[41] The existence of the pro-Common Market group assured HMG of a solid and powerful response, making Europe both practical and popular, while Beaverbrook and his allies sought to create and publicize popular revulsion against governmental policy. In general, the press exerted more of a vertical effect[42] (upon the

---

tudes towards Political, Economic and Military Integration (January, 1953), pp. 10-11. Cited in Jacques-René Rabier, "The European Idea and National Public Opinion," *Government and Opposition*, 2, no. 3 (April-July, 1967): 446.

[41] The predictive ability of the press could scarcely inspire any confidence in the accuracy of various claims to represent the public will. Individual journalists committed some astounding miscalculations about the major developments during the negotiation period. For example, in July 1962, Walter Farr of the *Daily Telegraph* referred to the Brussels negotiations as having reached the stage of putting the "finishing touches" on the entry agreement; on September 28, 1962, H. P. Boyne of the *Daily Telegraph* described Hugh Gaitskell as feeling "in his bones that Britain's place is inside Europe. . . ."; and on January 13, 1963 (one day before the de Gaulle veto) Nora Beloff assured *Observed* readers that it was certain de Gaulle would not veto Britain's entry.

[42] The conceptions of vertical and horizontal influence are discussed by Colin Seymour-Ure, "The Press and the British Political System." Paper presented at the annual conference of the Political Studies Association, Oxford, April 3-5, 1967.

public) than a horizontal one (upon governmental decision-makers) but even that influence had substantial limitations.

PUBLIC OPINION, POLLS, AND BY-ELECTIONS

Prior to July 1961 the British public remained relatively quiescent as far as European policy was concerned. So quiescent in fact that little significant shift of public opinion took place in the year prior to the Macmillan announcement. A Gallup poll taken in July 1960 found that 49 percent would approve of a Government decision to join the Common Market, while 13 percent would disapprove and 38 percent were undecided. A year later, similar polls taken six different times during the months of June and July showed figures of from 36 percent to 46 percent approval.[43] Thus rather than shifting in favor of entry, public sentiment actually moved slightly in the opposite direction. Since a substantial plurality of the public was prepared to accept a Common Market decision all along, it follows that any real shift of sentiment took place among the various opinion, institutional and political elites. During 1960-61, elite opinion did move dramatically, and it is this massive conversion in industry, the City, the media, Whitehall and, to some extent, Westminster which effectively set the stage for Macmillan's action.

DE-EMPHASIS OF THE EEC ISSUE

Substantial public debate began only after July 1961. What is somewhat surprising is that the Government made little effort to lead public opinion in the first year following this date. At the same time, it placed greater emphasis upon the economic rather than the political features of Europe. Macmillan's timetable provided for a major campaign on the issue once negotiations neared a successful termination and the General Election approached. Although this technique ulti-

---

[43] *Journal of Common Market Studies* (September, 1966) pp. 49-50.

mately proved counterproductive with the Europeans, who awaited evidence of genuine British conviction, there was a certain justification for this approach. Opinion polls indicated that there was widespread public support for a vague European connection, but that opposition increased when specific issues came to the foreground.[44] Thus as early as 1953, 58 percent of British respondents favored the unification of Western Europe, but only 41 percent remained in favor if it meant a risk to the interest of their own country.[45] In 1957, 64 percent favored European unity, but only 31 percent a European political federation in which final authority would lie with a central government.[46] In September 1961, only one-fourth of the public would support entry without satisfactory solutions being agreed to for such interests as farming, the Commonwealth, and EFTA,[47] and during 1962 the public indicated by a margin of about three to one that it would approve a Government decision not to enter the Common Market if the

[44] The structural characteristics of this situation are not unlike those noted by Prothro and Grigg in their study of Tallahassee, Florida, and Ann Arbor, Michigan, which found that overwhelming support existed for a broad conception such as freedom of speech, but that there was far less consensus when respondents were confronted with operational tests of this principle. See James W. Prothro and C. M. Grigg, "Fundamental Principles of democracy: bases of agreement and disagreement," *Journal of Politics*, 22 (May, 1960): 276-294.

[45] Rabier, *loc. cit.*, p. 445.

[46] USIA, *Attitudes Towards European Union, the Common Market and Euratom*, West European Public Opinion Barometer, Report 50 (August 12, 1957), quoted *ibid.*, p. 446.

[47] "Are any of these difficulties so overriding that you would not support Britain joining the European Common Market unless they agreed to a satisfactory solution?"

If Yes: Which of these difficulties do you regard of such importance?

"Yes: British farming interests	25 percent
The Commonwealth interests	39
The interests of other EFTA countries	4
No: None of them overriding	25
Don't Know	24

The public also continued to place the Commonwealth and then America ahead of Europe as the most important to Britain. The figures

desired terms were unattainable.[48] Similarly the British preferred an economic association to a political one; as late as
February 1963 the former was approved heavily, with 57 percent in favor and only 14 percent opposed, but the latter was
accepted by the narrow margin of only 39 percent to 28
percent.[49]

THE DEVELOPMENT OF PUBLIC SENTIMENT

The fluctuations of public opinion as measured by the polls
received a great deal of observation. One source of controversy was the discrepancy between various polls. For example,
the *Daily Express* and the National Opinion Poll (NOP) asked,
"Are you for or against Britain joining the Common Market?"[50] while Social Surveys Ltd. (Gallup) asked, "If the British Government were to decide that Britain's interest would
best be served by joining the European Common Market,
would you approve or disapprove?" The first method produced anti-EEC pluralities in June and December 1962, and
even a hostile majority (52.2 percent against, 37.8 percent for)
in early September.[51] During 1962 alone, responses to the
NOP question displayed swings of nearly 20 percent (high
of 47 percent in March, April, and October; a low of 28.2 percent in June). Meanwhile on the Gallup question, those disapproving never outnumbered those approving, and swings

---

for September 1961 were Commonwealth 48 percent, America 19 percent,
Europe 18 percent, Don't Know 15 percent.
    Gallup Poll, quoted in *Journal of Common Market Studies* (Septem-
ber, 1966), p. 53.
    [48] "If the British Government cannot get the terms they want and
decide not to enter the European Common Market, would you approve
or disapprove of the Government's decision?"

Approve	50 percent
Disapprove	18
Don't Know	29

    Gallup Poll, quoted *ibid.*, p. 51.
    [49] Gallup Poll, quoted *ibid.*, p. 60.
    [50] See, for example, *Daily Express*, August 29, 1961.
    [51] *Observer*, September 9, 1962.

were generally less. Opponents of entry criticized Gallup's question as loaded, but, as Windlesham observes, it was a factual description of the political situation.[52]

Initially, Macmillan's announcement brought forth a rise in pro-entry sentiment. From a Gallup poll figure of 39 percent approval immediately prior to July 31, support climbed to 52 percent in September (with only 18 percent disapproving) and then, following a brief decline in October, to a December 1961 peak of 53 percent.[53] From that time on, Common Market support underwent attrition, heading downward to a June 1962 low point of 36 percent approval versus 30 percent disapproval.[54] This decline is commonly attributed to the lack of pro-Common Market impetus by HMG, but as will be noted below, the decline also correlates with an exceptionally low point in Tory popularity. The polls later indicated a rise in pro-entry feeling. This recovery reached a peak in September-October, following the opening of a concerted Common Market campaign by the Prime Minister (who for the first time had presented the public with an unequivocal case for Common Market entry) and the subsequent meeting of the annual Conservative Conference. Eventually, the Gallup poll indicated a precipitous decline from a late October high of 49 percent to a late December nadir of 37 percent. (See Figure 1.) Indeed, a new Gallup question asking whether respondents favored joining on the existing facts found that support had dwindled to 24 percent, the same percentage expecting the Tories to win the next General Election.[55]

A salient characteristic of the eighteen months between July 1961 and January 1963 is the extent to which the fate of the Common Market became increasingly tied to that of the Conservative Party. The effect appears to have been a function of the increasing bipartisan disaccord over the issue. During the

---

[52] Windlesham, *op. cit.*, p. 158.

[53] *Gallup Political Index,* no. 24 (December, 1961), p. 8.

[54] *Ibid.*, no. 37 (January, 1963), p. 12.

[55] *Daily Telegraph,* December 12, 1962.

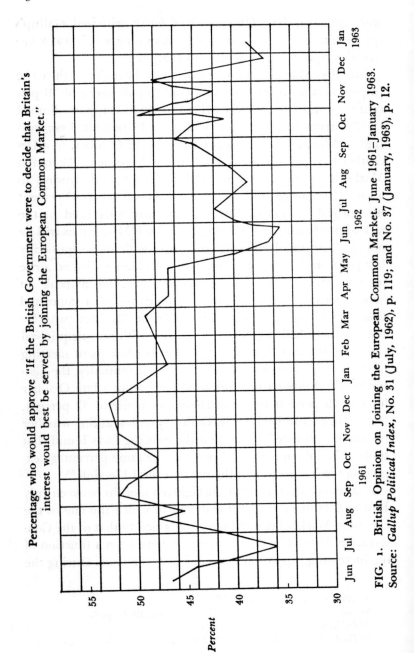

FIG. 1. British Opinion on Joining the European Common Market. June 1961–January 1963.
Source: *Gallup Political Index*, No. 31 (July, 1962), p. 119; and No. 37 (January, 1963), p. 12.

six months following July 1961, those who had voted Labour in 1959 favored the Common Market almost as heavily as Tory voters. At the time of the December 1961 peak in Common Market sympathy, 52 percent of Labour voters would have approved a Governmental decision to enter the Common Market (a figure only 4 percent lower than that of Tory voters) and a mere 20 percent disapproved.[56] The fact that Labour had in August taken the lead in polls of voting intention did not harm the prospects for Common Market entry at this time.

The position of the Tories then worsened drastically. After having obtained an increased share of the vote at successive General Elections in 1950, 1951, 1955, and 1959, the Party's fortunes had peaked in late 1960. The mean swing to the Conservatives in by-elections during that year had averaged 1.8 percent. From the middle of 1961 however, the Conservatives permanently trailed Labour in polls of voting intent, and the Party became increasingly "accident prone."[57] The by-election swing away from the Tories during 1961 equaled a fairly steady 6 percent, representing a potential Labour landslide since the actual results of the October 1964 General Election gave Labour a thin Parliamentary majority with a swing of only 2.9 percent.[58] Throughout 1962, the Tories fared even worse as Labour steadily increased its projected voting majority to about 12 percent at the close of the year. In July 1962, Macmillan's popularity fell to the lowest point of any Prime Minister since Chamberlain in 1940. Results of twelve by-elections from March through July 1962 produced a 10.0 percent mean swing away from the Tories, and five elections in November showed an only somewhat lesser loss of 7.8 percent.[59]

With the increased perception of Labour Party criticism

---

[56] *Gallup Political Index,* no. 24 (December, 1961), p. 8.

[57] The term is reminiscent of the "death wish" attributed to the 1950-51 Labour Government.

[58] The figure is computed by Butler and King, *op. cit.,* p. 305.

[59] *Ibid.,* p. 14 and p. 336. Computation of swing varies slightly depending on the presence of a third party candidate and the method em-

232   *The Common Market: Broader Public*

and then open hostility toward HMG's European policy, Labour voters' support for the Common Market fell precipitously. By April 1962, their margin of 52 percent to 20 percent preference had nearly vanished, and they supported a potential entry decision by only 38 percent to 33 percent. This contrasted sharply with Conservative sentiment, which preferred entry by a 58 percent to 22 percent margin. Following the 1962 Labour Conference, Labour support for Common Market entry dwindled further to a December figure of only 27 percent in favor and 36 percent opposed.

The Common Market remained more popular than Prime Minister Macmillan and his Party. Pluralities of British voters were pro-Common Market and pro-Labour at the same time. This disparity is accounted for by the Common Market support of some Labour and many Liberal voters.[60] Increased partisan disagreement had the effect of narrowing the difference by which the public supported EEC entry more than it did the Conservatives. In general, the swings in public sentiment vis-à-vis Europe tended to follow the pattern set by the overall popularity of the Conservative Party. Because the Prime Minister had succeeded in identifying himself with the

---

ployed. The most common explanation is the following:

Average of the difference in the Labour and Conservative share of votes comparing the present and the previous General Election.

i.e., $\dfrac{(L2 - L1) + (C1 - C2)}{2}$

When L1 = Labour percentage in previous election
L2 = Labour percentage in present election
C1 = Conservative percentage in previous election
C2 = Conservative percentage in present election

See *Election 1966, Gallup Analysis of the Voting Results* (London: The Daily Telegraph Ltd., 1966), p. 18.

[60] For example, in early October, Labour led the Conservatives by a percentage margin of 40 to 33.5, with 16.5 percent Liberal; 46 percent of the public approved a potential entry decision against only 30 percent disapproving. *Sunday Times,* October 7, 1962.

Ironically, some Anti-Common Market Conservatives chose to protest against the Party's position by transferring their allegiance to the Liberals (the most vociferously pro-European party of all).

Common Market, and in putting all the Conservatives' eggs
into the European basket, the fate of EEC entry became in-
extricable from that of the Government itself.

ELITE VERSUS PUBLIC SENTIMENT

HMG tested both elite and public opinion during the pre-
lude to and execution of its Common Market venture. As
noted earlier in this Chapter, informed elite opinion became
overwhelmingly pro-European[61] while the attitude of the
British public as a whole, as measured by opinion polls, stagnated and then became less favorable.

When, in the period 1960-61, HMG consulted the opinion
of various elites (that is, individuals in Parliament, upper
levels of the Civil Service, the press, industry, and the like)
they were becoming increasingly receptive to the idea of EEC
membership. Daniel Lerner indicates that in 1961, eight out
of every ten elite respondents felt Britain must join, and more
than half were ready, if forced to choose, to see the U.K. sacrifice some of its Commonwealth interests to promote European
ones.[62] The shift seems to have begun in late 1960 and early
1961, and a Labour critic of entry reports that by mid-1962
"the whole political, intellectual, and moral force of Britain's
Establishment was committed to the enterprise."[63] Critics also

---

[61] There is some evidence that British elites had assumed increasingly benevolent attitudes toward Europe since 1954. See Daniel Lerner,
As Britain Faces the Continent: How Its Leaders Weigh Their Choices
(Cambridge, Massachusetts: MIT, Center for International Studies,
1962), p. 6. (Mimeographed.)

[62] *Ibid.*

[63] Peter Shore, *Entitled to Know* (London: Macgibbon and Kee,
1966), p. 22. Certainly, large-scale British industry had become heavily
pro-EEC. A *Sunday Times* poll of leading industrialists found that "the
predominant weight of modern British industry, which actually has to
make the export sales, is strongly in favour of British entry. . . . " *Sunday
Times*, September 2, 1962, quoted in Windlesham, *op. cit.*, p. 156. At
nearly the same time, a poll of leading economists produced a margin of
about 4:1 in favor of entry on the existing terms. The breakdown was 12
against, 49 in favor, 22 balanced or uncommitted. *Observer*, October 14,
1962.

objected that much of the Common Market debate had been confined to a limited number of interested parties or experts, and R.H.S. Crossman claimed that "the British people had been scarcely affected by the sudden wholesale conversion of the Whitehall establishment."[64] This near-monopolization of the argument constituted one dimension of Hugh Gaitskell's antagonism, and in his October 1962 address to the Labour Conference he expressed anger at the desire of "top people" to arrogate to themselves the right of judgment.[65]

The general public paid little attention to Europe prior to July 1961 and, even afterward, opinion never became dramatically mobilized. It remained quiescent, a background force setting few explicit limits. To the extent that general opinion had any effect at all, it was via governmental anticipation of the public response. As far as the EEC was concerned, public opinion appears to have depended more on the Government than vice versa. It was informed elite opinion in itself, and as expressed in the various centers of power, which set the real limits on the domestic scene.

Even when the Common Market became relatively politicized in treatment, public involvement remained limited. As noted by Jean Blondel,[66] Max Beloff[67] and Kenneth Younger[68] there is little evidence of public partisanship in

---

[64] RHS Crossman, "British Labour Looks at Europe," *Foreign Affairs*, 41, no. 4 (July, 1963); 736. Also see Peter Nettl and David Shapiro, "Institutions Versus Realities—A British Approach," *Journal of Common Market Studies*, 2, no. 1 (July, 1963): 25.

[65] *The Guardian*, "The Labour Party Conference 1962," October 1-5, 1962.

[66] Jean Blondel, *Voters, Parties and Leaders* (Harmondsworth, Middlesex: Penguin, 1966), pp. 77-79.

[67] Max Beloff, *New Dimensions in Foreign Policy* (London: Allen & Unwin, 1961), p. 15.

[68] Kenneth Younger, "Public Opinion and British Foreign Policy," *International Affairs* (London), 40, no. 1 (January, 1964): 22-25. Younger takes a view which is widely shared by persons interviewed for the present study: "British public opinion rarely makes itself decisively felt as a separate force of which governments take account, but it is nevertheless

foreign affairs because the public concentrates—and votes—upon domestic issues, leaving foreign policy to an elite or oligarchic constituency. The public eventually did divide along party lines over the Common Market issue, but the divergence seems to have depended on voters taking their cues from the political parties. The effect of the limitation on the public's involvement was to preserve some leeway for the operation of sectional pressure groups and their leaders.

CONCLUSION

THE PRIME MINISTER AND THE PUBLIC

Perhaps the best explanation for the fact that public opinion remained relatively unchanged is that the Macmillan Government made no clear effort to rally it to the European cause. The Prime Minister's recognized temperamental preference for the avoidance of confrontation,[69] the belief that premature European enthusiasm would damage Britain's bargaining position at Brussels, and the desire to delay the European issue for use in a later campaign to peak at the time of a coming General Election explain why the Government adopted this course.

Until September 1962 the subject of membership in the European Community had remained substantially a political decision debated in economic terms.[70] Because of its emphasis on the conditions to be negotiated, HMG could not undertake a domestic promotional campaign until the Brussels talks had

---

there in the background setting limits to what a prudent government will attempt" (p. 31).

[69] Anthony Sampson analyses this facet of Macmillan's character in *Macmillan: A Study in Ambiguity* (London: Allen Lane, The Penguin Press, 1967), p. 212.

[70] As late as the middle of August, Edward Heath prefaced a Conservative Party pamphlet on Europe with the argument that Britain should join the Six in order first to expand her European markets, and second to be better able to support the Commonwealth. *Financial Times*, August 17, 1962.

shown what the details of membership would be. Not until a telecast on September 20, 1962, did Macmillan for the first time emphatically tell the British people that the U.K. must join the Common Market. The Conservative Party followed suit with a barrage of speakers and pamphlets, but this effort came too late to sway public opinion.

A major reason for the failure of this campaign was the drastic weakening of the Conservative Government. The decline of Macmillan and the Conservatives in opinion polls had been compounded by the July 1962 Cabinet shuffle, disastrous results in five November by-elections, American attacks on the EEC's agricultural agreements, de Gaulle's triumph in the French elections, and the cancellation of Skybolt. Insofar as it had become linked with the Tories' fate, support for the Common Market suffered as well.

In retrospect it appears that a much earlier and more dramatic appeal to the public, a Churchillian approach, could have offered distinct advantages. In mid-1961, Macmillan might have attempted to present the Common Market as a grand historical challenge to the British, one which demanded all their energies and attention in an enterprise seeking to unite the Western European peoples and thereby reorient their mutual destiny. A number of pro-Europeans in the Conservative Party did advise mobilization of the broader public. If successful, such an approach would have freed Macmillan's hands in regard to the detailed terms of entry, leaving him more room to concentrate on the broader considerations at Brussels.

The essence of the Prime Minister's problem was that in order to gain domestic approval for the European course, he had pledged himself to obtain safeguards which, if not wholly incompatible with membership, were at least unlikely to be obtainable. Macmillan had put a high price on Britain's entry because of his greater concern for the internal political problem of getting Common Market entry accepted at home than for the external international consideration of reaching agreement at Brussels. Ultimately the Government became trapped in a vicious circle partly of its own construction. The inescapable need for concessions to the Six[71] enabled the Beaverbrook Press and the Labour Party, as well as spokesmen for the NFU and the Commonwealth, to tell the public that Britain was now "negotiating on her knees." This further undermined the Government's domestic political position. In turn the Europeans gained the impression that Macmillan had staked everything on the EEC and would find it necessary to accept whatever conditions he could get. Accordingly, the French stiffened their agricultural demands, asking for the ending of the British deficiency payment system and the completion of transition arrangements by 1970.

COLLAPSE OF THE EUROPEAN VENTURE

On January 14, 1963, President de Gaulle held the press conference at which he asserted Britain was not yet ready for Common Market membership. Two weeks later, the Brussels negotiations were terminated. In the House of Commons post-mortem which followed, Conservative leaders argued that French objections were unjustified. Substantial progress had been made, Britain did accept the Treaty of Rome including its common institutions and external tariff, and negotiations had been at the point of success when abruptly broken off by France. Labour countered with the assertion that HMG was erecting a myth that an impending agreement had been ruptured by a sudden evil act. Instead, no agreement was yet in sight and the terms already negotiated amounted to a humiliating sellout of the interests of the Commonwealth, EFTA, and British agriculture.[72]

In fact, the actual situation in late January was neither so promising as the Government contended, nor quite so difficult

---

[71] Camps explores some of these points and notes the problem that Britain had not made it clear to the Europeans that she had intellectually and emotionally made her choice. *Op. cit.,* p. 370.

[72] See *Hansard,* Vol. 671 (February 11-12, 1963).

as Labour argued. Negotiations did not yet stand on the point of success. At the time, unresolved issues still included the status of the EFTA, transitional arrangements for agriculture, Britain's desire for nil tariffs on her imports of certain commodities (e.g., aluminium and newspulp), the status of temperate zone agricultural imports (especially those of New Zealand), the disposition of the expected income from agricultural import levies, and the question of voting arrangements. The formal report to the European Parliament by the European Commission implicitly refuted President de Gaulle's veto arguments by observing that the complex remaining problems could have been settled. However the Commission candidly stated that "what was needed for a solution was in some cases mainly a move from the British Government. . . ."[73]

British politics played a considerable part in the failure to reach agreement, especially by placing obstacles in the path of an early agreement. The slowness of Britain in making concessions to the Six may have been crucial; Miriam Camps believes that saving of six weeks in the summer of 1962 might have constituted the difference between success and failure.[74] This contention is not subject to verification, but it is at least true that the Government's effort to satisfy domestic demands prevented it from taking a more positive approach at Brussels.

The importance of the domestic situation did not lie exclusively in its shaping of the British bargaining position; it also facilitated the de Gaulle veto. The French President found Britain a threat to his own conception of Europe and to French primacy there. The worsening of Macmillan's position, the results of polls and by-elections, statements by Eden, Montgomery, and Attlee, and the opposition of Gaitskell all

---

[73] European Economic Community—Commission, *Report to the European Parliament on the State of the Negotiations with the United Kingdom* (Brussels, February 26, 1963), p. 110.

[74] Camps, *op. cit.*, p. 411.

put the prospect of British entry in doubt. The circumstances in Britain therefore made de Gaulle's task easier.

BROADER CONCLUSIONS

In theory, politicization of the Common Market issue should have taken the matter beyond the reach of sectional group demands. Active participation by the political parties, the removal of Europe from the economic ministries and the involvement of the broader public signaled the predominance of the process of party government. The absence of a settled and specialized policy, the existence of an issue transcending individual group interests and the unavailability of a closed relationship between sectional pressure group and ministry militated against the operation of the functional representation channel. And yet, after the initial political decision to seek Common Market entry had been taken, sectional demands nonetheless played a key role in the subsequent formulation of Britain's bargaining position vis-à-vis the EEC.

Hypothetically, the process of party government should have insured a relatively unhindered approach. However, politicization remained ineffective because Common Market entry was not treated as a supreme political issue. Such an approach derived not only from the Prime Minister's temperament, considerations of timing, and HMG's assessment of how to bargain at Brussels; it also gained substantial impetus from the state of the parties and of public opinion. As we have seen in Chapter 7, any decision to confront EEC membership as a dramatic political step faced intrinsic obstacles from within both the Conservative and Labour parties. These difficulties were compounded by the fact that public opinion was more favorable toward an economic association with Europe than a political one. Together, the elements of party and public preference created a propensity toward dealing with Europe as a matter of trade and economics. The subsequent treatment of Europe as a specialized economic issue, together with the necessity for encumbering the British position at Brussels in economic detail (due to the attempt to bargain for the Commonwealth and to negotiate *à sept* and in a "glass house" atmosphere) thus assured that, despite the dominance of party government, the channel of functional representation would remain open for the exercise of group influence.

Given the approach taken by HMG, even the process of party government provided a means of pressure group access. Hitherto specific group demands, especially in the case of agriculture, were assimilated by the public or the political parties. But more significantly, bipartisan disaccord increased the importance of sectional groups and the weight of the Tory agricultural and industrial constituency because, faced with Labour's mounting opposition, the Government needed to rally as much support as possible.

Thus the dominance of the party government mechanism was not in itself a sufficient determinant of the limitation of pressure group influence. In the next chapter, we shall see how the group interests were rendered insignificant during the Wilson Government's 1966–67 Common Market effort, where, accompanying effective politicization, we find an absence of most of the factors cited above as well as the presence of external international necessities which dictated an unimpeded approach.

Chapter 9

The Wilson Government and the Common Market

The de Gaulle veto had come as a traumatic climax to a truly profound shift in Britain's conception of her international role. A 1966 campaign polemic prepared by Peter Shore, head of Labour's Research Department, captured the impact of the French President's *"non"* in accurate, if somewhat pungent, terms. "It was as though an ageing virgin who had resisted all advances in her youth had at last brought herself to the moment of delicious surrender; one by one the garments had been taken. Naked, defenceless and loving, she awaits the final embrace—only to be told that she is not yet ready or fit for union!"[1]

Despite the disastrous set-back, Europeanism remained a latent force within Britain. After an interlude of more than two years, the Labour Government began another approach to Europe, which eventually culminated on May 2, 1967, with a statement to Parliament by Prime Minister Wilson that Britain would make formal application to join the EEC.

What differentiated the European policy of the Labour Government in 1966–67 from the Macmillan effort in the 1961–63 period was the effectiveness with which the issue be-

---

[1] Peter Shore, *Entitled to Know* (London: Macgibbon and Kee, 1966), p. 23.

came politicized. For the first time, the major sectional groups completely lost their concurrent majority powers. The minimized role for the functional representation channel permitted Wilson to formulate his European approach virtually unimpeded with conditions resulting from commitments to various domestic and pressure group interests.

THE RESUMPTION OF EUROPEANISM

It is no exaggeration to describe Europe as virtually absent from consideration in the October 1964 General Election. What had been the most salient political issue of 1962 received attention in the election address of only 11 percent of the Conservative candidates and 8 percent of the Labourites. Even among Liberal Party candidates, only 38 percent saw fit to make reference to the subjects of Europe, the Common Market or EFTA.[2] Labour's election manifesto condemned the Conservative Governments of Macmillan and Home for their readiness to negotiate entry under highly unfavorable terms, and stated that while it would seek "closer links with our European neighbors, the Labour Party is convinced that the first responsibility of a British Government is still to the Commonwealth."[3] In turn, the Conservative manifesto deemphasized Europe by stipulating that "entry into the EEC is not open to us in existing circumstances. . . ."[4]

Following the election, the Government of Sir Alec Douglas Home resigned and Harold Wilson became Prime Minister on the strength of a House of Commons majority of four seats. The new Labour Government kept its distance from Europe, but a few pro-Europeans predicted privately that it would take

---

[2] Analysis from a random sample of one-fourth of the constituencies in England, Scotland, and Wales. D. E. Butler and Anthony King, *The British General Election of 1964* (London: Macmillan, 1965), p. 143.

[3] Labour Party, *New Britain, Manifesto for the 1964 General Election* (London, 1964), p. 19.

[4] Butler and King, *op. cit.*, p. 131.

only eighteen months before Harold Wilson turned to the Common Market choice. Meanwhile, the Labour Government was absorbed with other matters. Its priorities were with domestic problems, the promotion of *détente,* and the development of the Commonwealth relationship.[5] Its initial policy statements offered little prospect of a resumption of the European venture. Speaking to the British Chamber of Commerce in Brussels on February 11, 1965, Foreign Secretary Michael Stewart described Britain's desire for closer cooperation between EFTA and the Common Market, but reaffirmed the country's role of Commonwealth leadership and observed that no choice was necessary between Atlantic and European orientations.[6] A few days later, Harold Wilson told Parliament that the Government would be prepared to negotiate "only if the necessary conditions relating to essential British and Commonwealth interests could be fulfilled."[7]

The Common Market question began to attract increasing attention during the spring and summer of 1965. Conservative and Liberal leaders resumed their enthusiastic advocacy, and Labour began to find that the opportunities presented by the Commonwealth, EFTA, *détente,* and the special relationship with the U.S. were less than satisfactory. By the autumn, the Foreign Secretary showed signs of softening the Five Conditions, which remained Labour's official policy. At the Party's Annual Conference, he criticized those reservations involving the Commonwealth and the problem of retaining independent foreign policy and economic planning capabilities, and in Parliament he described some of the conditions as easier to meet than previously.[8] By the end of 1965, the major re-

---

[5] Miriam Camps develops these points in her book, *European Unification in the Sixties* (New York: McGraw-Hill, 1966), pp. 140-141.

[6] "Extracts from a Speech by the Foreign Secretary, Mr. Michael Stewart to the British Chamber of Commerce at Brussels, February 11, 1965" (London: Labour Party Overseas Department, mimeographed).

[7] *Hansard, Parliamentary Debates* (Commons), Vol. 706 (February 16, 1965), c. 1003.

[8] *Ibid.,* Vol. 722 (December 20, 1965), c. 1723.

maining recognized difficulty with Common Market entry was the problem of agriculture.

The General Election which took place on March 31, 1966, gave Labour a parliamentary majority of ninety-seven seats. In contrast to the pattern of the previous election, Europe this time emerged as a more relevant political issue, at least for the opposition parties. References to the subject on the part of Conservative and Liberal candidates far surpassed the 1964 figures. Among Conservatives, 50 percent cited European matters in their speeches, while 67 percent of the Liberals raised the subject. On the other hand, Labour's persisting de-emphasis was reflected in a figure of only 9 percent.[9] The parties' election manifestoes offered a definite separation of views, although the division was less marked and less passionate than it had been in the autumn of 1962. Led for the first time in an election by Edward Heath, who had conducted the Brussels negotiations, the Conservatives made Europe the only foreign or defense issue among the five major themes in their campaign.[10] The Party pledged to "work energetically for entry into the European Common Market at the first favorable opportunity,"[11] and Heath flatly admitted the need for accepting the Six's Common Agricultural Policy.[12]

Labour, in turn, depicted the Opposition as ready to take

------

[9] Analysis from a random sample of one-fifth of the constituencies in England, Scotland, and Wales. A simple mention of any European topic was recorded. Butler and King, *The British General Election of 1966* (London: Macmillan, 1966), p. 103. Another and perhaps more comprehensive study found a somewhat higher percentage of references (Labour 16, Conservative 67, Liberal 81 percent). See *Attitudes to European Unity and World Institutions in the 1966 General Election* (London: Federal Trust for Education and Research, 1967), p. 14.

[10] The other four items were the economy, trade union reform, social services, and housing. See Butler and King, *General Election of 1966*, p. 92.

[11] Quoted in Conservative Research Department *Notes on Current Politics* (January 16, 1967).

[12] This contrasted with the Conservative Government's 1961-63 pledge that entry "depended upon . . . satisfactory arrangements being made in the Community which would assure the well-being of British

Britain into the Common Market "without any conditions or safeguards." The Party's position remained vague; it expressed a readiness, "in consultation with . . . EFTA partners . . . to enter the EEC, provided essential British and Commonwealth interests are safeguarded." The manifesto also spoke of maintaining close European contacts in industry, science and culture so as to produce the necessary understanding among the Six of Britain's position.[13] The overall party predisposition was not unsympathetic toward Europe, but Labour did appear unyielding in rejecting the Community's agricultural arrangement. The most favorable campaign statement on Europe came from George Brown, then Minister of Economic Affairs, who observed that going into the Common Market was not an issue between the parties. What was at issue was whether it was done "rationally or in a headlong manner."[14] The Labour leadership remained divided on the issue, and the one major policy statement by the Prime Minister presented a more or less reserved attitude. Speaking at Bristol on March 18, Wilson observed that the Labour Government would negotiate its way into Europe, not crawl. He scathingly contrasted Edward Heath's position: "Now one encouraging gesture from the French Government, which I welcome, and the Conservative leader rolls on his back like a spaniel. . . . Some of my best friends are spaniels, but I would not put them in charge of negotiations into the Common Market."[15]

More to the point, the Prime Minister had two serious reservations. First, that "we must be free to go on buying food and raw materials as we have for 100 years, in the cheapest markets—in Canada, Australia, New Zealand, and other Com-

agriculture." National Farmers' Union, "British Agriculture and the Common Market," March 24, 1966 (newsletter sent to NFU branches).

[13] Labour Party, *Time for Decision, Manifesto for the 1966 General Election* (London, 1966), pp. 21-22.

[14] Butler and King, *General Election of 1966,* p. 110.

[15] Quoted in *The Guardian* (London), March 19, 1966.

monwealth countries. . . ."[16] Second, that Britain rejected any supranational control of foreign and defense policies; the country's power and influence must never be confined to Europe. While Wilson's speech was widely regarded as anti-European, it is best interpreted in the light of the election campaign and as an effort to make points at the expense of the Conservatives. In practice, the Wilson Government did not for long adhere to the conditions enunciated in the Bristol speech.

Upon the opening of Parliament the following month, the Queen's speech included a mention of Britain's readiness to join the EEC provided her conditions were met. These conditions remained unspecified, and the Prime Minister observed that certain of the obstacles to entry had diminished. Wilson also took the important step of naming two of his prominent ministers, George Brown and George Thomson, to concentrate upon relations with Europe. Brown was to handle the economic aspects through the Department of Economic Affairs, Thomson to deal with the foreign policy elements. Subsequently the two men made it plain that Gaitskell's five conditions no longer possessed relevance, and Brown stipulated that the question was not whether Britain should join the EEC but when and on what terms.[17]

The Labour Government had, as Camps observes, recapitulated the Conservative stages on Europe. There had been first the flirtation with Commonwealth and EFTA alternatives, next the effort at bridge-building between Six and Seven, then the cautious acceptance of entry on conditions and with the political overtones de-emphasized.[18] Within a year, the Labour Government would enter still another phase, that of whole-hearted assertion of Europeanism.

During their Annual Party Conference in October 1966,

---

[16] *Ibid.*

[17] Statement on May 6, 1966. See Conservative Research Department, *Words For Eating* (London, 1966), p. 75.

[18] Camps, *op. cit.*, p. 194.

the Conservatives continued to place heavy emphasis on Europe. Alec Douglas Home laid special emphasis on the political advantages of membership for Britain's world influence and for European relations with the super-powers. Heath urged the acceptance of the EEC as is. The Conference debate as a whole was strongly pro-European with virtually no dissent.[19] The Labour Conference largely ignored the Common Market issue, in part because the Government was absorbed in probing the way toward possible EEC membership, in part because Brown and Wilson sought to avoid becoming entangled in an intraparty fight over the five conditions.

After a year and a half of quietly feeling its way toward the Six, the Wilson Government finally made its first dramatic step. Speaking to Parliament on November 10, 1966, the Prime Minister announced that, after a deep review of Britain's European relations, the Government had decided to embark on a series of discussions with the individual Heads of Government of the Six in order to establish "whether it appears likely that essential British and Commonwealth interests could be safeguarded if Britain were to accept the Treaty of Rome and join EEC."[20] However Wilson maintained his freedom of maneuver by refusing to define the nature of these essential British and Commonwealth interests. In reality, the Labour Government's European policy had undergone a remarkable political transformation. During the Parliamentary debate which followed, Home, Maudling, and Heath welcomed the changed attitude toward Europe and urged the Prime Minister to convince the Six that he was really in earnest.[21]

Armed with a parliamentary resolution, Wilson and Brown held a series of bilateral talks with leaders of the Six during

---

[19] See National Union of Conservative and Unionist Associations, *84th Annual Conservative Conference* (Blackpool, October 12-15, 1966), pp. 111-119.

[20] Quoted, *The Times* (London), November 11, 1966.

[21] See *ibid.*, November 18, 1966.

January, February, and March of 1967. In April, the Cabinet reviewed the matter thoroughly and the Labour leadership completed a lengthy consultative effort within the Parliamentary Labour Party. By the end of the month the Cabinet had made its decision. Wilson told a private meeting of the PLP that whatever the immediate and perhaps adverse economic effects of membership, there were vital unquantifiable long-term advantages of economic dynamism and technology. Furthermore, it was the political arguments which could be decisive.[22] *The Times* found the Prime Minister's emphasis "exactly right"; the economic case was important, but the political case was much more important.[23]

On May 2, Wilson announced to Parliament that HMG had decided to make formal application under Article 237 of the Rome Treaty for membership of the EEC, and parallel applications to the ECSC and Euratom. Only two major issues needed to be resolved during negotiations. One involved the Community's Common Agricultural Policy, specifically its financing arrangements and the necessity for an adequate transition. The second was provision for New Zealand agricultural exports and Commonwealth sugar producers. Nonetheless, there was nothing in the Rome Treaty or the practical operation of the EEC which made these or a few other problems insoluble.[24] The House of Commons debated the matter between May 8 and May 10. The Conservative and Liberal parties supported the Government, and Parliament approved the application by a margin of 488 to 62, with approximately 80 abstentions. 36 of the 358 Labour MP's defied a three-line whip to vote against the Government (also, about 50 abstained). This was a substantial rate of defection, but nonetheless was comparable to the desertion from Tory ranks by 26 of 259 MP's—or approximately 10 percent. Unlike the

---

[22] *European Community* (May, 1967), p. 16.

[23] *The Times,* May 1, 1967.

[24] See *Membership of the European Communities* (Cmnd. 3269, HMSO, May, 1967).

situation in 1961–63, rebels on the Government side had nowhere to turn because the opposition parties backed the Government's policy.

For the first time since the 1963 de Gaulle veto, Britain was actively seeking EEC membership. However, within days, the renewed approach encountered a staggering blow from President de Gaulle at his press conference of May 16, 1967. The French leader recited the obstacles to British entry and urged a delay until this "gifted" people had carried through a fundamental economic and political transformation.[25] Wilson refused to take "no" for an answer, and by October Britain gained the approval of the European Commission for the opening of negotiations.[26] This time the French President left no ambiguity. On November 27, he categorically refused to acquiesce in the initiation of negotiations, as these would open the door to "tricks" which would threaten the existence of the European edifice.[27] Once again, Britain's approach to Europe would be held in abeyance.

The remainder of this chapter seeks to deal not with the details of international maneuver, but with the circumstances of domestic policy-making which permitted the Prime Minister to launch a European approach remarkably free from conditions and unimpeded by the previous requirements of pressure group politics.

POLITICIZATION: THE INDICATORS

It will be recalled that the major indicators reflected a political treatment of Common Market policy during 1961–63. Broadly speaking, similar indications were present in the period leading up to Wilson's May 1967 declaration. This politicization was reflected in a non-monopolization of the issue by the economic ministries, in the involvement of the

---

25 See *European Community* (June, 1967).
26 *The Times,* October 5, 1967.
27 *New York Times,* November 28, 1967.

political parties, and in the participation of the broader public as evidenced by promotional groups, the press, and opinion polls.

THE ADMINISTRATION

While the Department of Economic Affairs (DEA), and to a lesser extent the Treasury and the BOT, assumed important roles in the formulation of the details of European policy, the Foreign Office also played a critical part. Indeed, during the time that Michael Stewart held the position of Foreign Secretary, the Foreign Office civil servants seem to have had considerable influence in shaping his view that Common Market entry was desirable. After George Brown moved from the DEA to become Foreign Secretary in mid-1966, the Foreign Office had at its head an especially committed and passionate pro-European of political importance within the Cabinet and Labour Party.

From the middle of 1965 onward, the various ministries became occupied with the "spadework" of renewed European contacts and the exploration of the implications of potential Common Market membership. This activity intensified in early 1966, when, it is widely reported, the Prime Minister surprised George Brown by informing him that Britain was going into the Common Market and that Brown would lead the effort. What is important is that European matters were not treated, as they had been in 1956–60, as primarily of a specialized economic nature, nor were they left to the exclusive attention of the BOT. As will be discussed, the broader international implications were what stood out prominently among the criteria for decision, and this implied extensive and active involvement by the Foreign Office and the Cabinet.

THE PARTIES

The second of the indicators of politicization was the involvement of the political parties. The critical difference from the Macmillan period was that this time the Government of the day possessed the resource of Opposition support.

Wilson's original Cabinet was unsympathetic toward another Common Market venture. While civil servants, the major business leaders and the press held strongly pro-European views, the renewed approach only became a possibility once the balance within the Cabinet shifted. This change was partly a function of personalities and partly one of conviction. The early replacement of Patrick Gordon Walker by Michael Stewart, and the entry of Roy Jenkins and Anthony Crosland, modified the balance within the Cabinet; and while Wilson himself never had been passionately attached to the anti-Common Market group within the Party, his own attitude underwent fundamental alteration during the early portion of his tenure as Prime Minister. By December 1965, Wilson advised a group of young pro-European MP's that there was no point in their pushing a campaign within the Party. The effort could only be divisive, and they would find that things would ultimately go their way in any case.[28]

A host of factors favored the reorientation of the PLP toward approval or acceptance of the Common Market. The "new intake" of younger, more internationalist members elected in the Labour victories of 1964 and 1966 brought in MP's more sympathetic toward Common Market entry, and the continued efforts of pro-Common Market organizers such as John Hynd and R. E. Winterbottom produced some conversions. A certain amount of the pre-existing anti-Common Market passion had owed its force to the opportunity of opposing a policy put forward by the Conservative Government; with this factor gone, there was still another reason for weakened antagonism. Some MP's changed their attitudes for reasons similar to those affecting Wilson: worsening economic problems, the increased independence of Europe, the depar-

---

[28] See article by Nora Beloff, *Observer*, October 13, 1966.

ture of Adenauer, and the perception of a lack of alternatives which the experience of governing had brought; but above all there was the fact that the Prime Minister himself was opting for Europe. Approximately 120 Labour MP's belonged to the Government in one capacity or another and were effectively bound to support the Prime Minister's policy; of the remaining 240, a third were pro-Common Market, another third flexible or willing to follow Wilson's leadership, and only one-third resolutely opposed. In sum, conviction, opportunism, and circumstance combined to make Common Market entry relatively acceptable within the Parliamentary Labour Party.

While the bulk of the Left remained deeply suspicious of Wilson's pledge that nothing would be decided without prior consultations, its members found themselves at a disadvantage because the balance within the Party had shifted against them on the European issue. Indeed the Left itself was not uniformly opposed. Eric Heffer and perhaps a score of other MP's were staunch pro-Europeans, arguing that two years of Labour Government should have been enough to convince anyone that they would never build Socialism in Britain alone. Leftist energies were also partially absorbed in attacking the Government's policies on incomes, Vietnam, and Rhodesia.

The general policy position of the Labour anti's no longer emphasized the Cold War aspect of the Common Market. Four more years of de Gaulle's independent foreign policy had taken care of that. Their main theme tended to be one of opposition to the EEC's "doctrinal adherence to private competition".[29] There was also an undercurrent of insularity or nationalism, often latent in pronouncements of the need to maintain British independence. It remains true, however, that an anti-Common Market Manifesto signed by 74 Labour MP's criticized the prospect of Common Market entry as *not*

---

[29] *Tribune* manifesto, quoted in *The Times,* May 8, 1967.

being a step toward a wider European or World Government,[30] and many younger opponents of entry claimed to oppose the Common Market as "international Socialists" rather than as "British nationalists."

The membership of the anti-Common Market group consisted of from 80 to 100 of the 363 Labour MP's, and suffered from a lack of strong leadership. The more prominent members were elderly, somewhat anti-foreign, politicians of "memory" rather than of "hope": Emanuel Shinwell (age 82), Lord Blyton (67), and even Lord Attlee (84). The younger and more internationalist opponents such as John Mendelson and Mrs. Renee Short lacked prominence as leaders. Finally, within the Cabinet, the seven of twenty-one Ministers hostile to Europe differed so widely in their reasons that they could not operate as a team.

In the same manner as Macmillan five years before, Wilson utilized prime ministerial leverage to shape the choices so as to minimize opportunities for successful opposition within the Cabinet. In February 1967, Douglas Jay received wide publicity when he addressed one in a series of back-bench PLP meetings arranged by the Labour leadership and unveiled a projected 10-14 percent rise in domestic food prices and a £175-250 million annual drain on the balance of payments.[31] While these figures were damaging, the Prime Minister succeeded in putting them in the context of broader economic and political considerations. Ultimately he edged Jay out of the Cabinet. A substantial portion of the Cabinet remained cool toward the EEC, but only a few Ministers (Jay, Peart, perhaps Castle and Greenwood) would have considered resignation. However, they faced the difficulty that it was not an appropriate resigning question. Their objections rested more on the terms than the principles of entry, and resignation in May 1967 would have had to be based on the uncertain guess

---

[30] *Ibid.*
[31] *The Times*, February 16, 1967.

that satisfactory terms could not be negotiated.[32] Thus when seven Parliamentary Private Secretaries (including those of Jay and Peart) abstained on May 10 despite the three-line whip, Wilson forced their dismissal with relative ease.

In formulating his European policy, the Prime Minister had virtually ignored Labour's NEC and the Party Conference. Only in the fall of 1967, with Government and Parliament already committed, did he seek the endorsement of these bodies. At that time he succeeded in obtaining virtually unconditional support from the NEC;[33] and, despite Shinwell's oath of "I support the egalitarian society and damn the Common Market,"[34] the Annual Conference itself endorsed the Government's Common Market application by a margin of more than two to one.

The importance of Conservative support for the Government's policy can scarcely be exaggerated. In 1961-62, Macmillan faced the requirement to carry his Party as solidly as possible because of Labour hostility. This necessitated reassurances on agriculture, the Commonwealth and sovereignty, which proved an embarrassment at Brussels. By 1966, the more receptive attitude of British farmers, the decreasingly attractive circumstances of the Commonwealth, and the independence of France within the EEC had largely dispelled the reservations among those Tories previously critical of Europe.[35] Conservative leaders not only tended to take a broader approach to Europe than they had previously, but they also made it clear that they backed Wilson to the hilt.[36]

---

[32] See the comments by David Wood, political correspondent, in *The Times*, April 24, 1967.

[33] The NEC resolution stated, "The Labour Party fully supports Britain's application to enter the EEC." See *The Times*, October 2, 1967.

[34] *New York Times*, October 8, 1967.

[35] See, for example, article by Ronald Butt, *Financial Times* (London), November 4, 1966.

[36] Conservatives placed nearly as much stress on the roles Britain could play in Europe and the world, as on economic factors. See Federal Trust, *op. cit.*

THE BROADER PUBLIC

Circumstances here resembled those during the earlier phase, the difference being that the center of gravity had shifted in a pro-European direction. There was less passionate intensity among the opponents of Europe, although attention and argument remained plentiful. A chief complaint of opponents was that, despite Wilson's November 1966 call for a "great debate," little debate actually took place. They argued that the party channels, press, and broadcasting were already committed in favor, and that the anti-Common Market forces lacked effective means for putting their case.[37] While it is true that much of the large volume of comment was pro-EEC, the opposite case did receive substantial expression.

Among the press, the *Express, Mirror,* and *Sun* went out of their way to make Europe prominent in the 1966 election campaign.[38] On the anti-entry side, the *Express* maintained its strong stand, even after the death of Lord Beaverbrook. However, the newspaper's tone became less strident. Even *The Times* gave some critical coverage, as in economic articles by the son of Douglas Jay during the spring of 1967. On the pro-Common Market side, the *Daily Mirror* and the *Sun* strove to promote entry. For the *Mirror,* Europe was *the* issue, and the paper aggressively sought to convert the Labour Government to Europeanism. It criticized Wilson's Bristol speech, and indeed waited until the last moment before endorsing Labour with the headline: "Give Wilson A Good Majority So That, This Time, There Can Be No Alibis."[39] Later, when the time came for Wilson to change his course, such all-out backing strengthened his hand against those groups which might have sought special conditions.

Nowhere was the shift in the center of gravity more evident

---

[37] See, for example, letters to *The Times* by Arthur Bryant *et al.*, January 20, 1967; and by Fred Hoyle, March 27, 1967.

[38] Butler and King, *General Election of 1966,* pp. 166-167.

[39] *Ibid.*, p. 162.

than in the sphere of promotional pressure group operation. There, vigorous activity took place, but predominantly on the pro-entry side. The groups favorable to Europe were well-organized, well-financed and frequently possessed a prominent and overlapping membership. One bloc of organizations came under the umbrella of the British Council of the European Movement. Its associated groups, many of them operating out of shared headquarters, included the following: United Europe Association, United Europe Movement, Federal Union, European League for Economic Cooperation, British Section of the Council of European Municipalities, European Luncheon Club, U.K. Section of the European Association of Teachers, European Atlantic Group, and Committee of Student European Associations.[40] The peak group included 332 MP's in its political section. Its chairman was Sir Edward Beddington-Behrens, and its various members and officers included prominent politicians, businessmen, and academics. The British Council groups were usually all-party organizations, with an open membership, their purpose being "to strengthen public support for British membership." Typical of their efforts was an Albert Hall Rally held by the British Council of the European Movement; it was attended by 3000 people and was addressed by prominent figures including George Brown (then Foreign Secretary and Deputy Prime Minister), Reginald Maudling (deputy leader of the Conservatives), and Sir Paul Chambers (Chairman of ICI).

There were other important groups on the pro-Europe side as well. The all-party Campaign for a European Political Community revived the 1961 Common Market Campaign. Under the chairmanship of Lord Gladwyn, it enlisted the support of numerous MP's, academics, civic leaders, and lawyers, and it undertook a national educational campaign, supplying speakers for party organizations, unions, and pro-

---

[40] For further details see information pamphlet of the British Council of the European Movement, *The European Movement in Britain* (London, 1967).

fessional groups. Finally there was the Labour Committee for Europe, which enlisted about 100 MP's plus peers and trade union leaders. It too called on HMG to apply for membership in the period prior to Britain's May 1967 commitment.

Only two bodies of any consequence remained on the anti-EEC side. One organization was John Paul's Anti-Common Market League, operating as it had during the Macmillan period, but much reduced in money, staff, and supporters. In the 1964 General Election it had run anti-Common Market Conservatives in three Tory-held constituencies, but polled an average of less than 3 percent of the vote and had no impact on the results. Since then the ACML had kept barely alive. Its resumed campaign could never approach the proportions of the 1962 effort and in any event would have had scant impact on the Labour Government. Furthermore, the Conservative Party had screened out opponents of the Common Market from among its parliamentary candidates and the right-wing anti-Common Market forces in Parliament had dwindled.

The other major anti-Common Market organization occupied an entrenched position within the PLP. Duly registered with the Party's Chief Whip, Britain and the Common Market had reconstituted itself along the lines of an earlier grouping, but without those members (e.g., Castle, Jay, Marsh) who had since entered the Government. Led by Lord Blyton, Alfred Morris, and Raymond Fletcher, it operated strictly within the Parliamentary Party, claiming 114 MP's as members, plus others in the House of Lords and tacit supporters within the Government. The organization placed great stress on observing the five conditions of September 1962, and on the preservation of British sovereignty, especially parliamentary sovereignty. It also reflected the variety of anti-European positions long held on the Labour left. As an alternative to the Common Market, some members of the group preferred ties to the EFTA and Commonwealth countries. However they were not primarily concerned with other options, for, in the words of John Mendelson, "The alternative to suicide is not to commit it."[41] The group operated an educational campaign and also provided a focus for opposition. For the basic reasons already cited as affecting the balance of forces within the PLP, the organization was unable to prevent Britain's application or to extract specific conditions.

During the three years following the January 1963 debacle, public and elite opinion in Britain became increasingly receptive to the prospect of Common Market entry. By the beginning of 1966, 66 percent of the public indicated it would approve a Government decision to join the Common Market, and throughout the year a consistent two-thirds or more maintained this disposition. Indeed, these respondents outnumbered those disapproving by margins ranging from at least four to one to as much as seven to one.[42] Elite sentiment was even stronger, ranging from 75 percent to perhaps 90 percent in favor.[43]

In the period preceding his November 1966 announcement, Wilson thus obtained reinforcement for the Common Market option. Public approval of entry stood anywhere from twenty to thirty-five percentage points higher than it had at the time Macmillan formulated his policy. Such solid approval implied a decided advantage for Wilson in dealing with domestic dissidents and special interests.

This support did not however stem from a deep-seated popular conviction. A detailed survey taken for *New Society*

---

[41] Interview, May 18, 1967.

[42] The peak came in May 1966 (approve, 70 percent; disapprove, 10 percent; don't know, 20 percent). *Gallup Political Index,* no. 73 (May, 1966), p. 65.

[43] Daniel Lerner and Morton Gorden, "A Decade of Challenge: The Responses of European Leaders" (Cambridge Mass.: MIT, Center for International Studies, August 1967), p. iv-6. (Mimeographed.) Also see Uwe Kitzinger, "Britain and Europe—today," *The Listener,* Vol. 77, no. 1977 (February 16, 1967). An October 1966 Gallup Poll of 411 persons drawn from *Who's Who* found that 90 percent approved of Common Market entry and only 6 percent disapproved. *Daily Telegraph,* October 24, 1966, cited in David Calleo, *Britain's Future* (New York: Horizon, 1968), p. 202.

in mid-1966 revealed that "the very substantial and increasing rock of opinion in favour of entry does not yet rest on a solid substratum of emotional commitment to Europe."[44] What this study revealed was that the attraction to Europe was economic rather than emotional. Issues such as damage to the Commonwealth, increased food costs, and perhaps the diminution of sovereignty presented definite dangers. While 66 percent expressed a general preference for EEC entry, the support fell sharply when specific matters were raised. Thus only 39 percent remained in favor if joining the Common Market would cause food prices to rise by 10 percent, and only 25 percent would still be in favor if it meant a weakening of ties with the Commonwealth. Other figures indicated that the British public preferred the Americans as allies, and trusted India more than the European countries, and France scarcely more than Russia.[45] Events proved confirmation of the *New Society* poll's implications. From January 1967 public support began to recede in the face of the increased salience of the issue. In March, about the time the Prime Minister was making his final decision, the margin of approval had declined to two to one (57 percent approving, 27 percent disapproving). But even this seemingly substantial preference evaporated, and following the Government's formal commitment on May 2, 1967, and the subsequent Parliamentary de

---

[44] Humphrey Taylor and Timothy Raison, "Britain Into Europe—General Attitudes," *New Society* (June 23, 1966), p. 8.

[45] Respondents were asked how much they trusted various countries. "Completely" (scored 1.0), "quite a lot" (.75), "don't know" (.5), "not very much" (.25), "not at all" (0.0). The following were the results:

Australia	0.87	Germany	0.38
Sweden	.73	Nigeria	.38
U.S.	.71	France	.26
India	.50	U.S.S.R.	.25
Italy	.39		

Ibid., June 16, 1966, pp. 6-7; also June 23, 1966. For more information on how the British elite viewed Europe in a relatively apolitical fashion, compared with French and German elites, see Lerner and Gorden, *op. cit.*, pp. iv-14 to iv-27; pp. vi-8 to vi-15.

bate, support for Common Market entry dropped to its lowest point in nearly five years: only 36 percent approved, while, for the first time in seven years of polling by the Gallup organization, a plurality of the public (41 percent) now disapproved.

A perhaps startling aspect of the public turnabout was the distribution of sentiment by political party. The Gallup figures indicated that a majority of Conservative voters (50 percent versus 32 percent) disapproved of entry, as did a plurality of the Liberals (45 percent versus 31 percent). In a reversal of the 1962 relationship, only Labour voters favored the Government's policy (45 percent for, 29 percent against.)[46] The implication is that Prime Minister Wilson had successfully stolen the European clothing of the other two parties; almost too successfully since the public now identified him as closely with Common Market entry as they had Macmillan in 1962. Fortunately for Wilson's freedom of manuever, the parliamentary opposition remained faithful to the Common Market policy. Without its support, the Prime Minister's position vis-à-vis various domestic interests and opponents would have lacked the reinforcement which sustained his relatively free hand.

TICIZATION: THE CAUSES

mbination of external events and conscious choices thrust Common Market option forward and caused it to be eated in a political manner. The urgency of the events, especially the collapse of alternatives, produced a propensity toward politicization, and the nature of Wilson's choices, particularly the decision to treat the European commitment as a major national departure, resulted in a politicization which was effective.

---

[46] *Daily Telegraph* (London), May 18, 1967.

EXTERNAL EVENTS

For the Labour Government, the progression toward Europe was a story of collapsing alternatives. Nowhere was this more evident than in the case of the Commonwealth. During 1962, the heart of Labour's opposition toward Macmillan's European effort had been a preference for the Commonwealth. This was especially manifest in Gaitskell's speeches during the autumn of 1962, and in Labour's 1964 General Election manifesto. However, a series of events combined to shatter Labour's almost mystical devotion to Commonwealth solutions. In April 1965 and again in September, fighting broke out between India and Pakistan. This damaged the existing fragile notion of Commonwealth unity, and the settlement to the conflict was later arranged not by the British as leaders of the Commonwealth, but by the Russians at Tashkent. In August 1965, the Labour Government aroused antagonism by making plans to limit Commonwealth immigration, and in the same month Singapore quit the Federation of Malaysia amid racial bitterness. In November, Rhodesia issued its Unilateral Declaration of Independence. When Britain failed to bring down the Smith regime by the method of economic sanctions, she met with bitter abuse from the African Commonwealth members, some of whom broke diplomatic relations with the U.K. over the issue. In early 1966, the first Nigerian coup took place, followed several months later by a second coup and then civil war, and in February 1966 the Ghanaian army took power while Nkrumah was on a visit to China. Adding to these happenings, Britain's own trade with the Commonwealth continued to decline. Prior to the 1964 election, Labour had criticized the Conservative Government for allowing the Commonwealth share of Britain's trade to fall from 44 to 30 percent, and pledged to seek a re-expansion,[47] yet by the year 1966, Britain's exports to the

[47] The Labour Party, *New Britain,* p. 19.

Commonwealth had fallen to a figure of 25.8 percent of her total exports, compared with 33.7 percent for EFTA and the EEC.[48] The Government's disillusion with Commonwealth possibilities in trade and as an influential world grouping was not long in coming. The March 1966 Labour manifesto contrasted strongly with the October 1964 document in its de-emphasis of the Commonwealth's importance.[49]

Another alternative conception had been the promotion of better relations with Eastern Europe. In 1964, Labour came to power with the notion of "Left talking to Left." Presumably a democratic socialist British government could communicate more readily with the Communist governments of Eastern Europe. Little developed from this notion, especially since Britain's importance in this sphere depended on her special relationship with the U.S. The transatlantic tie had weakened further with the coming to power of the Johnson Administration, hence the Russians and their allies had less use for Britain's cooperation. Wilson was making the same discovery as Macmillan: Britain possessed less and less ability to deal with the U.S. on a basis of partnership rather than subordination.

Finally, events in Western Europe also pointed in the direction of the Common Market option. Among the EFTA countries, the emergency imposition by Britain of a 15 percent surcharge on all imports created substantial resentment. The action was taken without prior consultation, and the head of the EFTA organization, a former British civil servant, was reported to have protested so vigorously against the surcharge that he was later edged out of his post. Simultaneously, British exports to the EEC, which had been increasing strongly despite the Community's unified tariff barriers, began to level off. This increase in exports, which had been 14 percent in 1963, fell to 3 percent in 1964 and 0.5 percent in 1965.

---

[48] *The Times,* May 1, 1967.
[49] Labour Party, *Time for Decision,* pp. 22-23.

Plainly, the U.K. could not hope to take further advantage of trading opportunities within the Common Market without becoming a member.

WILSON'S CHOICES

Just as Macmillan had done, Prime Minister Wilson exhausted other options before turning toward the EEC. In 1964, Labour had come to power with its own variant of the three circles conception of Winston Churchill. But the Commonwealth, Eastern Europe, and the Atlantic relationship proved to offer few possibilities. The realities of governing presented a different perspective than the realities of winning power. As oppositions are prone to do almost everywhere, the pre-1964 Labour Party had overestimated the freedom of maneuver open to the Government.[50] It did not take Wilson long to judge that the most realistic position for Britain to adopt was that of a European rather than a world power. In addition, seizing the European option offered Wilson the chance to "dish" the Tories by pre-empting an issue which Heath had been monopolizing, and the opportunity of appealing to certain social groups (e.g., technocrats) whose support Labour sought to attract.

The country's economic crisis lent urgency to the need for a reorientation of roles. Labour's most prominent election appeal had been that it was best qualified to modernize and to manage Britain's economic growth. Yet on taking office, the Labour Government faced a critical balance of payments

---

[50] James Callaghan, then Chancellor of the Exchequer, frankly admitted this point in his remarks during the May 1967 Common Market debate: "My experience over the last two and a half years has led me to the conclusion more and more that nations are not free at the moment to take their own decisions. This is becoming increasingly true, as I have observed in financial, economic and political matters . . . I have been struck by the effect of the international forums in the world today on the policies of individual countries, an effect which is much more than I had assumed before I took office. . . . " *Hansard,* Vol. 724 (May 9, 1967), c. 1302.

problem which forced it borrow heavily in order to support the pound. Then, in July 1966, the Government chose to sacrifice the National Plan and the Party's social priorities in order to prevent devaluation. Thus failing in the national context, it appeared logical to seize the possibility of attempting to break through the existing difficulties by joining with the Six. Wilson construed the economic question in a general sense, putting great stress on the new dynamic or "élan" that membership might create and on the broader base for technologically oriented industries with their massive research and development programs.[51] By contrast, the economic motivations of the Conservative Government during the late 1950's and early 1960's had been the narrower aims of avoiding trade discrimination and of competing on the basis of equality within the growing markets of the Six.[52]

As pressing as the economic reasons were, they did not constitute the fundamental basis of the case for entry. Indeed, Wilson specifically denied that British entry could provide an automatic solution to economic problems.[53] For Wilson and George Brown, the real impetus was political. This was the choice which set apart Wilson's approach from Macmillan's, and which determined the effective politicization of the Common Market issue. Wilson had made a conscious choice to emphasize Europe, not to disguise it as a commercial deal. In his statement of May 2, the Prime Minister made this quite obvious:

But whatever the economic arguments, the House will realise that, as I have repeatedly made clear, the Government's purpose derives above all from our recognition that Europe is now faced with the opportunity of a great move forward in political unity and that we can—and indeed we must—play our full part in it.[54]

---

[51] See the comments by Harold Wilson, *Hansard,* Vol. 724 (May 8, 1967), c. 1082.

[52] Camps, *op. cit.,* pp. 158-159.

[53] *Hansard,* Vol. 724 (May 8, 1967) c. 1062-1063.

[54] Cmnd. 3269, p. 5.

On another occasion he reaffirmed the political motive and conceived of Britain playing a leading part in "an independent Europe able to exert far more influence in world affairs than at any time in our generation."[55] The Foreign Secretary further emphasized this commitment during a Parliamentary debate, observing that, "In the last analysis, our decision to negotiate our entry into the European Communities is basically a political one."[56]

POLITICIZATION: THE EFFECTS

THE ATROPHY OF FUNCTIONAL REPRESENTATION

Sectional pressure groups normally occupied a formidable political position. The Labour Government consistently based its domestic actions on intimate consultations with non-parliamentary groups such as the CBI and TUC. The only groups that received no consultation appeared to be the Labour back-bench MP's and the Party's National Executive Committee. For instance, when proposals on incomes policy were put forward, these were so settled by the process of bargaining that almost no room remained for MP's to exercise any influence short of bringing down the Government.[57] And yet despite their virtually unparalleled ascendency in domestic economic policy, the sectional pressure groups found themselves in a position of unprecedented weakness when it came to influencing Britain's European policy.

The foremost example of this changed relationship was shown by the National Farmers' Union, an organization which had played an intimate role in European policy during 1956-58 and a decreased but still significant part in 1961-62. By 1966, the NFU encountered a serious erosion of its political position, caused by bipartisan agreement, the existence of a

---

55 *Hansard,* Vol. 724 (May 8, 1967), c. 1094.

56 *Ibid.* (May 10, 1967), c. 1516.

57 See especially *The Times,* February 24, 1967; also April 17, 1967.

Labour Government, and, above all, the enhanced and effective political importance of Europe as a national issue. Since it appeared increasingly evident that the Government would have wide support if it decided to seek accession to the Common Market, the NFU was faced with the necessity of coming to terms as best it could. Britain's agricultural support system seemed likely to undergo basic changes regardless of the European question, and the highly enthusiastic report of the CBI threatened to leave the NFU out on a limb. Conviction as well as self-interest predisposed the organization to alter its policy. Larger farmers, younger men, and producers of corn and beef now tended to see definite advantages for themselves should Britain enter the Common Market. Another important change was that G. T. Williams replaced a resolute anti-European, Sir Harold Woolley, as President during the spring of 1966.

Accommodating itself to HMG's policy, the NFU issued a report during November 1966 in which the President emphasized that the group was not opposed to British membership nor sought changes in the Rome Treaty. Williams pledged that the NFU would be "realistic and constructive" in its approach and would "certainly not obstruct the national interest."[58] Instead, the NFU's main concern was in altering the regulations which the Six had adopted to suit their own agricultural needs. It was the Union's view that "acceptance of the present EEC regulations would have grave consequences for large sections of British agriculture."[59]

More than any other single factor, the NFU feared loss of influence. This fear was evident in its memorandum issued

---

[58] National Farmers' Union Information Service, *British Agriculture and the Common Market* (London, November, 1966), pp. 1-2.

[59] *Ibid.*, pp. 34-35. Italics in original. The NFU identified the following disadvantages: (1) greater price fluctuations; (2) ending of direct production grants; (3) increased grain costs for animal feed; (4) damage to large sectors of horticulture; (5) no regulation for potatoes, sheep and wool; (6) "the opportunity for the industry to influence the formulation and execution of agricultural policy would be greatly diminished."

during the March 1966 General Election and was explicit in the November statement, which urged that the enlarged Common Market incorporate an annual review. Even more than in 1962, the Union also sought to tie its own interest in with that of the nation. Rather than concentrating on the damage to sectors such as horticulture, it focused on the balance of payments problem and on the expected rise in consumer food prices of 25 shillings per week for a family of four (with the effect this would have on living and wage costs and export competitiveness).[60] Yet despite efforts to come to terms with HMG on the Common Market issue, and close consultation with the Minister of Agriculture, who shared the NFU's reservations, the Union failed to extract any specific pledge concerning modifications in EEC agricultural regulations. As noted below, the NFU, along with the other major interest groups, was fobbed off on a DEA Consultative Committee which proved to be of little value as a channel for influencing policy.

Another major sectional group, the TUC, had never played a powerful role in prior European deliberations of the Conservative Government, but had obtained detailed and intimate consultations. During 1962 its policy had been more favorable toward Europe than that of the Labour Party, and the ensuing four years had somewhat augmented this attitude. While the trade unions remained divided on the European question, most members of the TUC's Economic Committee saw the European inhibitions as outdated. Those concerns which the TUC did express involved details of capital movement, regional planning, food prices, labor mobility, and social

---

[60] The NFU position reflected the realities. An independent study by a British agricultural economist concluded, "Taken as a whole, British farmers have little to fear . . . though some of them may suffer while others gain substantially." The balance of payments, not farmer income, was the main agricultural stumbling block. T. Kempinski, "Entry Into the European Common Market and British Agricultural Income," University of Manchester, Department of Agricultural Economics, Bulletin no. 114, November 1966, p. 19.

services, rather than the general wisdom of Common Market entry.

TUC consultations on prices and incomes policy had involved genuine negotiations and actual alteration of White Papers before these were presented by the Government. No such situation existed for the Common Market question. The trade unions were less concerned with Europe—George Woodcock, the General Secretary, described his own feeling as "passionless"[61]—and the Government was not inclined to grant them a major role. During 1965-66, members of the Economic Committee met occasionally with individual ministers to discuss specific policy concerns, and in late 1966 five trade union leaders joined the Industrial Consultative Committee attached to the DEA. The effectiveness of these governmental consultations was limited; they did not result in any significant alteration of the Government's European application. The TUC may have found as much relevance in its representation on the CBI body studying the industrial effects of joining the Common Market, and in developing its ties with the Six's trade union organization, the European Community Trade Union Secretariat (ECTUS). Eventually, despite the fact that its consultations with the Government involved little in the nature of bargaining, the TUC Economic Committee supported the Common Market application.[62]

The Confederation of British Industries, which had been formed by the 1965 merger of the FBI, BEC, and NUM, had few reservations to press upon the Government. Rather it was in the position of urging the Government to adopt the policy of Common Market entry. The CBI leadership held an enthusiastic pro-European attitude, which was especially manifest in the important and highly publicized report the organization issued in December 1966. The main conclusions were that entry would entail a "clear and progressive balance of

---

[61] *The Guardian,* September 8, 1967.
[62] Trades Union Congress, *Industrial News,* May 10, 1967.

advantage" for British industry, that the Treaty of Rome and the Community's method of operation were acceptable given a reasonable transition, and that entry should be negotiated as soon as possible. The report found potential advantages of dynamic growth, technological cooperation, size of market, investment, and competitive stimulus. There would be a short-term problem of increased costs and competition at home, and possible difficulties with the agricultural levy system, but these and other problems could be dealt with satisfactorily.[63] British industry appeared to have agreed with these conclusions; within two months, eleven of twelve regional councils had debated the report, all of them supporting it by overwhelming majorities.[64] The content and fervor of industry's position thus committed it so overwhelmingly to Common Market entry that the Government had little compulsion for seeking to bargain in detail.

The general predicament of the sectional groups was reflected in the creation and operation of the Industrial Consultative Committee on the Approach to Europe. This body originated in a speech by the Prime Minister at the Lord Mayor of London's banquet a few days after his November 10, 1966 announcement of exploratory talks with the Six. Wilson said that the coming European moves would require "the closest cooperation and consultation with industry";[65] therefore, he had instructed Michael Stewart to approach representative bodies in industry for the purpose of establishing a committee through the DEA. Within a few weeks, prominent individuals were nominated by the CBI, TUC, ABCC, Cooperative Union, and other economic and financial bodies. Of twenty-one Committee members, two were Government

[63] Confederation of British Industries, *Britain and Europe—Volume I: An Industrial Reappraisal* (London, December, 1966).

[64] Letter from Stephen Brown, President of the CBI, to *The Times*, February 18, 1967.

[65] Department of Economic Affairs, Press Notice, no. 231, December 8, 1966.

Ministers, seven represented the leading business and financial institutions, four were trade unionists, two were heads of nationalized industries (coal and steel), and one each came from the leadership of the NEDC, CBI, NFU, TUC, Cooperative Union, and London Chamber of Commerce.

The Committee's prestigious participants gathered a total of three times between early December 1966 and late March 1967. While their function might have been the two-way exchange of views implicit in Wilson's description of "closest cooperation and consultation," the enterprise became scarcely more than an exercise in high-level briefing and hand-holding. The first meeting entailed a Ministerial explanation of what the Common Market probe entailed, while the two subsequent meetings were further progress reports on the visits to Common Market capitals by the Prime Minister and Foreign Secretary. Obviously the Committee was too large for any meaningful exchanges to take place. Thus, TUC representatives expressed frustration at the lack of information given out by Michael Stewart, and one union official commenting on the size of the group observed that "it represents every organization but the National Society of Dog Catchers."[66] Other representatives described the consultations as unsatisfactory and meaningless. Not surprisingly the Committee lapsed into disuse following its third session. HMG had been willing and able to occupy the sectional interests with this harmless activity in order to keep its hands free in the preliminary contacts with the Six and in the initial formulation of Britain's bargaining position. Eventually, whatever technical consultations were necessary would take place through Ministerial contacts with individual representatives, or through the production department system in the BOT or Treasury.[67] These contacts would inevitably involve technical

____

[66] *The Times,* April 10, 1967.

[67] The production department system was especially used during World War II, enabling each trade association to have a "pigeon-hole" in one of the ministries. In Common Market negotiations, the Government

minutiae and not the making of policy or the imposition of conditions.

CONDITIONS OF MEMBERSHIP

The most important change in European policy compared with 1961 was the ability of HMG to make its application relatively free of restrictive conditions. The erosion of the Conservative Government's three conditions of 1961 (EFTA, Commonwealth, and agriculture), and of Labour's five conditions of 1962 (the above three plus independence in foreign policy and economic planning), reflects this shift. What then was the residual status of these conditions? First, the concern for an independent foreign policy had largely evaporated. De Gaulle's freedom, increasing *détente,* and the demise of the supranational element (especially after the 1966 Luxembourg Declaration)[68] satisfied even many critics of Common Market entry. Second, the EFTA problem had also faded. In the 1961 London Declaration, Britain had pledged not to join the Common Market unless arrangements were made to meet the needs of the Seven. However, at a London meeting on December 5, 1966, the leaders of EFTA countries agreed only to close consultation and coordination of their approaches to the EEC. Among the members, Denmark and Norway sought Common Market entry, with the other countries being interested in some form of associational agreement. In April 1967 the London Declaration was allowed to lapse by mutual agreement, even though Britain refused to pledge that she would not later agree to tariff discrimination against her former partners.[69] A third condition, the right to independent management of the economy remained a concern of the *Tribune*

---

would be likely to explore these channels in order to learn how various proposals under negotiation would affect various sectors of industry.

[68] The Luxemburg Declaration of the Six came in response to French pressures and provided that no member could be overruled on a majority vote where a question of genuine national interest was involved.

[69] *The Times,* April 27 and 29, 1967. A compromise arrangement stated that the UK would grant the Seven "sufficient transitional periods"

group, but for Wilson and Brown the spirit of the Rome Treaty, the existence of French indicative planning, and the inevitable limitations caused by international monetary problems and by membershp of EFTA made this no cause for special attention. Fourth, even the Commonwealth no longer presented the kind of obstacle previously considered. The series of events since 1963 had produced a pervasive disenchantment, and this implied less need for special arrangements should Britain enter the EEC. This fifth and final point, agriculture, constituted the only remaining major item among the original five conditions. While the adoption of the Community's Common Agricultural Policy and accompanying system of operation would not necessarily harm British farmers, it would eventually create a 10 to 14 percent rise in domestic food prices (hence a 2.5–3.5 percent increase in living costs) and a harmful drain on the balance of payments of £175–250 million per year.

HMG made few specific commitments prior to the negotiations. Having opted for EEC entry, Wilson was absolutely determined in his course, and in essence predisposed to accept almost any conditions in order to gain membership. Thus in announcing Britain's outright application, Wilson cited as objects of negotiations only a "small number of really important issues . . . on which agreement should be reached if the House and the country are to be satisfied that essential British and Commonwealth interests will be safeguarded."[70] The most central of these issues was the Common Agricultural Policy, but on this, Wilson's main request was for an adequate transitional period. He made no pledge to seek the retention of the British system of deficiency payments, nor to prevent the demise of domestic horticulture. He also stated that the financial arrangements for agriculture would involve an "inequitable" sharing of costs and a burden on Britain's balance

---

before participating fully in the Common Market should they need reasonable opportunity to conclude their own negotiations.

[70] Cmnd. 3269, p. 4.

of payments which she should not in fairness be asked to bear.[71] For the Commonwealth, which in 1961 had elicited from Heath a country by country listing and an insistence on the principle of "comparative outlets," the Prime Minister pledged only to seek safeguards for New Zealand and for countries covered by the Commonwealth Sugar Agreement. He also made passing reference to the problems of capital movement and regional policies. Unlike the relatively negative tone of Macmillan's July 1961 announcement and of prior Labour Party pronouncements, the Government's attitude was not one which implied that entry would be impossible unless certain British conditions were satisfied; rather, Wilson affirmed that while these were major issues, "I . . . believe that there is nothing either in the Treaty of Rome or in the practical working of the Community which need make them insoluble."[72] The basically unqualified nature of the British application was best characterized by the Foreign Minister, George Brown, on the last day of Parliamentary debate. "We shall make our application short, clear, positive and to the point. In the application there will be no 'ifs' and 'buts', no conditions or stipulations. We shall apply to join."[73]

CONCLUSION

One lesson suggested by analysis of the 1966-67 period is that the perceived precedence of external–international factors dictated that the European approach would be unimpeded by conditions. During the first effort at EEC entry the Macmillan Government acknowledged no such predominance in the external sphere and devoted more attention to domestic "con-

---

[71] *Ibid.*, pp. 3-4. Britain would have been required to exact levies on all her agricultural imports from non-EEC countries, then pay 90 percent of these revenues into the European Agricultural Guidance and Guarantee Fund. As a heavy importer of food, Britain's contribution to the Fund would have been twice as great as that of any other member.

[72] *Ibid.*, p. 5.

[73] *Hansard*, Vol. 724 (May 10, 1967), c. 1513-1514.

sensus" than to international "compatibility."[74] In the case of the Wilson approach, the necessity to avoid giving de Gaulle a genuine pretext for another veto meant that considerations in the domestic sphere had to be relegated to a lesser role, which implied the demise of functional representation. Several factors facilitated this domestic de-emphasis. To begin with, the situation within the parties was far more favorable than it had been in 1961. The erosion of the five conditions and accompanying change of attitude had left the Labour Party willing to accept a bid for Common Market entry. In turn, the Conservatives were completely committed to Europe, a policy on which they had campaigned in the 1966 General Election. Because of these attitudes—especially the assurance of Opposition support—Prime Minister Wilson's hand was greatly strengthened. He did not need to seek every possible bit of extra backing which the pressure groups could supply, and he faced no necessity for encumbering Britain's application with safeguards and conditions in order to bid for the support of these and other domestic blocs. In addition, Wilson himself, as a Labourite, was not burdened with a party constituency in which agriculture and business occupied positions of prominence. Finally, elite sentiment was overwhelmingly favorable, and public opinion had become conditioned to the prospect of membership. This allowed a more direct treatment of Common Market entry with less need to disguise its political implications.

Labelling the changed treatment as effective politicization implies that a broadly construed national interest became the dominant concern, and as such transcended the previous pattern whereby sectional pressure groups had enjoyed a concurrent majority status or at least exercised effective bargaining power in a situation where Britain's national interest seemed

---

[74] The terms are those of Wolfram F. Hanrieder, "Compatibility and Consensus: A Proposal for the Conceptual Linkage of External and Internal Dimensions of Foreign Policy," *American Political Science Review*, 61, no. 4 (December, 1967): 971-982.

a more diffuse consideration. As in the case of the 1961 Common Market application, political authorities had again made the crucial decision in advance of, or without real regard for, the sectional pressure groups' strong articulation of their positions. Unlike the earlier application, however, politicization continued beyond the initial decision period and thus shaped the context in which the actual terms of the application were formulated.

Chapter 10

Conclusion

Before going on to reconsider the status of the theoretical propositions set forth at the start of this work, it will be useful to review the salient points which emerge from the actual events in the successive periods of Britain's European policy-making.

THE CONTEXT OF POLICY FORMULATION

During the period of policy-making for the Free Trade Area and then the European Free Trade Association, neither external events nor the choices of party or governmental leaders compelled a political treatment of the European issues. In these years, from 1956 to 1960, the three indicators reflected this lack of politicization. First, at the administrative level, policy formation and international negotiations were undertaken primarily by the Board of Trade with some participation by the Treasury. The Foreign Office did not take part. Second, generalized debate and participation by the broader public were largely absent. The mass press gave only minor coverage to the FTA and EFTA compared with its later handling of the Common Market question. Even promotional groups played little role. Third, the parties remained largely uninvolved. This was the case for several reasons; among them the tendency of the parties to share similar official attitudes, and widespread perception of the subject of European unity as economic in content.[1]

In the formation of its European policy, the British Government functioned between two sets of constraints. One was the international situation, especially the attitude of the Six and the position of France; the other, the interplay of domestic pressures. Between 1956 and 1958 (the FTA period), the Government concentrated on the domestic side. Because the more usual foreign policy constituency of parties, the press, and public opinion remained relatively uninvolved, policy thus proceeded through the channel of functional representation rather than that of party government. The Government saw as its main task the need to bargain for the cooperation of the major sectional interests, and as was normally the case in domestic matters, the FBI, NFU, and TUC enjoyed concurrent majority status, a position which they had been remarkably explicit in demanding.[2] The making of European policy went forward on a relatively economic and technical plane, with the Government choosing to exclude agriculture from the proposed FTA, a course strongly urged by the NFU and supported by the FBI, and seeking a relatively limited European arrangement. Most of the European countries wanted Britain in Europe for political reasons, but France was unwilling to pay Britain's price. The question then is why the U.K. required such a price, which was ultimately to preclude the successful establishment of a European-wide FTA. The

---

[1] For example, Edward Heath told the 1960 Conservative Conference that the Government had sought to create the FTA and EFTA "for economic reasons." National Union of Conservative and Unionist Associations, *79th Annual Conservative Conference* (October 12-15, 1960), p. 62.

[2] E.g., the TUC General Council stated on one occasion, with reference to the sending of a policy document to the government: "Observance of these principles is necessary *if there is to be in this country that measure of national agreement which a long term commitment of this kind requires.*" TUC, *Report of Proceedings at the 90th Annual Trades Union Congress* (1958), pp. 446-447; italics added.

answer is to be found in the requirements of British pressure group politics.

From 1958 to 1960 (the EFTA period), the sectional organizations again played an intimate role in the shaping of policy, one which went well beyond a mere veto power. The FBI actually had a prominent role in organizing the EFTA with its Scandinavian counterparts during the winter of 1958-59 before Government officials stepped into the picture. The NFU also cooperated intimately in this undertaking. While the groups did not exert a negative force, they did contribute to the formulation of a policy perhaps not entirely in Britain's interest. That is, the EFTA was put together on a largely technical basis with scant regard for its long-range political implications, both positive and negative. A more searching political judgment would have been desirable at this time in order to make these calculations. Had HMG placed less emphasis on domestic concerns than international ones, it might have found it advantageous to include agriculture in the original FTA proposal and perhaps not to undertake creation of the EFTA.

In the case of Britain's first Common Market application, during the period 1961-63, the subject of European unity did become relatively politicized in treatment. Thus we find that, first, the European negotiations were no longer handled by ministers with primarily economic departmental responsibilities, but by Edward Heath, then second in command at the Foreign Office. Second, the broader public was drawn into the debate. Promotional pressure group activity became widespread; mass circulation papers such as the *Daily Mirror* and *Daily Express* launched strident campaigns for and against entry; and polls and by-elections reflected the Common Market's position as a highly visible subject of debate. Third, the political parties became deeply involved and even made Europe a matter of partisan contention.

Given the nature of these symptoms of active politicization, the sectional groups should theoretically have been inactive or unimportant. Yet, following Macmillan's political decision to negotiate for EEC entry, they managed to reassert their role in the post-July 1961 phase. One logical explanation for this unexpected development is that while the party government channel became the dominant means of communication between government and society on the Common Market subject during 1961-63, the channel of functional representation continued to operate as a pathway for sectional interests.

Several factors facilitated the persistence of functional representation. To begin with, the Government sought to negotiate as though Britain were a participant in the Common Market at the time of its inception, that is *à sept,* rather than as an individual country facing a more or less unified group of six. The implication of this was an exaggerated emphasis on technical details of trade and commerce—a natural area for specialized sectional pressure group attention. Next, the Commonwealth myth remained exceedingly powerful at this time. This required that Britain negotiate for the Commonwealth at Brussels; a further factor producing protracted and specialized bargaining. Finally, the Government conducted negotiations in a "glass house" atmosphere. The resultant publicity required Britain's chief negotiator to exchange memoranda and meetings with aggrieved groups following each detailed arrangement adversely affecting their interests.

Surprisingly, the party government process also functioned to facilitate the assertion of group interest. Normally, British sectional pressure groups concentrate their efforts upon the administration; however, in this instance they were able to exert influence via the parties as well. Because the Conservative constituency was composed very considerably of the agricultural, industrial, and commercial portions of the society, this made it possible to supplement the voice those sectors would normally have had through functional channels. More fundamentally, the increasing opposition to Common Market entry by the Labour Party enhanced the significance of sectional demands because, lacking bipartisan reinforcement for a major foreign policy departure, the Government needed to gather as much other backing as possible.

Prime Minister Macmillan made a series of choices which had much to do with the creation of these circumstances. The most important of his decisions was to treat Common Market entry as a more or less economic issue, de-emphasizing its fundamental political implications, especially the basic re-orientation of Britain away from the U.S. and Commonwealth and toward much closer ties with France and Germany. This is not to say that Macmillan, and Conservative leaders, were unaware of these implications,[3] for, as we have seen, the actual decision to seek entry was treated as highly political, and was made before sectional pressure groups strongly articulated their own interests. However Macmillan tried to edge the Common Market decision past domestic opposition "by disguising his strategic choice as a commercial deal."[4] The consequence of this approach was to preserve a certain amount of group access via functional representation. While it is also true that the absence of bipartisanship encouraged group access via the party government process,[5] the fact remains that the Prime Minister himself bore some responsibility for this because he made little effort to carry the Labour Party with him.

Why did Macmillan choose to de-emphasize the Common Market issue? One reason was that he had been accustomed to

---

[3] There have been numerous assertions of the political motivation. For example, Edward Heath has explicitly stated that the impetus for the Common Market application was political. *The Times* (London), March 22, 1967.

[4] Richard E. Neustadt, "Whitehouse and Whitehall," Paper delivered at the 1965 Annual Meeting of the American Political Science Association, Washington, D.C., September 8-11, p. 9.

[5] Finer describes this kind of situation, where there is straight party alignment, as one where the chances of pressure group success are indeterminate. Had there been bipartisan agreement in support of the Government, there would be no prospect of success for a pressure group opposed to ministerial policy. *Anonymous Empire* (London: Pall Mall Press, 1958), pp. 75-81.

leading the Tories forward by backing into new policies and by temperament or choice did not seek to cast the European issue as a great break with the past. The attribution of this kind of approach to Macmillan is not merely an effort to second-guess the tactics of a shrewd politician. The fact is that respondents interviewed for the present study agreed overwhelmingly that the Prime Minister characteristically preferred to avoid direct confrontations. What seems additionally significant here is the convergence of various viewpoints. Respondents sympathetic to Harold Macmillan referred to him as a man of consummate "subtlety," while critics judged him to be "devious." These characterizations reflect different evaluations of a single underlying dimension, and the Prime Minister's record in the liquidation of the Suez enterprise, the retreat from Africa, and the introduction of economic planning provide concrete illustrations. Still another reason for Macmillan's choice was that he faced the prospect of some reluctance on the part of the two major parties. His own Conservatives were wary of policy departures which would affect such items of deep-seated party attachment as the Commonwealth, sovereignty and agriculture. The opposition Labourites could be expected to display distrust toward a European structure which some of them viewed as Conservative, Catholic, and capitalistic. Hence an approach to Europe which de-emphasized the broader political implications offered the opportunity for keeping the issue on what appeared to be an easier, more economic, plane. Finally, the Prime Minister feared that the British bargaining position at Brussels would be damaged if the Government appeared overly eager for Common Market membership. In any event, it was not until September 1962 that he undertook to treat Common Market entry as an issue of transcendent national importance, and attempted a systematic mobilization of public opinion.

The relationship between domestic and international forces is especially visible in the 1961–1963 period, where Macmillan became increasingly trapped between domestic

Conclusion

political needs and the necessities of the Brussels negotiations. An easier domestic situation would have allowed the Government to accept the Rome Treaty more unreservedly. This in turn would have facilitated mutual concessions by the Six and the possibility of a speedier course for the negotiations. However, as Kenneth Waltz has observed, Macmillan failed to confront the European issue as one which went against long-existing national notions.[6] Instead, in order to gain domestic approval for Common Market entry, he pledged to obtain safeguards which were virtually incompatible with full British membership in the EEC.[7] Public opinion did not dictate the British reservations; they were established on the basis of consultations with the major interests.[8] The consequences of this approach were to hinder the negotiations at Brussels, and then to undercut the Government's domestic position because the necessary retreat from the initial conditions was interpreted at home as a series of surrenders. These difficulties facilitated the subsequent de Gaulle veto.

Lest this explanation appear too determinist, there is a third dimension which requires mention. This was the sphere of the Government's room for maneuver between the constraints imposed by the domestic and international circumstances. Here Macmillan and the Government made a series of mistakes which worsened the situation. Initially, they were late in realizing the importance and the dynamic of the whole European movement. They delayed in taking the Six seriously and for a long time viewed the European movement on a mainly economic basis. In addition, they seriously overestimated their bargaining position. Efforts to separate the Five

---

[6] *Foreign Policy and Democratic Politics: The American and British Experience* (Boston: Little Brown, 1967), p. 266.

[7] For example, the agricultural terms which Heath asked for at Paris on October 10, 1961. These included a 12- to 15-year transition period, protection of horticulture, and British retention of the right to safeguard agricultural standards of living. (See Chap. 5.)

[8] Lord Windlesham makes this point effectively. *Communication and Political Power* (London: Jonathan Cape, 1966), p. 158.

from France during negotiations were a failure, and made the
Six less willing to offer concessions. Next, the Government
made its own concessions late and often surreptitiously. These
were frequently done too begrudgingly to suit what the Europeans saw as obvious requirements of membership in the
EEC, and at the same time irritated interests within Britain.
Finally, when entry was decided upon, a recognition of the
implications of becoming "European" should have required
that Britain re-evaluate her transatlantic ties. However this
was not done, and the Nassau Agreements of December 1962
called special attention to Britain's American connection,
providing still another impetus for de Gaulle's veto.

During the period following the actual decision to seek
EEC entry, the sectional groups managed to maintain a role
approximating a concurrent majority. While the FBI neither
caused nor obstructed the Common Market decision and negotiations, outright hostility on the part of business would
definitely have prevented the undertaking of the Common
Market venture. The TUC was not deeply involved, and
while it lacked a bargaining relationship with HMG, it did
obtain substantial consultation. The NFU, havng the most to
lose, exerted the greatest influence upon the British position.
While the farmers could not veto entry in itself, they did
succeed in shaping the conditions under which the Government sought that entry, thereby contributing substantially to
delays at Brussels and to the eventual undermining of the
Government's position. Had the NFU been pro-Common
Market, HMG's freedom of maneuver would have been far
greater. While no major group sought to prevent the decision
to seek entry, groups did play a major role once this decision
had been taken and the negotiating position was being established. Although politicization assured the dominance of the
party government mechanism, this did not prevent substantial pressure group influence. Because of politicization the
interests could only lay direct claim to portions of the European issue (trade, full employment, agricultural arrange-

ments) rather than an inherent involvement in the central political issue of whether Britain should merge her destiny with that of the Europeans. But due to the incomplete nature of this politicization, these groups still managed to exercise a concurrent majority role in the formulation of Britain's negotiating policy.

The orientation of the Wilson Government toward Europe offers some useful contrasts to the 1956–60 and 1961–63 periods. During the 1966–67 attempt at Common Market entry, the effectiveness of politicization rendered group interests insignificant. Unlike Macmillan's effort, Harold Wilson's approach to Europe was thus unimpeded by the requirements of pressure group politics.

This difference of approach resulted from a combination of external events and conscious choices. The urgency of the events, especially the collapse of alternatives, produced a strong propensity toward politicization; and the nature of Wilson's choices, particularly the decision to treat the European commitment as a major national departure, resulted in a politicization which was effective.

Sectional pressure groups therefore found themselves in a position of unprecedented weakness. Effective politicization essentially had closed the channel of functional representation, and a number of conditions, the most important of which was the existence of bipartisan agreement over European policy, discouraged group access through the channel of party government. Unlike Macmillan, Wilson made no pledges to pressure groups; he also sought entry with far fewer conditions. The sectional interests found themselves fobbed off upon a consultative committee operating through the Department of Economic Affairs, and providing them with occasional briefings and only *pro forma* consultation rather than genuine bargaining. Groups could still influence lesser technicalities but they were left without a vestige of concurrent majority powers.

POLITICIZATION AND GROUP INFLUENCE

In the light of the empirical evidence, let us examine the theoretical conceptions put forward in Chapter 1. First, does the sectional pressure groups' domestic corporatist role, as expressed by the concurrent majority notion, carry over into the making of foreign policy? The evidence from successive phases of European policy making between 1956 and 1967 is that it does unless the issue becomes politicized. However the relationship between group influence and politicization is somewhat more complex than was initially assumed. In particular, the presence of all three indicators of politicization does not in itself determine whether politicization will actually be effective. The evidence of the period following Macmillan's July 1961 announcement is that if political authorities do not consciously choose to treat the issue as broadly political, so that considerations of broad national interest take precedence, the sectional interests are likely to reassert their involvement in a situation where cost and benefit calculations of the effect on various groupings become important criteria for judgment.

The question of bipartisanship also assumes a somewhat greater importance in the limitation of group influence than had been expected. As we have seen, Macmillan's hand was weakened by the lack of Labour Party backing in 1961–63 This situation forced him to seek additional support by making a succession of pledges, and it generally facilitated a measure of pressure group access via the party government process (as opposed to the normal concentration of these groups on the administrative departments of government by means of functional representation). In contrast, Prime Minister Wilson was strengthened by Opposition support for Common Market entry in 1966–67.[9] Nonetheless, it would be

---

[9] Indeed, Conservative Party support was still more significant at the time Wilson began the 1969-70 application because public opinion had become at least temporarily hostile to Common Market entry.

wrong to conclude from this that simple bipartisanship, rather than the more complex hypothesis involving politicization, best accounts for restricted pressure group access. The simpler explanation proves inadequate when applied to the entire 1956–60 period, when bipartisanship coexisted with an exceedingly high group access. To put the question of bipartisan accord into perspective, it must be recognized that bipartisanship is one of several elements which determine whether politicization in a given situation will be effective.

At this point it may be useful to express more systematically the relationship between group influence and politicization. The most obvious fact is that there exists a continuum of declining pressure group influence in the period analyzed here. The groups' high standing in the first phase, that of FTA and EFTA in 1956–60[10] corresponds with non-politicization and is quite similar to their customary influence in domestic politics (e.g., in the operation of the National Health Service, NHS). In the second phase, Macmillan's 1961–63 Common Market application, the groups preserved substantial influence in a setting which was not effectively politicized. Finally, with the Wilson approach, groups were deprived of their power in a setting of effective politicization. The relationship is perhaps more clearly expressed by the comparison of group influence and politicization in Figure 2.

Variations according to one criterion largely coincide with those according to the other; that is, group influence is inversely proportional to politicization.

In an effort to be more precise, it is also worth trying to gauge the magnitude of the decline in sectional pressure group influence over the three successive phases of European policy-making in order to suggest some quantitative support for the proposition that sectional pressure groups lose their concurrent majority power with the onset of effective politicization.

---

[10] The 1956-58 and 1958-60 periods are grouped together since the basic relationships in both are quite similar.

One promising line of approach is offered by the definition
of power which Robert Dahl suggests in the hope that it may
possess enough rigor for operational use.[11] Dahl defines power
as the capacity to shift the probability of outcomes. This
definition presents the opportunity for at least a crude calculation of individual or group power. Being careful to observe
the necessity for distinguishing association from cause, Dahl
represents the amount of an actor's power by a probability

		No	*Politicization* Yes, but Ineffective	Complete
Group Influence	High	Normal domestic (*e.g.NHS*) FTA & EFTA 1956-60	XXXX	XXXX
	Medium	XXXX	EEC 1961-62	XXXX
	Low	XXXX	XXXX	EEC 1966-67

(Figure 2)

statement. He defines the actor's power as equal to the difference in the probability of an event, given some action by him,
and the probability of an event given no such action.[12] Thus
if the probability that the U.S. Senate will vote to increase
taxes if the President makes a nationally televised appeal for

[11] Robert Dahl, "The Concept of Power," *Behavioral Science*, 2
(1957): 201-215.
[12] "The power of an actor, A, would seem to be adequately defined
by the measure M which is the difference in the probability of an event,
given certain action by A, and the probability of the event given no such
action by A," *ibid.*, p. 214.

a tax increase is 0.4, and the probability if he does not make the appeal is 0.1, then the President's "power" equals 0.4 minus 0.1, or 0.3.[13]

Attempting to apply this scheme in the British context, it is useful to examine the clearest case of group influence, that of the NFU. Let us assume that the probability of HMG adopting the exclusion of agriculture from European arrangements during the 1956–58 period if the NFU made a strong appeal for this course was perhaps 0.9, and the probability had the NFU not made such an appeal was 0.3. Thus the NFU's power during that period was in the order of 0.9 minus 0.3, or 0.6. Of course these figures are in no way precise, but they do reflect relative orders of magnitude and therefore possess at least heuristic value.[14] The above figure of 0.9 reflects the fact that the exclusion of agriculture from the FTA was highly likely (in fact, that is what occurred). The figure of 0.3 also has some validity, since a disinterested appraisal of Britain's overall interests at the time could well have produced the conclusion that agriculture should have been included because the Europeans (especially the French) wanted this, and their support was necessary for the creation of the FTA. Finally, the calculation of 0.6 as the indicator of NFU power means that the British farming community[15] exerted a very considerable influence. (A figure of 1.0 would have reflected absolute determination of the outcome, a figure of 0.0 a state of absolute powerlessness.)

---

[13] *Ibid.*, p. 204.

[14] While these assignments of probability are obviously arbitrary, an effective case for the practice of pinning numbers on ordered categories has been made by Edward Tuftee, "Improving Data Analysis in Political Science," *World Politics*, 21, no. 4 (July, 1969) 644-646. He argues that "the researcher often knows more about the phenomenon than the mere ordering of observations implies; thus assigning numbers helps to build that additional information into measurement. . . . Of course it is arbitrary. The point, as Tukey has put it, is to be *wisely* arbitrary" (p. 645).

[15] With little exaggeration the NFU can be described as synonymous with the British farming community.

Now to apply this test to the 1961 and 1966 phases. In 1961 the probability of HMG initially seeking special arrangements for British agriculture (e.g., safeguards for horticulture and a 12 to 15 year transition period) if the NFU made a strong appeal was perhaps 0.6, and the probability had the NFU not made such an appeal was about 0.2. Therefore the NFU's power at that time can be computed as 0.6 minus 0.2, or 0.4. During 1966–67, the probability of Britain adopting a strong policy favoring revision of EEC agricultural regulations and retention of the annual review if the NFU made a strong appeal fell to perhaps 0.2, and the probability had the NFU not urged such a course was about 0.1. The net power of the NFU in this period was thus only 0.1. For the first time, the NFU had exerted pressure but failed to get its way even partially.

Based on these calculations, we now have a measure of the decline of NFU influence in the face of increasing politicization during the three stages of European policy making: 1956–58 equals 0.6, 1961 equals 0.4, 1966–67 equals 0.1. The standing of pressure group influence in these stages corresponds to first, non-politicization; second, politicization which was not wholly effective; and third, effective politicization.

The causal nexus is such that politicization, the independent variable, causes a decline in pressure group influence, the dependent variable. But why should this relationship hold? What is there about politicization which determines the direction of causation? The answer lies in the fact that effective politicization prevents the operation of the functional representation process, through which groups customarily exercise their role. And it is here that the three indicators of politicization assume their importance. The first of these, the shift of the issue from economic to political ministry, is significant in that it reflects the movement of policy-making from a ministry such as the Board of Trade, which is organized on the basis of consultation between civil servants and their opposite numbers in the sectional groups, to one such as the

Foreign Office, which has no such provision. Routine consultation and bargaining for cooperation are central to the functional representation process; the shift of attention away from the economic ministries tends to prevent their operation. The importance of the second indicator, public involvement, lies in the fact that public scrutiny, whether direct or mediated by the communications media, interferes with the necessarily private bargaining process which makes up functional representation.[16] Third, the involvement of political parties becomes critical because they do not allow the assertion of undiluted sectional interests. This is not only because parties are organized around some distinctive conception of the common good —no matter how vague or vestigial—but also because those interests which the parties do heed in their search for support and in bidding for votes must of necessity be aggregated with numerous other interests. Inherently this aggregation implies dilution.

There is a normative implication here involving a preference for parties, rather than pressure groups, to play the greater role in the making of public policy. Yet in the context of European policy-making outlined in this study, can it be said that parties are constituted so as to create sufficient discretionary powers for leaders to make independent judgments on the basis of some broad interpretation of the national interest? There are some who take the view that parties are simply unsuited for the task.[17] Nonetheless, if parties are judged in the context of being just one major component of a broadly politicized setting, they do play an important part in creating at least the opportunity for political leaders to make such

---

[16] This is one reason why various proposals in Western European countries for a second legislative chamber based on economic representation are unlikely to come to fruition.

[17] E.g., J. R. Pennock rejects the classic view of the British system of responsible government that the government will seek majority support by acting in the public interest and that pressure groups will be less able to obtain a definition of the public interest on their own terms. Instead, he argues that the all-or-none nature of party competition may sensitize

judgments. And the European case certainly gives evidence that political judgments ultimately do get made. Thus, regardless of the group role in the actual negotiation phase of the first attempt at EEC entry, the actual decision of the Macmillan Government to seek Common Market entry was made on a political basis in advance of the groups strongly asserting their interests. Not only did this reflect the existence of policy powers insulated from the influence of pressure groups, no matter how corporatist the political setting, but it also illustrated the way in which a political interpretation of the national interest can take precedence over the sort of profit and loss calculations involving sectional interests. The fact that following the Macmillan decision the situation shifted to provide the groups with greater influence merely highlights the existence and importance of the political component. At a minimum it also confirms that political powers are not a mere chimera in the spheres of legislative or administrative policymaking. The Wilson Government's approach to Europe in 1966–67 provides further evidence of the significance of political decision-making.

The European case also provides support for the assertion that policy-making in an industrial democracy where corporatist politics exists should not be reducible to an interplay among organized interests. In the formation of European policy from 1956 to 1960 the political constituency was quiescent. While political leaders exercised final authority, constraints were imposed mainly by the sectional groups, which enjoyed a major role because of their expertise in what was treated as a technical and commercial matter. In this period it was logical that HMG saw its main task to be one of winning

leaders to the demands of pressure groups, and party discipline may be used to suppress those in the party who would resist group demands. " 'Responsible Government,' Separated Powers, and Special Interests: Agricultural Subsidies in Britain and America," *American Political Science Review*, 56, no. 3 (September, 1962): 621 and 631. Also see H. H. Wilson, *Pressure Group: The Campaign for Commercial Television* (London: Secker and Warburg, 1961), pp. 210-211.

over business, agriculture, and labor. Hence the groups claimed and were accorded the role they ordinarily played in the domestic politics of the Managed Economy and Welfare state. But a critical difference existed: the issue was not one of agricultural price supports or National Health Service arrangements affecting a particular sector of the polity; rather it was one of foreign policy, involving the long-range national interest and having potentially broad repercussions for the entire nation. The effect of group influence was seriously to complicate British efforts to come to terms with developments in European integration. Again during 1961 to 1963 Britain's European policy was shaped in substantial measure through a process of consultation and bargaining between government and sectional interests. The result was to provide less articulation for a broader, long-range, national interest than would have been the case had the party government channel been completely dominant. Basically, a major role in the choice was not appropriately the prerogative of the sectional interest groups, but as a consequence of group involvement those intimate in the process of policy determination were non-elective, not responsible to the public, and concerned to maximize values less broad than those of the country as a whole.[18] In contrast, effective politicization in 1966–67 eliminated the concurrent majority previously exercised by pressure groups and enabled the assertion of a generalized public interest—in this case the necessity of seeking Common Market membership without impediment.

Finally, the fact that political authority, moved by considerations other than material advantage, exercised at least the

---

[18] Sigmund Neumann called attention to the danger of the modern state "deteriorating into a neofeudalism of powerful interest groups" when the parties do not succeed in the primary task of fitting specific interests into a national framework. *Modern Political Parties* (Chicago: University of Chicago Press, 1956), p. 397. S. E. Finer finds the "lobby" to be tolerable but notes certain distortions of the democratic process which need to be offset by a strengthening of the "numerical majority" as opposed to the "concurrent majority" *op. cit.,* pp. 126-129.

ultimate responsibility for policy toward Europe offers certain implications for theories of political integration. While any lengthy consideration of this relationship goes beyond the scope of the present study, a few points deserve mention. First, as noted in passing in Chapter 1, the conclusions of this study imply real difficulty for the functionalist theory that de-politicization and a technical or functional treatment offer the best route to integration.[19] During the period 1956–60, and again following the Macmillan decision in 1961–62, Britain's relationship to Europe did evolve on such a level, but quite unsuccessfully as far as progress toward integration was concerned. Second, the British experience tends to confirm the view put forward by Stanley Hoffmann indicating the importance of an irreducible political core which is not susceptible to gradual erosion through step-by-step functional or spillover processes.[20] While Ernst Haas has acknowledged the limitations of his original assumption that step-by-step economic decisions are permanently superior to crucial political choices,[21] he does maintain that "in the absence of the statesman who can weld disparate publics together with the force of his own vision . . . we have no alternative, if we wish to integrate a region, but to resort to gradualism, to indirection, to functionalism."[22] Yet at least in the problem of enlarging

---

[19] The seminal work is David Mitrany's *A Working Peace System* (London: Oxford University Press, 1943).

[20] E.g., Hoffman takes issue with Ernst Haas' view that there no longer exists a distinctly political function separate from economics, welfare, or education. Stanley Hoffman, "European Process at Atlantic Cross-purposes," *Journal of Common Market Studies,* 3, no. 2 (February, 1965), p. 92. Elsewhere he has used an analogy based on the artichoke: peeling away the numerous leaves (steps toward economic unity) ultimately brings one to the very different heart (the separate and intractable problem of political sovereignty).

[21] Ernst B. Haas, " 'The Uniting of Europe' and the Uniting of Latin America," *Journal of Common Market Studies,* 5, no. 4 (June, 1967): 327.

[22] *Ibid.,* p. 328. Haas and Philippe Schmitter have also argued that economic integration of a group of nations does ultimately lead to

the geographic area of integration, if not in expanding that integration once a grouping already exists, the complex history of Britain's relation to European unity is such as to indicate that there is an inescapable and conscious political decision which must first be made before there can be an opportunity for any process of integration to get under way.

---

political unity, along a continuum. They find that "Integration can be conceived as involving the gradual politicization of the actors' purposes which were initially considered 'technical' or 'noncontroversial.' " "Economics and Differential Patterns of Political Integration: Projections about Unity in Latin America," reprinted and revised from *International Organization*, 18, no. 4 (Autumn, 1964) in *International Political Communities* (Garden City, New York: Anchor, 1966), p. 262.

Bibliography

GENERAL WORKS

POLITICS AND BRITISH POLITICS

Almond, Gabriel, and Powell, G. Bingham, Jr. *Comparative Politics: A Developmental Approach.* Boston: Little Brown, 1966.

Attitudes to European Unity and World Institutions in the 1966 General Election. London: Federal Trust for Education and Research, 1967.

Beavan, John. *The Press and the Public.* London: The Fabian Society, Tract no. 338, July, 1962.

Beer, Samuel H. *British Politics in the Collectivist Age.* New York: Knopf, 1965.

Beloff, Max. *New Dimensions in Foreign Policy: A Study in British Administrative Experience, 1947-59.* London: Allen & Unwin, 1961.

Blondel, Jean. *Voters, Parties and Leaders.* Rev. ed. Harmondsworth, Middlesex: Penguin, 1966.

Brittan, Samuel. *The Treasury Under the Tories. 1951-64.* Harmondsworth, Middlesex: Penguin, 1964.

Butler, D. E., and King, Anthony. *The British General Election of 1964.* London: Macmillan, 1965.

———. *The British General Election of 1966.* London: Macmillan, 1966.

Dahl, Robert. "The Concept of Power," *Behavioral Science,* 2 (1957): 201-215.

Election '66, Gallup Analysis of the Voting Results. London: Daily Telegraph, 1966.

Epstein, Leon D. *British Politics in the Suez Crisis.* London: Pall Mall Press, 1964.

Gallup Political Index. London: Social Surveys Limited, no. 1 (January, 1960)—no. 91. (November, 1967).

Hanrieder, Wolfram E. "Compatibility and Consensus: A Proposal for the Conceptual Linkage of External and Internal

Dimensions of Foreign Policy." *American Political Science Review* 61, no. 4 (December, 1957): 971-982.

McKenzie, Robert. "Between Two Elections (II)." *Encounter* 26, no. 2 (February, 1966): 21-29.

Mitchell, B. R., and Boehm, Klaus. *British Parliamentary Election Results, 1950-64.* Cambridge: Cambridge University Press, 1966.

Neumann, Sigmund. "Toward a Comparative Study of Political Parties." In *Modern Political Parties,* edited by Sigmund Neumann, pp. 395-421. Chicago: University of Chicago Press, 1956.

Neustadt, Richard E. "Whitehouse and Whitehall." Paper delivered at the 1965 Annual Meeting of the American Political Science Association, Washington, D.C., September 8-11.

Sampson, Anthony. *Anatomy of Britain.* London: Hodder & Stoughton, 1962.

———. *Macmillan, A Study in Ambiguity.* London: Allen Lane, The Penguin Press, 1967.

Seymour-Ure, Colin. "The Press and the British Political System." Paper delivered at the annual conference of the Political Studies Association, Oxford, April 3-5, 1967.

Shanks, Michael. *The Stagnant Society.* Baltimore: Penguin, 1961.

Shonfield, Andrew. *British Economic Policy Since the War.* Harmondsworth, Middlesex: Penguin, 1958.

———. *Modern Capitalism: The Changing Balance of Public and Private Power.* New York: Oxford University Press, 1965.

Waltz, Kenneth N. *Foreign Policy and Democratic Politics: The American and British Experience.* Boston: Little Brown, 1957.

Windlesham, Lord (G. R. J. Hennessy). *Communication and Political Power.* London: Jonathan Cape, 1966.

Younger, Kenneth. "Public Opinion and British Foreign Policy." *International Affairs* 40, no. 1 (January, 1964): 22-33.

PRESSURE GROUP POLITICS

Beer, Samuel H. "Group Representation in Britain and the U.S." In *Comparative Politics,* edited by Roy C. Macridis and Bernard Brown, pp. 130-140. Rev. ed. Homewood, Illinois: Dorsey Press, 1964.

Christoph, James B. *Capital Punishment and British Politics.* London: Allen & Unwin, 1962.

Eckstein, Harry. "Group Theory and the Comparative Study of Pressure Groups." In *Comparative Politics,* edited by Harry

Eckstein and David E. Apter, pp. 384-397. Glencoe, Illinois: The Free Press, 1963.

———. *Pressure Group Politics.* Stanford: Stanford University Press, 1960.

Finer, Samuel E. *Anonymous Empire: A Study of the Lobby in Great Britain.* London: Pall Mall Press, 1958.

LaPalombara, Joseph. "The Utility and Limitations of Interest Group Theory in Non-American Field Situations." In *Comparative Politics,* edited by Harry Eckstein and David E. Apter, pp. 421-430.

McKenzie, Robert. "Parties, Pressure Groups and the British Political Process." *Political Quarterly* 29, no. 1 (January-March, 1958).

Political and Economic Planning. *Advisory Committees in British Government.* London: Allen & Unwin, 1960.

Potter, Allen. "Attitude Groups." *Political Quarterly* 29, no. 1 (January-March, 1958).

———. *Organized Groups in British National Politics.* London: Faber and Faber, 1961.

Wilson, H. H. *Pressure Group: The Campaign for Commercial Television.* London: Secker & Warburg, 1961.

BRITAIN AND EUROPE

Abrams, Mark. "British Elite Attitudes and the European Common Market," *Public Opinion Quarterly,* 29, no. 2 (Summer, 1965): 236-246.

Anderson, Perry and Hall, Stuart. "Politics of the Common Market," *New Left Review,* no. 10 (July-August 1961), pp. 1-14.

Beloff, Nora. *The General Says No.* Baltimore: Penguin, 1963.

Calleo, David. *Britain's Future.* New York: Horizon Press, 1968.

Camps, Miriam. *Britain and the European Community, 1955-1963.* Princeton: Princeton University Press, 1964.

———. "Britain and the European Crisis." *International Affairs* 42, no. 1 (January, 1966): 45-54.

———. *European Unification in the Sixties.* New York: McGraw-Hill, 1966.

———. *What Kind of Europe? The Community Since de Gaulle's Veto.* London: Oxford University Press, 1965.

European Economic Community-Commission. *Report to the European Parliament on the State of the Negotiations with the United Kingdom.* Brussels, February 26, 1963.

"The Free Trade Area: A Challenge to British Industry." *The World Today* 14 (August, 1958): 338-356.

Great Britain. *Background to the Negotiations: Britain and the European Communities.* London: HMSO, 1962.

———. *Britain and the EEC, The Economic Background.* London: HMSO, May, 1967.

———. *Britain's Standpoint in the Common Market Negotiations.* Text of a statement to Ministers of Common Market Countries, by the Lord Privy Seal, Rt. Hon. Edward Heath, Paris, October 10, 1961.

———. *The Common Agricultural Policy of the European Economic Community.* Cmnd. 3274. London: HMSO, May, 1967.

———. *Commonwealth Consultations on Britain's Relations with the European Economic Community.* Cmnd. 1449. London: HMSO, July 1961.

———. *A European Free Trade Area.* Cmnd. 72. London: HMSO, February, 1957.

———. *Membership of the European Community.* Presented to Parliament by the Prime Minister. Cmnd. 3269. London: HMSO, May, 1967.

———. *The Modern Commonwealth.* Prepared for the Commonwealth Relations Office by the Central Office of Information. London: HMSO, January, 1962.

———. Paymaster General's Office. *Negotiations for a European Free Trade Area: Report on the Course of Negotiations up to December, 1958.* Cmnd. 648. London: HMSO, January, 1959.

———. *Negotiations for a European Free Trade Area: Documents Relating to the Negotiations from July, 1956, to December, 1958.* Cmnd. 641. London: HMSO, January, 1959.

Heiser, Hans J. *British Policy with Regard to the Unification Efforts on the European Continent.* Leyden, The Netherlands: Sythoff, 1959.

Hogg, Quintin. "Britain Looks Forward." *Foreign Affairs* 43, no. 3 (April, 1965): 409-425.

Journal of Common Market Studies. "The Future of Britain's Relations with Europe," a symposium including articles by John Bowyer, François Duchêne, David Howell, John Lambert, Christopher Layton, Richard Mayne, John Pinder, Roy Pryce, Noel Salter, Dennis Thomson. Vol. 3, No. 3 (July, 1965).

Kitzinger, Uwe. "Britain and Europe: The Multivalence of the British Decision." In *The European Yearbook,* Vol. 9 (1962), pp. 38-55.

————. *The Challenge of the Common Market.* 4th ed. Oxford: Basil Blackwell, 1962.

————. *The Second Try: Labour and the EEC.* Oxford: Pergamon Press, 1968.

Lerner, Daniel. *As Britain Faces the Continent: How Its Leaders Weigh Their Choices.* Cambridge, Massachusetts: MIT, Center for International Studies, 1962.

Lerner, Daniel, and Gorden, Morton. *A Decade of Challenge: The Responses of European Leaders.* Cambridge, Massachusetts: MIT, Center for International Studies, August, 1967. (Mimeographed.)

Miller, J. D. "Britain Without Europe." In *Europe Without Britain,* edited by Coral Bell, Melbourne, Australia: F. W. Cheshire, 1963, pp. 27-44.

Nettl, Peter, and Shapiro, David. "Institutions Versus Realities—A British Approach." *Journal of Common Market Studies* 2, no. 1 (July, 1963): 24-36.

Pfaltzgraff, Robert L. "The Common Market Debate in Britain." *Orbis* 7, no. 2 (Summer, 1963): 278-299.

Pickles, William. "The Choice and the Facts." *Journal of Common Market Studies* 4, no. 1 (October, 1965): 22-35.

Pinder, John. *Britain and the Common Market.* London: Crescent Press, 1961.

Political Quarterly. "When Britain Joins: A Symposium." 34, no. 1 (January-March, 1963).

Rabier, Jacques-René. "The European Idea and National Public Opinion." *Government and Opposition,* 2, no. 3 (April-July, 1967): 443-454.

Robinson, Geoffrey. *Europe: Problems of Negotiation.* London: Fabian Research Series, no. 263, September, 1967.

Robinson, James A. "Legislative Influence on Foreign Policy: Britain Considers the Common Market." Unpublished essay drawn in part from an earlier paper written with Roland Young and presented at the annual meeting of the American Political Science Association, Washington, D.C., September 6, 1962.

Sahm, Ulrich. "Britain and Europe, 1950." *International Affairs* 43, no. 1 (January, 1967).

Shanks, Michael, and Lambert, John. *Britain and the New Europe.* London: Chatto & Windus, 1962.

————. (ed.) "John Bull on the Brink," *The Sunday Times,* August 26, 1962.

Shonfield, Andrew. "Second Thoughts on Western Europe," *The Listener,* Vol. 56, no. 1437 (October 11, 1956).

Taylor, Humphrey, and Raison, Timothy. "Britain Into Europe? —General Attitudes." *New Society,* June 16 and 23, 1966.

Thorneycroft, Peter. "The European Idea." *Foreign Affairs,* 36, no. 3 (April, 1958): 472-479.

The Times. *The Common Market: A Survey.* 2d ed. London, February, 1962.

THE PARTIES

CONSERVATIVE

Bow Group. *Britain Into Europe.* London: Conservative Political Centre, August, 1962.

——. *No Tame or Minor Role.* London, September, 1963.

Conservative Political Centre. "The Commonwealth and the Common Market." A brief for CPC discussion groups, January, 1962.

——. *The New Europe.* London, August, 1962.

Conservative Research Department. *Words for Eating.* London, 1966.

The Guardian. *The Conservative Conference 1967.*

Macmillan, Harold. *Britain, the Commonwealth and Europe.* London: Conservative and Unionist Central Office, October, 1962.

National Union of Conservative and Unionist Associations, *Annual Conference* (report of proceedings), 1956-66.

Notes on Current Politics. Conservative Research Department (ed.). "Britain's Trade Policy," no. 13 (July 11, 1960).

——. "European Unity—The Political Issues," no. 16 (August 8, 1960).

——. "Agriculture and Allied Topics," no. 13 (July 3, 1961).

——. "Britain and the Common Market," no. 16 (August 28, 1961).

——. "The UK and the EEC," no. 3 (February 5, 1962).

——. "Agriculture," no. 3 (April 16, 1962).

——. "Debate on the Common Market," no. 13 (June 25, 1962).

——. "Commonwealth and Common Market," no. 19 (October 8, 1962).

——. "Britain and Europe," no. 5 (March 4, 1963).

——. "Labour, TUC and Liberal Conferences," no. 19 (October 24, 1966).

——. "Conservative Party Conference 1966," no. 20 (October 31, 1966).

——. "Britain and Europe," no. 1 (January 16, 1967).

LABOUR

Beloff, Max. "Labour and Europe: Unreal Romanticism." *Time & Tide* (May 3, 1962).

Crossman, R.H.S. "British Labour Looks at Europe." *Foreign Affairs*, 41, no. 4 (July, 1963): 732-743.

The Guardian. *The Labour Party Conference 1962.*

——. *The Labour Party Conference 1966.*

——. *The Labour Party Conference 1967.*

Labour Party. *European Unity, A Statement by the National Executive Committee.* May, 1950.

——. *Feet on the Ground: A Study of Western Union,* September, 1948.

——. *The European Commitment.* Home Policy Committee. July, 1961.

——. *Labour and the Common Market,* A Statement by the National Executive Committee, September 29, 1962.

——. *New Britain: Manifesto for the 1964 General Election.* London, 1964.

——. *Report of the Annual Conference,* 1957-1966.

——. *Time for Decision: Manifesto for the 1966 General Election.* London, 1966.

Labour Party Research Department. *Twelve Wasted Years.* London, 1963.

Rodgers, William T. (ed.). *Hugh Gaitskell, 1906-1963.* London: Thames and Hudson, 1964.

Shore, Peter. *Entitled to Know.* London: Macgibbon and Kee, 1966.

PRESSURE GROUPS

PROMOTIONAL GROUPS

British Council of the European Movement. *The European Movement in Britain.* London, 1967.

Bryant, Arthur. *A Choice for Destiny: Commonwealth and Common Market.* London: Collins, 1962.

Common Market Campaign. *Forward Britain Into Europe: The Case for Britain Joining the Common Market.* Essay by Sir Anthony Meyer, with questions and answers by Norman J. Hart. London, 1962.

———. *Common Market Broadsheet*, 1961-62.

Corbett, R. Hugh (ed.). *Britain, Not Europe*. London: Anti-Common Market League, May, 1962.

Forward Britain Movement. *Britain Should Stay Out*. Report of the Britain-Commonwealth-EFTA Conference held at the House of Commons, Westminster, on July 16-19, 1962.

———. *The Case Now Against Britain's Entry into the Common Market*. London, 1962.

Jay, Douglas. *The Truth About the Common Market*. London: Forward Britain Movement, August, 1962.

Jay, Douglas, and Jenkins, Roy. *The Common Market Debate*. London: Fabian Tract No. 341, November, 1962.

Labour Common Market Committee. *Commonsense About the Common Market: Questions and Answers for Trade Unionists and Socialists*. London, August, 1962.

Leighton, Ron. *What Next For Britain?* London: Forward Britain Movement, 1963.

Luard, Evan. *Britain and Europe*. London: Fabian International Bureau, Tract no. 330, January, 1961.

MacDougall, Sir Donald. *Britain and the Common Market*. London: Rotterdamsche Bank, Review no. 4, December, 1961.

"Mr. Michael Mason Attacks Common Market Entry Plan." *Witney Gazette*, December 28, 1962, pp. 2-3.

Pickles, William. *Britain and Europe—How Much Has Changed?* Oxford: Basil Blackwell, 1967.

———. *Not With Europe: the political case for staying out*. London: Fabian International Bureau, Tract No. 336, April, 1962.

UK Council of the European Movement. *The Cost of Labour in the UK and the Six*. Reprinted from the *Financial Times*, October 5, 1962.

Walker-Smith, Derek, and Walker, Peter. *A Call to the Commonwealth*. London, n.d.

Woodburn, Arhur. *A Commonsense View of the Common Market*. London: UK Council of the European Movement, n.d.

SECTIONAL GROUPS

FBI/CBI and Industry

Confederation of British Industries, Britain and Europe—Volume 1: An Industrial Reappraisal, London, December, 1966.

Federation of British Industries *39th Annual Report of the FBI for the Year Ending December 31, 1955.* Yearly volumes through the 48th *Annual Report,* 1964.

———. *The British Commonwealth, Commonwealth Preference and the Sterling Area.* London, July, 1958.

———. *Director General's Aide Memoire to the Chief Official of Member Trade Associations.* 1955 to 1961.

———. Grand Council Papers, October, 1956 and February–September, 1957.

———. *European Free Trade Area, A Survey for Industrialists.* London, April, 1957.

———. *Free Trade in Western Europe, A Joint Statement by the Industrial Federations and Employers' Organizations of Austria, Denmark, Norway, Sweden, Switzerland, the United Kingdom.* Paris, April 14, 1958.

———. *Overseas Circular.* no. 1 (October, 1961)–no. 28 (February, 1964).

———. *Report by Sir William Palmer's Working Party to the FBI, ABCC and NUM.* D/2203. August 22, 1957 (Mimeographed.)

———. *UK Trade with Scandinavia and Finland. A Report of Conferences held in London, Birmingham, and Glasgow on May 20-22, 1959.*

———. *ABCC, NUM. A Joint Report on the European Free Trade Area.* London, September, 1957.

FBI Review. no. 58 (January, 1955–no. 163 (December, 1963).

Finer, Samuel E. "The Federation of British Industries." *Political Studies,* 4, no. 1 (February, 1956): 61-84.

———. *Private Industry and Political Power.* London: Pall Mall Pamphlet no. 3, 1958.

Monthly Bulletin. Empire Industries Association (later the Commonwealth Industries Association), No. 191 (March, 1957)–no. 265 (May, 1963).

The Director. Institute of Directors, Vol. 7, no. 1 (October, 1955)–Vol. 14, No. 1 (July, 1961).

The Times Review of Industry. New Series, Vol. 11, no. 120 (January, 1957)–Vol. 17, no. 193 (February, 1963).

NFU and Agriculture

Beynon, V. H., and Harrison, J. E. *The Political Significance of the British Agricultural Vote.* Newton Abbot, Devon: University of Exeter, Report no. 134, July, 1962.

British Farmer. (New Series) Weekly journal of the National Farmers' Union of England and Wales.

Hallett, Graham. *British Agriculture and Europe.* Pamphlet written for *Crossbow,* The Bow Group quarterly, Supplement to spring issue, 1961.

Holmes, R. A. "The National Farmers' Union and the British Negotiations for Membership in the European Economic Community." *Res Publica* 5, no. 3 (1963): 276-287.

Kempinski, T. "Entry Into the European Common Market and British Agriculture Income." Manchester: University of Manchester, Department of Agricultural Economics, Bulletin no. 114, Nov. 1966.

National Farmers' Union of England and Wales. "Annual Report," for 1958, see *British Farmer* (New Series), No. 59, January 10, 1959; for 1959, No. 111, January 9, 1960; for 1960, No. 163, January 7, 1961; for 1961, No. 215, January 6, 1962; for 1962, No. 268, January 12, 1963; for 1963, No. 321, January 11, 1964; for 1964, No. 374, January 9, 1965.

————. *British Agriculture and the Common Market: A policy statement by the NFU.* London, July, 1961.

————. *British Agriculture Looks Ahead.* London, September, 1964.

————. *A Farm and Food Plan.* London, August, 1962.

————. *Year Book,* "Annual Report," 1955-58. NFU Information Service. "Agriculture in the Community." Vol. 16, No. 2 (1961).

————. *British Agriculture and the Common Market,* Published jointly by the NFU, National Farmers' Union of Scotland, and the Ulster Farmers' Union. London, November, 1966.

Pennock, J. Roland. "The Political Power of British Agriculture." *Political Studies,* 7, no. 3 (October, 1959): 291-296.

————. " 'Responsible Government,' Separated Powers, and Special Interests: Agricultural Subsidies in Britain and America." *American Political Science Review,* 56, no. 3 (September, 1962): 621-633.

Redmayne, G. B. "The Common Market and British Agriculture." *Westminster Bank Review,* August, 1966.

Self, Peter and Storing, Herbert J. *The State and the Farmer.* London: Allen & Unwin, 1962.

Winegarten, Asher. "Agriculture—In or Out?" *The Statist,* December 14, 1962, pp. 742-744.

   TUC and Trade Unions

Beever, R. Colin. "Trade Union Re-Thinking." *Journal of Common Market Studies,* 2, No. 2 (November, 1963): 140-154.

Feather, Victor. "British Trade Unions and the Common Market." *New Commonwealth,* 33 No. 6 (March 18, 1957): 254-257.

Pelling, Henry. *A History of British Trade Unionism*. Baltimore: Penguin, 1963.

Trades Union Congress. *ABC of the TUC*. London, 1965.

————. *Industrial News,* for the use of the press. Appears approximately twice per month. 1956-1963.

————. *Report of Proceedings at the Annual Trades Union Congress,* 1955 to 1966.

INTERVIEWS

During the course of my research, I interviewed 55 people, all of them significantly involved in the organizations and events relevant to this work. My meetings with these individuals took place in London during the 1966-67 academic year. The sessions were open-ended, but were based on specific sets of questions. Most of the meetings ranged from one to two hours in length. There were also a number of repeat interviews.

As a rule, the value of each session was inversely proportional to the willingness of the respondent to be quoted. Because of this, and because of the recentness of events and the continued participation of a great majority of the interviewees in Government, politics, and pressure group activity, it has been necessary to list these persons by category rather than by name. The positions cited below are those held at the time of the interviewees' involvement within the years 1956-67. The list totals 59 to allow for overlap of positions in four cases (e.g., an individual who was both a trade union leader and leader of a promotional group).

Civil Servants 9
  Administrative Class 8
  Other 1
Conservatives 12
  Cabinet Ministers 5
  Party Leadership 2
  Party Organization or Staff 4
  MP 1
Labourites 9
  Junior Minsters 4
  Staff 5
  MP 2
Sectional Pressure Group Leaders 16
  FBI/CBI 5

NFU 3
TUC and trade union leaders 8
Promotional Pressure Group Leaders 6
Journalists 4
Academicians 3

OTHER MATERIALS

Great Britain. *Parliamentary Debates* (5th Series). (Commons).
Daily Express (London).
Daily Telegraph (London).
Financial Times (London).
The Guardian (London).
Observer (London).
Sunday Times (London).
The Times (London).

Index